Elections in America

Recent Titles in the

CONTEMPORARY WORLD ISSUES

Series

First Amendment Freedoms: A Reference Handbook
Michael C. LeMay

Medicare and Medicaid: A Reference Handbook
Greg M. Shaw

Organic Food and Farming: A Reference Handbook
Shauna M. McIntyre

Civil Rights and Civil Liberties in America: A Reference Handbook
Michael C. LeMay

GMO Food: A Reference Handbook, Second Edition
David E. Newton

Pregnancy and Birth: A Reference Handbook
Keisha L. Goode and Barbara Katz Rothman

Hate Groups: A Reference Handbook
David E. Newton

Plastics and Microplastics: A Reference Handbook
David E. Newton

Prescription Drugs: A Reference Handbook
David E. Newton

The U.S.-Mexico Border: A Reference Handbook
Michael C. LeMay

Homelessness in America: A Reference Handbook
Michele Wakin

The Judicial System: A Reference Handbook
Michael C. LeMay

Foster Care in America: A Reference Handbook
Christina G. Villegas

Women in Media: A Reference Handbook
Amy M. Damico

Books in the **Contemporary World Issues** series address vital issues in today's society such as genetic engineering, pollution, and biodiversity. Written by professional writers, scholars, and nonacademic experts, these books are authoritative, clearly written, up-to-date, and objective. They provide a good starting point for research by high school and college students, scholars, and general readers as well as by legislators, businesspeople, activists, and others.

Each book, carefully organized and easy to use, contains an overview of the subject, a detailed chronology, biographical sketches, facts and data and/or documents and other primary source material, a forum of authoritative perspective essays, annotated lists of print and nonprint resources, and an index.

Readers of books in the Contemporary World Issues series will find the information they need in order to have a better understanding of the social, political, environmental, and economic issues facing the world today.

CONTEMPORARY WORLD ISSUES

Elections in America

A REFERENCE HANDBOOK

Michael C. LeMay

ABC-CLIO®

An Imprint of ABC-CLIO, LLC
Santa Barbara, California • Denver, Colorado

Library of Congress Cataloging-in-Publication Data

Names: LeMay, Michael C., 1941- author.
Title: Elections in America : a reference handbook / Michael C. LeMay.
Description: First Edition. | Santa Barbara, California : ABC-CLIO, [2022] | Series: Contemporary World Issues | Includes bibliographical references and index.
Identifiers: LCCN 2022008513 | ISBN 9781440876493 (Hardcover : acid-free paper) | ISBN 9781440876509 (eBook)
Subjects: LCSH: Elections—United States—Handbooks, manuals, etc.
Classification: LCC JK1976 .L37 2022 | DDC 324.973—dc23/eng/20220416
LC record available at https://lccn.loc.gov/2022008513

ISBN: 978-1-4408-7649-3 (print)
978-1-4408-7650-9 (ebook)

26 25 24 23 22 1 2 3 4 5

This book is also available as an eBook.

ABC-CLIO
An Imprint of ABC-CLIO, LLC

ABC-CLIO, LLC
147 Castilian Drive
Santa Barbara, California 93117
www.abc-clio.com

This book is printed on acid-free paper ∞

Manufactured in the United States of America

Preface

Elections in America: A Reference Handbook examines the more than 200-year history of electoral politics in the United States. The book details and documents the great diversity and complexity that characterize U.S. elections. Some of that complexity is related to the federal system of government established by the U.S. Constitution and its Article I provision that reserves the power of election management to the states. The actual function of elections in America is further determined by the extensive demographic diversity of the United States, arguably the most ethnically, racially, and religiously diverse society of any nation on the face of the earth.

Another theme of the book is how the eventual establishment of the two-major-party system shaped American electoral politics in profound ways. So, too, the vast array of interest groups active in American electoral politics in various capacities has played an increasingly significant role in electoral politics. Yet another theme of the book is how and why the franchise was expanded, but only after considerable political struggle by persons and groups that fought to be included in elections and thus share political power.

Laws enacted by national, state, and local governments have often expanded—but sometimes have limited—who may run for office, who may vote, and how those votes are counted. A plethora of laws are discussed and analyzed herein as to their impact, intended or unintended, on U.S. elections.

The book discusses numerous landmark court decisions that have dealt with the right to vote and to participate in U.S.

elections in various ways. Some Supreme Court decisions have had the practical effect of diminishing voting rights, while other decisions have expanded the franchise forward for new groups of individuals in the electorate. The book explains the structure and types of elections used in American electoral politics and illuminates how the types and levels of electoral contests influence voter turnout and impact the relative political influence of political parties and interest groups.

The book follows the format used by every book in the Contemporary World Issues series. Chapter 1 discusses the historical background of the topic, describing the establishment and evolution of American elections. The historical background presents its narrative in an evenhanded manner to better enable readers to form their own judgments as to the many issues raised.

Chapter 2 describes and discusses the most vexing and contentious problems evident in American electoral politics. The chapter explores electoral controversies associated with each of the problem areas. It describes efforts by advocates, government agencies, and officials to address and resolve these problems through laws, administrative regulations, and legal challenges.

Chapter 3 presents nine original essays by scholars and activists in electoral politics to add their voices and perspective to that of this author. The contributors represent diverse disciplinary perspectives, and their contributions enrich our understanding of various facets of American electoral politics.

Chapter 4 presents profiles of an array of organizations and individuals involved as stakeholders in electoral politics. Featured organizations include government agencies, nonprofits, major and minor political parties, nonpartisan organizations, and research organizations. It then presents profiles of individuals who have played or continue to play important roles in the evolution of America's electoral politics.

Chapter 5 presents data and documents on elections in America. Data are presented in accessible tables. These data enable readers to better assess and understand critical issues raised in the book's opening two chapters. The data section is followed by a documents section that presents (in full or in excerpts) 12 primary documents: six acts of the U.S. Congress and six landmark U.S. Supreme Court decisions.

Chapter 6 is a resource chapter that provides an annotated list of scholarly books that showcase the variety of academic literature on American elections. It then lists numerous academic journals that readers are encouraged to consult for further original research articles on American electoral politics. Finally, the resources chapter closes with a list of useful websites for readers to visit and consult for further research and eight documentary films that examine aspects of electoral politics in America.

A chronology of key events in the history of elections in America is presented in chapter 7, followed by a glossary of key terms to help readers navigate legal or academic jargon that often accompanies discussion of elections and voting rights. The book closes with an extensive and helpful subject index.

Elections in America

HARPER'S WEEKLY
A JOURNAL OF CIVILIZATION

VOL. XI.—No. 568.] NEW YORK, SATURDAY, NOVEMBER 16, 1867. [SINGLE COPIES TEN CE[NTS.] $4.00 PER YEAR IN ADV[ANCE.]

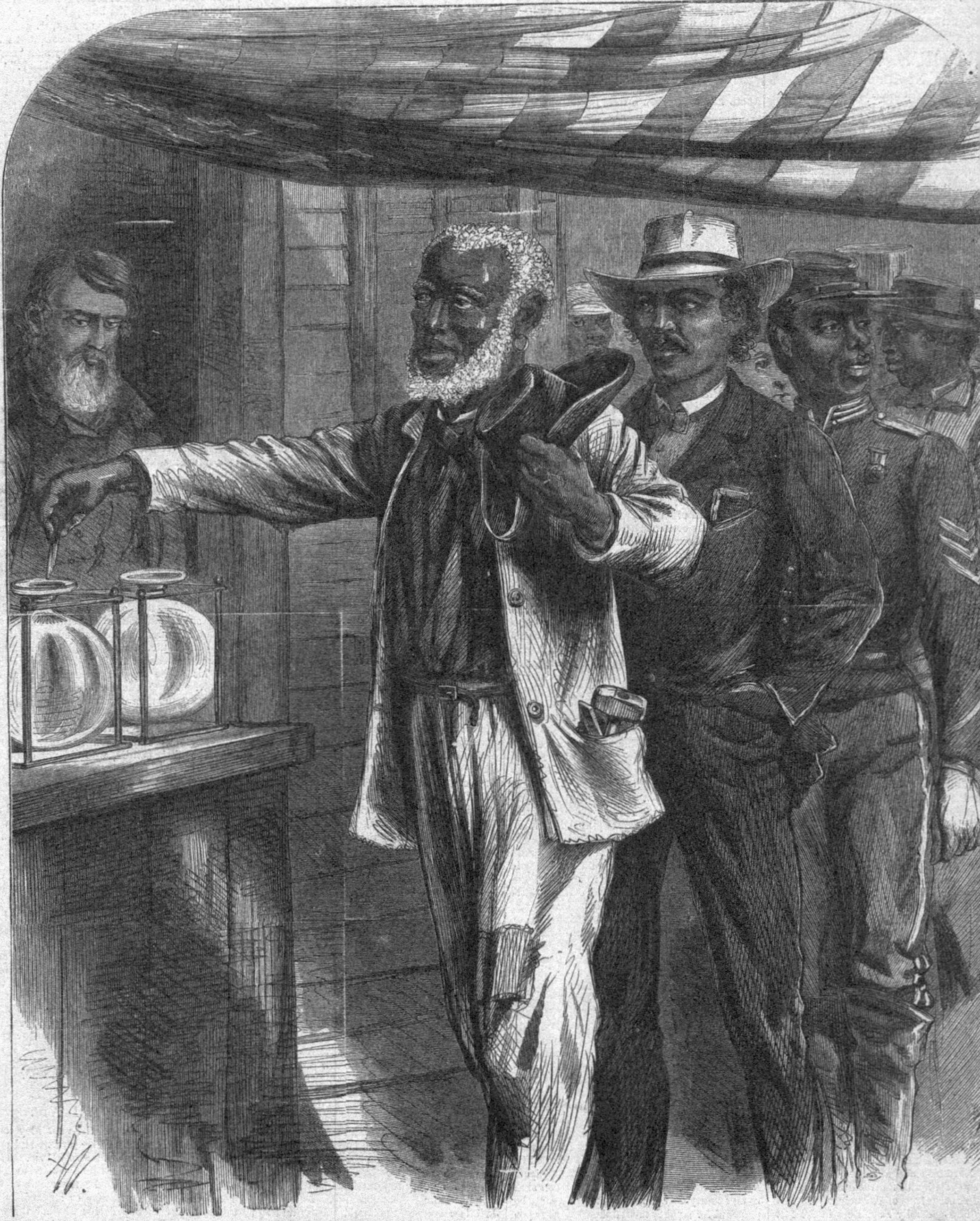

"THE FIRST VOTE."—DRAWN BY A. R. WAUD.—[SEE NEXT PAGE.]

1 Background and History

Introduction: Determinants of the Great Diversity of U.S. Elections

Elections

Elections in the United States are quite diverse and can be almost bewilderingly complex. This complexity and diversity stem to a great extent from structural aspects of the federal system used in American politics, as established by the U.S. Constitution. In fact, the United States does not have a single electoral system. By its foundational design, it has 50 systems of elections (LeMay 2017, 86).

In addition to the constitutional/legal framework governing U.S. elections, the actual functioning of elections is further greatly determined by regional political cultures, demographic factors and trends, the development and evolution of political parties in American politics, organized interest groups that have arisen in the body politic, and unique socioeconomic structures found within the 50 U.S. states.

Throughout its history, the United States has greatly expanded voting rights—but only after considerable political struggle over who should be allowed to participate in elections and hold political power. Through numerous laws enacted at

---

African Americans were legally able to vote (Black suffrage) by the Fifteenth Amendment. Due to Jim Crow laws and extensive intimidation, however, they were not able to vote in significant numbers until after enactment of the 1965 Voting Rights Act. (Library of Congress)

the national, state, and local levels, and through several landmark federal court decisions, the right to vote and to participate in elections in various ways has expanded over the course of generations. Many observers worry, however, that these hard-fought gains are in jeopardy today.

This chapter discusses elections at the national, state, and local levels. A defining theme of the chapter is the expansion of the franchise in practice, by state and national legislation, by national and state constitutional amendments, and by court decisions at both the federal and state levels concerning the conduct of elections.

To better understand and illustrate the complexity of elections and electoral politics in the United States, this chapter also details the variety of elections that are held. These include, for example, primary elections that may be direct or runoff elections, general elections versus special elections, presidential-year versus midterm elections, national versus statewide versus local elections, partisan versus nonpartisan elections, and winner-take-all versus proportional elections.

The results of these elections are shaped not only by laws and court decisions impacting voting but by a variety of nonlegal factors. For example, the attention given elections by the media, by political parties and interest groups, and by the general voting public varies dramatically by the level of office being contested. Not surprisingly, the greatest media attention and highest voter turnout is for the offices of president and vice president. This is followed by the elections for seats in the U.S. Senate and then the U.S. House of Representatives.

The amount of attention given to elections, both from the media and the voting public, declines for most nonfederal elected offices, although gubernatorial elections typically attract considerable interest, especially if the outcome is likely to be close.

Other elections for statewide offices, seats in state legislatures, or judicial offices typically garner less attention. The lowest levels of attention and turnout are for special elections, runoff elections, referendum issues, and recall elections. For such elections, a turnout rate as low as 15 percent of the eligible voters is common. Exceptions to this pattern abound, however. For example, more than 55 percent of eligible Californians voted in September 2021 in a recall election of Governor Gavin Newsom (who decisively beat back the GOP-led recall effort and remained in office).

Constitutional Provisions Regarding Elections in America

The power to administer elections is one of the powers reserved in the U.S. Constitution for the individual states. There are, however, some provisions pertaining to national-level elections that are constitutionally specified. Article I, Section 4 states, "The Times, Places and Manner of holding Elections for Senators and Representatives, shall be prescribed in each State by the Legislature thereof; but the Congress may at any time by Law make or alter such Regulations, except as to the Places of chusing Senators."

Similarly, Article II, Section 1 specifies the selection of members of the Electoral College to be used for the election of the offices of the president and vice president. The Constitution originally gave the power to appoint electors to the respective state legislatures. It further states, "The Congress may determine the Time of chusing the Electors, and the Day on which they shall give their Votes, which Day shall be the same throughout the United States." In addition, Article IV, Section 4 provides that "the United States shall guarantee to every State in the Union a Republican Form of Government."

Several of the amendments to the U.S. Constitution address issues important to elections as well. The 10th Amendment, adopted on December 15, 1791, specifies, "The powers not delegated to the United States by the Constitution, nor prohibited by it to the States, are reserved to the States respectively, or to the people." The conduct and management of elections in the United States constitute one such reserved power, and the states have had the primary role in determining the administration of elections ever since the 10th Amendment became the law of the land.

The 15th Amendment addresses the right of Black suffrage. Ratified on February 3, 1870, it was the last of what became known as the Civil War Amendments. It reads as follows: "Section 1. The right of citizens of the United States to vote shall not be denied or abridged by the United States or by any State on account of race, color, or previous condition of servitude. Section 2. The Congress shall have the power to enforce this article by appropriate legislation."

The 17th Amendment, which was ratified on April 8, 1913, stipulated the direct election of U.S. senators by voters (rather than by state legislatures, which previously held this power):

> The Senate of the United States shall be composed of two Senators from each State, elected by the people thereof, for six years, and each Senator shall have one vote. The electors in each State shall have the qualifications requisite for electors of the most numerous branch of the State legislatures. When vacancies happen in the representation of any State in the Senate, the executive authority of such State shall issue writs of election to fill such vacancies: Provided, That the legislature of any State may empower the executive thereof to make temporary appointments until the people fill the vacancies by election as the legislature may direct. This amendment shall not be so construed as to affect the election or terms of any Senator chosen before it becomes valid as part of the Constitution.

The 19th Amendment was ratified on August 15, 1920, giving women the right to vote. It stipulates women's suffrage as follows: "The right of citizens of the United States to vote shall not be denied or abridged by the United States or by any State on account of sex. Congress shall have power to enforce this article by appropriate legislation."

The 23rd Amendment was ratified on March 26, 1961. It granted suffrage to citizens of the District of Columbia as follows:

> Section 1. The District constituting the seat of the Government of the United States shall appoint in such manner as the Congress may direct: A number of electors of President and Vice President equal to the whole number of Senators and Representatives in Congress to which the District would be entitled if it were a State, but they shall be considered for the purposes of the election of the President and Vice President, to be electors appointed by a State, and they shall meet in the District and perform such duties as provided by the twelfth article of the amendment. Section 2. The Congress shall have power to enforce this article by appropriate legislation.

The 24th Amendment, which was ratified on January 23, 1964, banned poll taxes, which had been used across the Jim Crow South for the better part of a century to keep Blacks from voting. It reads as follows: "Section 1. The right of citizens of the United States to vote in any primary or other election for President or Vice President, or for Senator or Representative in Congress, shall not be denied or abridged by the United States or any State by reason of failure to pay poll tax or other tax. Section 2. The Congress shall have power to enforce this article by appropriate legislation."

Finally, the 26th Amendment, ratified on March 23, 1971, granted the right to vote to 18-year-olds: "Section 1. The right of citizens of the United States, who are eighteen years of age or older, to vote shall not be denied or abridged by the United States or by any State on account of age. Section 2. The Congress shall have the power to enforce this article by appropriate legislation."

Elections at the National Level

The quadrennial elections for president and vice president are held on the first Tuesday of November. The members of Congress are elected on the same day. All members of the U.S. House of Representatives are chosen, since House seats have only two-year terms. In addition, one-third of seats in the U.S. Senate (which have six-year terms) come up for election every two years.

If an election is held during a year when the presidency is not at stake, it is known as a midterm or off-presidential-year election. Whether an election year includes a presidential election influences voter turnout for that election. In addition, votes for the "head of the ticket" (candidates for president and vice president) during presidential campaigns can influence down-ticket races in what is often referred to as the "presidential coattails effect." Turnout in midterm elections often declines by as much as 15 percent versus the turnout in presidential years. Typically, the party of the sitting president loses seats in the Congress during those midterm election years.

From 1789 until 1800, political parties did not exist as we know them today. During President George Washington's two terms, Alexander Hamilton was the leading voice in organizing within the Washington administration the nucleus of the Federalist Party, which gradually resulted in informal state organizations that performed some of the functions of a modern political party (Witcover 2003, 8). John Adams became the most noted Federalist politician and the only man elected president under that party's banner (LeMay 2017, 5). Washington's secretary of state, fellow Virginian Thomas Jefferson, became the leading opponent to the Federalists and to Hamilton's policy programs. Thomas Jefferson joined with another founding father, James Madison, to form what became the Jeffersonian Democratic-Republican Party, which can be considered the first true national political party in U.S. history. The Democratic-Republican Party maintained organizations in each of the then

13 states. These state-level organizations performed electoral activities to get out the vote, endorsed candidates for various offices, and raised funds to help finance campaigns. Many of them created newspapers, flyers, and other materials to promote candidates. Those candidates were identified on election ballot as representatives of the Democratic-Republican Party.

The Constitution did not provide for a mechanism to identify candidates for the presidency. Article II describes the Electoral College, with members selected by state legislatures. This arrangement was intended to serve as a buffer between the people and the president by blunting tendencies toward partisanship and demagoguery in presidential selection. Congressional caucuses were significant in the identification of potential presidential candidates, and national party conventions linking the federal and state parties together did not develop until the 1830s.

Origins of the Two-Party System

In the 1800 presidential election, Thomas Jefferson won the office in part due to the efforts of the Democratic-Republican Party, which James Madison helped create. That election marked the beginning of what political scientists have described as the first political party system, with the Democratic-Republican Party establishing essentially one-party rule (LeMay 2017, 13). The Anti-Masonic Party, the first U.S. "third party" (minor party distinguishable from the two major parties), held the first presidential-nominating convention and introduced the concept of the party "platform," a formal statement of party values and policy priorities (Epstein 2012).

The Constitution and the U.S. Congress were silent on the issue of political parties (at the time referred to as "factions") and enacted no laws regulating their involvement in federal elections. Until 1828, the two major political parties were rather loose coalitions of party-like organizations at the state level.

The presidential election of 1828 was a transformative one, marking the beginning of the rise of the mass party system in which party organizations operating in each of the states activated voter drives, endorsed candidates, and rallied the "masses" of ordinary citizens to become politically active. Martin Van Buren and Andrew Jackson forged the Jacksonian Democratic Party that dominated American politics until 1860. The Whig Party and the Anti-Masonic Party were unable to obtain majority party status.

During this same period, the population of the United States tripled, from fewer than 10 million to more than 30 million. States vied for immigrants to increase their populations, and some even allowed resident aliens—immigrants who had not yet naturalized as American citizens—to vote in local elections. In 1846, for example, Wisconsin extended the franchise to aliens who intended to naturalize and who had lived in the state for a year. In 1850, Michigan adopted a similar law. By the late 19th century, 18 states were allowing aliens to vote in state or local elections (Ueda 1980, 737–40).

Some scholars posit that the election of Andrew Jackson in 1828 marked the beginning of America's two-party political system (though it was called a "second party system" in the mid-19th century). The Democratic Party, which emerged from the Jeffersonian Democratic-Republican Party, battled the Federalist Party and its successor party, the Whigs. This politicization created new opportunities for nominations, patronage, and political careers in return for party loyalty. Modeled after Van Buren's Albany Regency, a political club that became a dominant statewide party organization based in Albany, New York, the Jacksonian Democratic Party established party discipline to check the abuses of personal power sometimes seen from politicians with no party affiliation.

The mass party system characterized the modern political party system in American politics, with two major parties nationally organized down to the most basic level. This system emphasized participation in politics throughout the country.

The parties developed rallies to increase party enthusiasm and expanded the use of caucuses and then statewide conventions to select candidates for office and policy proposals and priorities in the party platform.

The Democratic Party, for example, held its first national convention in 1832. The party used the national convention as a coordinating body to raise resources, coordinate efforts, and oversee investment in building state- and local-level party organizations (the "grass roots" of the party). The growing strength of political parties dramatically increased voter turnout. Turnout increased from 26.5 percent of eligible voters in 1824 to 56.3 percent in 1828. When the Whig Party developed in the late 1830s, it followed the model of the Democrats, and the mass party system matured, resulting in greater democratization around the country. The Whigs held their first national convention in 1839.

A central theme of the Democratic Party in the 1840s and 1850s was aggressive western expansion. Many party members subscribed to the idea of "Manifest Destiny," the belief that it was ordained by God that the United States would expand its territory until it spanned from the Atlantic to the Pacific. The Democratic Party, for example, advocated for the admission of the Republic of Texas to the Union. In 1848, the Democratic Party established the Democratic National Committee (DNC) at its national convention, thereby completing the mass party structure.

The primary opposition to the Democratic Party was the Whig Party, home to Puritan Protestants and based in New England. The Whig Party collapsed in 1852, however, as divisions over slavery and nativism took their toll. In 1854, the Democrats became the de facto proslavery party in American politics (Zolberg 2006, 139; Barone 1990). The rapid immigration of Europeans to America in the mid-1840s was seen by both Republicans and Democrats as an opportunity to add to their ranks, and Irish immigrants were soon trending toward the Democratic Party at the same time that German immigrants became part of the newly emerging Republican Party.

Competing to Replace the Whigs

Massive immigration to America during the 19th century triggered the rise of an anti-immigrant social movement, the Secret Order of the Star-Spangled Banner. This group subsequently evolved into the American Party, which became more commonly known as the Know Nothing Party. Members advocated ending immigration and enacting stringent naturalization laws, to include increasing the waiting period for citizenship from 5 years to 21 years. In their political campaigns, Know Nothing Party members advocated enactment of a literacy test for citizenship and English-language qualification for voting (Zolberg 2006, 160). They became the temporary home for voters unwilling to cast their vote for either the Democrats or the Whigs. The nativist Know Nothing Party feared an increasingly political threat as the electoral clout of the immigrant voting bloc became evident with the beginnings of the urban political machine.

To attract new voters and politicians to their party, leading Democratic Party officials embraced what came to be called the "party spoils system," as in the cliché "To the victor belong the spoils of the enemy"—the "enemy" being the opposition party in this case. The party spoils system (also sometimes known as patronage) refers to the systematic distribution of goods (such as lucrative government contracts), positions in government and other offices, and other favors and benefits to reward loyal party members and punish members of other parties.

In 1854, the Republican Party was established in Ripon, Wisconsin, with an antislavery platform, essentially filling the political vacuum left by the Whigs. The Republican Party was first organized to oppose the Kansas-Nebraska Act, which extended slavery into the territories. It held its first national convention in 1856 in Philadelphia, attracting former Whigs and Free-Soil Democrats. Its members included white

Protestants, businessmen, professionals, factory workers, and African Americans, and it constituted the majority party in nearly every Northern state with the election of Abraham Lincoln in 1860.

The Republican Party was notably pro-business, supporting banks, hard money (that is, the gold standard), railroads, and high tariffs to protect industrial workers and industry. It supported giving free western land to farmers ("free soil"), the expansion of banking, and more railroads and factories. The party established a coalition of ethnic and religious groups that became Republican Party voting blocs, advocating purging society of alcoholism, polygamy, and slavery. Geographically, the party came to dominate New England, upstate New York, and the upper Midwest. Religiously, they received strong support from Congregationalists, Presbyterians, Methodists, Scandinavian Lutherans, and Quakers. Lincoln, like many antislavery Whig Party members, migrated to the newly emerging Republican Party as the Whig Party declined. The Whigs were split into Northern and Southern factions over the slavery question that resulted in the outbreak of the U.S. Civil War in 1861.

The transformative election of Abraham Lincoln in 1860 established the Republican Party as the party of the North and firmly abolitionist. Lincoln was reelected in 1864. His assassination on April 15, 1865, is commonly held as marking the beginning of the Reconstruction period (1865–1877). The Republican Party was factionalized on what "Reconstruction" policies to adopt to bring the former secessionist states back into the Union.

On April 6, 1866, the 13th Amendment (also known as the Civil Rights Act) was passed, and in 1868, the 14th Amendment was ratified. The 15th Amendment, the last of what has become known as the Civil War Amendments, was ratified in 1870. These amendments were passed on the strength of Republican votes over strong objections from Democrats in the South who had supported both slavery and secession. The amendments had been written to protect the rights of Blacks to vote and participate in electoral politics.

A further attempt by the federal government to ensure the civil rights of citizens was enacted on March 3, 1875. This "Enforcement Act" was a federal law passed during the Reconstruction era in response to civil rights violations against African Americans. The Enforcement Act made it a crime for operators of hotels, theaters, and other public accommodations to discriminate based on race. In the Civil Rights Cases (1883), however, the U.S. Supreme Court struck down the law as unconstitutional, holding that Congress did not have the power to enact a broad ban on the actions of private persons or businesses. On October 15, 1883, in an 8–1 decision, the Court ruled that the 13th Amendment prohibited discrimination by state and local governments but not by private individuals or organizations.

From the mid-1870s to the mid-1880s, anti-immigration organizations targeted first Chinese and then other Asian immigrants, whom many whites regarded as competition for jobs and as helping keep wages artificially low. The economic depression known as the Panic of 1873 further spurred white fears of "the Yellow Peril." By 1880, anti-Chinese sentiment was so strong on the West Coast that it became virtual political suicide for any lawmaker to support Chinese immigration.

Congress reacted to the rise of this xenophobic movement by passing the Chinese Exclusion Act of 1879. The 1879 bill was vetoed by President Chester Arthur on the grounds that the law violated the Burlingame-Seward Treaty of 1868. A new treaty was ratified in 1881, however, and Congress subsequently passed what became known as the Chinese Exclusion Act of 1882. Arthur signed that measure, which stopped virtually all Chinese immigration for 10 years and expressly prohibited their naturalization, effectively denying them to right to vote and to participate in American elections.

During the Reconstruction era, the Republican Party became the dominant majority party in the United States. Both the Republican and Democratic parties became more complex during this period, developing grassroots organizations at the precinct level in a growing number of large cities.

The period from the mid-1870s to the mid-1880s also saw the emergence of several third parties. One such party was the American Party (1876–1890), an anti-immigration party that ran candidates for the presidency in 1876, 1880, 1884, and 1888. The agrarian-based Greenback Party (1874–1884) was a single-issue party that opposed the Republican Party's hard-money policies (maintaining the use of gold coins) and advocated the use of paper currency. The Prohibition Party (1869–1884), which focused on the evils of alcohol, ran presidential candidates in 1872, 1876, 1880, and 1884. The Equal Rights Party (1884–1929), founded in San Francisco, advocated suffrage and equal property rights for women. It also supported a moderately protective tariff policy, prohibition of the sale of alcohol, civil service reform, and the sale of homestead lands only to actual settlers (as opposed to land speculators blamed for rising farmland prices). By contrast, the Socialist Party (1876–1890) used naturalized immigrants as its grassroots supporters. First known as the Socialist Labor Party, it fought for labor rights and was strongly anti-capitalist in its ideology.

Arguably the most successful third party of the period was the People's Party (1876–1896), a coalition of farmers, laborers, and middle-class activists who opposed the growing power of corporations over the national economy. It advocated for the direct election of senators as well as voting measures that included the initiative and the referendum. The initiative allows voters to put legislative proposals on the ballot for consideration by the public; if the proposal garners a majority of votes, it becomes law, thereby bypassing the legislature. The referendum is the actual public vote on a proposed law.

During this period, the Democratic Party became a somewhat regional party, benefiting from the resentment that many white Southerners felt for Republicans after the Civil War. The depression of 1873 (then known as the Panic of 1873) helped the Democrats take control of the U.S. House of Representatives from 1874 to 1877. The South became the "solid South," with states of the former Confederacy voting for Democrats in nearly every presidential election from 1880 to 1960. Democrat Grover Cleveland won the White House in 1884 and again in 1892. Cleveland led the Bourbon Democratic wing of the party, a pro-business faction that supported banks, railroads, and other business interests as part of its enthusiasm for *laissez-faire* capitalism (the economic policy or attitude of the abstention by governments from interfering in the workings of the free market). The Democrats, however, were largely blamed for poor economic conditions that allowed the Republican Party to become the dominant majority party during the period.

From Reconstruction to the Progressive Era

Reconstruction came to an end in the highly contested 1876 election. A special electoral commission that was convened due to Electoral College disputes in Florida, Louisiana, South Carolina, and Oregon awarded the presidency to Republican Rutherford B. Hayes, who, as promised, promptly withdrew federal troops from the South. Once the troops left, the states of the former Confederacy became the "Solid South," giving overwhelmingly majorities of Electoral College votes and congressional seats in those states to segregationist Democrats. These white Southerners also passed numerous Jim Crow laws at the state level to keep Blacks from voting and thus preserve their political power.

Meanwhile, the Republican Party, nicknamed the GOP for "Grand Old Party," became divided into various factions, including the stalwarts (who favored the spoils system), the half-breeds (against the spoils system), and the mugwumps (who coalesced around anti-corruption reforms). The mugwumps eventually broke ranks with the party and helped elect Democrat Grover Cleveland in 1884 (Gould 2003). During the Gilded Age (1877–1890), the Republicans became further divided between supporters of Prohibition and "wet

Republicans," who opposed such measures. The wet Republicans included German Americans, a key voting bloc of the party that included many brewers and nationalized German Americans who worked in the brewery industry. The wet Republicans broke ranks with their party in 1892, enabling Cleveland to return once again to the White House.

The Supreme Court further restricted civil rights laws in 1896 with its infamous *Plessy v. Ferguson* decision. *Plessy* established the "separate but equal" doctrine that justified legal segregation and gave legal cover to Jim Crow laws throughout the South. The Jim Crow era was also characterized by shocking levels of violence and intimidation to suppress Black voters from participating in elections at local, state, and even the national levels.

The 1896 election of Republican William McKinley to the White House set the stage for what many political scientists and historians refer to as the Progressive Era. Historians differ on the actual years of the Progressive Era, with end dates ranging from 1920 all the way to 1932. But scholars do agree that the Progressive Era was one driven by major social and political reforms.

Ten domestic issues were central to the Progressive Era: (1) regulation of the railroads and large corporations; (2) the gold standard versus silver as the base for American currency; (3) the degree to which the protective tariff was employed; (4) the role of labor unions and child labor; (5) the need for a new banking system; (6) reform of corrupt party politics through such structural reforms as primary elections, the direct election of senators, the initiative, and the referendum; (7) reducing or ending racial segregation; (8) government efficiency and civil service reform; (9) women's suffrage; and (10) control of immigration.

The dominant political leaders of the Progressive Era were Republican presidents William McKinley (who served from 1896–1901) and Theodore Roosevelt (1901–1908), and Democrat president Woodrow Wilson (1912–1920). Two other notable progressive leaders were unsuccessful candidates for the presidency: three-time Democratic candidate William Jennings Bryan and Wisconsin's Progressive Republican senator Robert La Follette (Sanders 1999).

One of the crowning achievements of the Progressive movement came in 1920, when the 19th Amendment was ratified, giving women the right to vote. On September 22, 1922, Congress passed the Cable Act, which restored citizenship to women who had married noncitizen husbands (the anti-immigrant Expatriation Act of 1907 had previously stripped such women of their U.S. citizenship). The provisions of the Cable Act, however, did not restore citizenship to women who married foreigners who were legally prohibited from becoming U.S. citizens—namely, Asian immigrants. In *Ozawa v. United States* (260 U.S. 178, 1922), the Court ruled that the law banning Japanese immigrants from naturalization was constitutional. In *United States v. Bhagat Singh Thind* (261 U.S. 204, 1923) the Supreme Court ruled that a "free white person"—someone who would qualify for citizenship—referred to individuals who *looked* white. Although East Indians are Caucasian, because of their dark skin they were not thought to look white and therefore could not naturalize.

On June 4, 1924, Congress passed the Act of June 4, "Citizenship for Noncitizen Indians." Noncitizenship Indians were Native American Indians who were living off-reservations. It was passed in recognition of their service in World War I. In 1935, Congress passed the Act of June 24 that allowed for naturalization of aliens who were veterans of World War I, explicitly granting citizenship to Asian veterans.

Great Depression Ushers in New Political Era

A stock market crash in 1929 led to a most severe economic depression in U.S. history—known as the Great Depression—during which time as many as one out of four members of the labor force could not find work. The election of Democrat Franklin Delano Roosevelt as president in 1932 and his overwhelming reelection in 1936 were considered realigning elections. Roosevelt's presidency led to the establishment of a recognizably modern bureaucracy and the introduction of an ambitious set of national welfare and economic programs collectively known as the New Deal.

The Great Depression and the Roosevelt administration's New Deal response to that economic pain and turmoil produced a new coalition of voting blocs that gave Roosevelt unprecedented dominance. His election ended the majority status of the Republican Party and broadened the popularity of his own Democratic Party. Roosevelt's years in the White House signaled a realignment of voting groups that reshaped the political landscape, redefining American liberalism and conservatism in the process (Safire 1978). For example, Roosevelt's aggressive New Deal reforms and programs kept Democrats happy while also attracting Republican Progressives (James 2000).

Roosevelt's New Deal included such reforms as the Social Security Act of 1935 and the Wagner Act of 1935, which won the firm allegiance of organized labor to the Democratic Party. The Roosevelt administration's urban policies also solidified his standing in America's big cities, especially among Blacks. Blacks voted largely Democratic in 1936 and have done so in consistent numbers ever since. In the meantime, Roosevelt won substantial support from rural farming families and communities with the Rural Electrification Act of 1936, the establishment of the Tennessee Valley Authority, and the introduction of agricultural price supports for struggling ranchers and farmers. All told, the Roosevelt administration enacted 14 major programs between 1933 and 1938 (Freidel 1990).

By 1938, a clear majority of the electorate identified with the Democratic Party and signaled a fundamental shift that reshaped American life, forming an enduring political coalition tied to activist and expansive central government that lasted for decades. Roosevelt also greatly expanded presidential executive powers during his years in the White House, and the American public took a more expansive view of what the president could and could not do (Barone 1990; Freidel 1990).

Voting Reforms amid Political Change

During the 1960s, America's voting and election laws were transformed by the civil rights movement, which sought to break down racial discrimination and segregation that was pervasive in many parts of the United States and especially in the South. Congress responded to this pressure by passing the 1960 Civil Rights Act, which banned the poll tax and set up conditions for federal voter registration efforts. That set the stage for the passage of the Civil Rights Act of 1964 and the Civil Rights Act of 1965 (also known as the Voting Rights Act). Those were followed by the Civil Rights Act of 1968, which addressed discrimination in housing and included several provisions collectively known as the Indian Civil Rights Act that expanded voting rights for Native American Indians.

In 1968, the Vietnam War divided the nation. Richard Nixon won the Republican nomination, and the Democrats were so deeply divided over the war and civil rights issues that Nixon won the presidency although the Democrats retained control of Congress. Southern Democrats had so abandoned the Democratic Party that Nixon's "southern strategy" gradually shifted the region to be the "Solid South" for Republicans in national, especially presidential, electoral politics. Nixon's southern strategy was to make a special effort to attract white Southerners upset with the national Democratic Party's support for African American civil rights policies. The GOP's southern strategy proved effective over the course of decades, and even working-class whites who had benefited from Democratic economic policies increasingly shifted their allegiance to the Republican Party.

Nixon won the 1972 election in a landslide, but a corruption scandal forced Vice President Spiro Agnew to resign, and Nixon appointed Representative Gerald Ford (R, MI) as vice president. The Watergate scandal forced Nixon to resign the presidency, and Ford pardoned him. That unpopular pardon, the corruption of the Nixon administration, and a high rate of inflation coupled with an economic recession enabled the Democrats to win back the White House in 1976 with Georgia governor Jimmy Carter.

The economy continued to struggle during Carter's presidency, however, and foreign policy setbacks such as the Iran hostage crisis (in which Iranian militants held more than 50 American diplomats and citizens captive for 444 days) and the Soviet invasion of Afghanistan damaged the Carter White House as well. When Carter ran for reelection in 1980, he was easily defeated by California's Republican governor, Ronald Reagan.

The 1980 election was another transformative one, but this time it led to a period of conservative ascendancy. Reagan's landslide election victories in 1980 and 1984 marked a realignment of American voting patterns and allegiances. He won over voters who came to be known as "Reagan Democrats," drawn to his social conservatism on issues such as abortion, and his anti-communism foreign policy. Those largely white, blue-collar voters remained Republican voters through the Bush presidencies. Meanwhile, Black voters increased their support for Democrats throughout the Reagan years and beyond.

In 1992, the Democrats reclaimed the White House when Arkansas governor Bill Clinton and his running mate, Tennessee senator Al Gore, defeated incumbent Republican president George H. W. Bush and vice president Dan Quayle. Clinton won reelection comfortably in 1996. In 2000, Republican governor George W. Bush (son of former president George H. W. Bush), of Texas, defeated Gore in a highly disputed election that ended only after the U.S. Supreme Court sided with Bush in *Bush v. Gore* (531 U.S. 98, 2000). The Court's controversial decision gave the Electoral College edge to Bush, who lost the popular vote to Gore.

In 1993, Congress passed the National Voter Registration Act—also known as the "Motor Voter" Act—which allowed for people to register to vote when they obtained their motor vehicle license. Making it easier to register to vote increased the number of eligible voters and produced a slight increase in voter turnout in subsequent elections, which traditionally has been viewed as benefiting the Democrats.

In 2008, Democratic presidential nominee Barack Obama defeated GOP nominee John McCain to become America's first Black president. Obama won 95 percent of Black men and 96 percent of Black women, who constituted 13 percent of the electorate that year. He lost the white vote overall, but he carried 54 percent of white voters in the 18–29 age bracket, 67 percent of the Hispanic vote (then nearly 10 percent of the electorate), 62 percent of the Asian American vote, and 79 percent of the Jewish vote. Obama rode a similar coalition to reelection in 2012, when he defeated Republican nominee Mitt Romney.

Republican Donald Trump won the presidency in 2016, garnering 306 Electoral College votes to Hillary Clinton's 232 (270 Electoral College votes are necessary to win). He did this despite losing the popular vote by about three million votes (46.2 percent of all legal ballots cast, compared to Clinton's 48.3 percent). Trump performed best among senior voters, men, and white voters without a college education.

Trump and Vice President Mike Pence were defeated for reelection in 2020 by the Democratic ticket of Joe Biden and Kamala Harris, who won states totaling 306 Electoral College votes. Biden and Harris also won the popular vote by more than seven million, tallying 51.3 percent of the vote compared to 46.8 percent for Trump-Pence. Trump and his allies repeatedly made false claims that the results showed widespread voter fraud, but they never presented any evidence in support of these assertions in dozens of court cases challenging elections in the swing states and ultimately dismissed for lack of evidence.

The results of the 2020 presidential election showed that the two tickets and their parties had decisive strengths and major weaknesses among various subgroups of the voting public. Exit polls indicated that Biden won 60 percent of the votes among 18- to 29-year-old voters and 52 percent among the 30- to 44-year-old voters; whereas Trump narrowly won among the 45- to 64-year-old voters, 50 percent to 49 percent, and won the 65+ age voters 52 percent to 47 percent. The exit polls categorizing respondents by race showed that Trump won 58 percent of white voters, but Biden won 89 percent of Black voters, 65 percent of Latino voters, 61 percent of Asian voters, and 55 percent among "other" race voters. In terms of area type, Biden won the urban vote 60 percent to 38 percent and the suburban vote by 50 percent to 48 percent, but Trump won among the rural vote, 57 percent to 42 percent. The election results also confirmed the continued existence of a decisive gender gap between the two parties, with Biden getting 55 percent of the women's vote but only 48 percent of the men's vote.

These election results demonstrate that the United States now has two ideologically distinct political parties: a liberal Democratic Party and a conservative Republican Party that is undergoing a marked shift to populist nationalism.

Elections at the State Level

The administration of elections is highly decentralized. Primary responsibility for the *administration* of elections lies at the county or city/town level, but state and federal election *laws* govern many aspects of those elections.

As a result, no two states administer elections in precisely the same way, and there is considerable variation even within states. An important historical factor influencing how states organize and administer their elections is the date on which each state joined the Union (see table 5.1). Elections within the 13 original states were administered by county officials and were not time-consuming affairs. Several states allowed noncitizens to vote in local elections. Voters were not required to register in advance, and voting was often done by voice rather than paper ballots. After the late 1880s, elections became more complex, with the adoption of voter registration and the move from ballots provided by political parties to secret ballots provided by election officials. Those changes required additional preparation and resources, and with the widespread adoption of voting machines in major urban centers in the 1930s and 1940s, the state election officials had to provide for required maintenance and storage.

State legislatures began to formalize election policy in statute to provide greater uniformity within the states. State election offices had to interpret increasingly complex procedures and manage growing technological needs. Each state's elections grew organically as the administration of elections became an increasingly complex task (Hale, Montjoy, and Brown 2015; NCSL 2022).

Currently, the administration of elections in any given state is the responsibility of a chief election official (see table 5.2). Twenty-four states have an elected secretary of state as the chief election official. Two states have an elected lieutenant governor as their chief election official. Three states have a chief election official appointed by the state legislature. In five states, the chief election official is appointed by the governor. Nine states use a board or commission to oversee elections, with their members appointed by the governor and confirmed by the state senate, and structured to be bipartisan, with some members selected by the two major political parties. Finally, seven states use a combination of a chief election official and a board or commission.

The duties of the chief election official or officials typically include the following: ballot design and coding, sending out mail ballots, certifying candidates, overseeing the procurement and maintenance of voting equipment and precinct tabulators, the delivery of them to each city/town before the elections, troubleshooting technical issues on Election Day, and the receiving and final (official) tabulation and certification of statewide results (NCSL 2022).

The state office of elections ensures that election laws are followed by local officials, administers the statewide voter registration database, aids local election officials by providing training courses, provides materials on running elections in the state, and provides for the testing and certification of voting equipment. Some state offices provide certification programs for local election officials on procedures and may pay for a portion of the expenses for certain types of elections.

As elections have become more complex and reliant on technology, statewide election officials have professionalized and become more like information technology (IT) managers. States and various other organizations provide training and support for election officials. Every state office provides some level of support to local officials, from publishing election-law digests to training of volunteers to full certification programs. Most states are equipped with a statewide association of election officials that meet to discuss election procedures and advocate for them in the state legislature.

The U.S. Election Assistance Commission serves as a national clearinghouse of information on election administration and provides resources to election officials, including election management guidelines, webinars, best-practices guidelines, and forums for local election officials. The Election Center of the National Association of Election Officials conducts conferences, workshops, and seminars and runs the Certification of Elections/Registration Administrator program with faculty from Auburn University's public administration program. Likewise, the University of Minnesota's Humphrey School of Public Affairs provides an online certification program in election administration.

The National Association of Secretaries of State and the National Association of State Election Directors provide forums for state election officials to exchange information and best practices. The International Association of Government Officials is a newly established organization that merged the International Association of Clerks, Recorders, Election

Officials and Treasurers with the National Association of County Recorders, Election Officials and Clerks. It holds special events and provides information in support of local election officials (NCSL 2022).

There is quite a variety of elected state constitutional offices, each of which is elected in a statewide race and most commonly on a partisan basis. The most common statewide office is the state chief executive, or governor. This elected office can be found in all 50 states and in the five U.S. territories (American Samoa, Guam, Northern Mariana Islands, Puerto Rico, and the U.S. Virgin Islands). Other statewide offices that exist in at least one state are lieutenant governors (in 47 states), attorneys general (46 states), state treasurers (36), secretaries of state (35), state auditors/comptrollers (34), state superintendents of public education (13), agriculture commissioners (12), insurance commissioners (10), labor commissioners (4), land commissioners (4), tax commissioner (1), and inspector of mines (1) (USA.gov 2021).

State Governorships

Gubernatorial elections are statewide elections to select the governor of a state as the state's chief executive officer. All 50 states hold gubernatorial elections, but the frequency and timing of elections vary from state to state. Two states (Vermont and New Hampshire) hold gubernatorial elections every two years, while the other 48 hold them every four years. Five states purposely elect their governors in off-presidential years: Kentucky, Louisiana, Mississippi, New Jersey, and Virginia. Kentucky, Louisiana, and Mississippi hold their gubernatorial elections in the year before a presidential election, and New Jersey and Virginia do so in the year after a presidential election. These stipulations reflected the political culture in those states at the time they were imposed. Supporters of off-year gubernatorial elections held that it was important for state's rights and policy independence to hold their elections in off-years specifically to avoid the "presidential coattails effect." In

36 states, governors are limited to two consecutive terms. As of 2021, there were 22 states with Democratic governors and 28 with Republican governors.

The state governor is both the head of the state and the head (chief executive) of the state's executive branch. Governors manage the state's bureaucratic agencies and departments, except those headed by a state constitutional office. In part because of their political visibility and name recognition, the office of governor has often been used as a stepping-stone to a run for president, and governors of large states with presidential ambitions often tout their administrative and problem-solving experience as governor as an important qualification for the White House.

Secretaries of state commonly have responsibilities in addition to the management of elections. They may administer business filings and licensing, for example, and commonly act as keeper of the state seal. They often enforce state campaign regulations. Since winning election to one of the state constitutional offices gives that officer a degree of statewide visibility, the offices of lieutenant governor, attorney general, and secretary of state are quite often used as stepping-stones to the state governorship or to national-level elective office in the U.S. House of Representatives or U.S. Senate.

Until the 2020 presidential election, voting officials carried out most of their responsibilities without incident, and determining election results was routine and noncontroversial. President Trump's unfounded assertion that the 2020 election was "stolen" from him has raised those offices of election officials to a level of partisan political controversy. In 2021, state legislatures controlled by Republicans proposed dozens of bills to curtail the authority of those election officials to certify election results, shifting the power or authority to do so to the state legislature. Republican elected officials in those states justify those laws or proposals as necessary to ensure election integrity, but Democratic critics point out that voter fraud is virtually nonexistent in American elections. They contend that such bills and laws are clearly intended as devices for voter suppression targeted at racial and ethnic minorities and young voters, who are more likely to support Democratic candidates.

A Brennan Center report on such state voting proposals found that as of late March 2021, legislators have introduced 361 bills with restrictive provisions in 47 states. These measures have begun to be enacted. Five restrictive bills have been signed into law, and 55 restrictive bills are moving through state legislatures. Twenty-nine bills have passed at least one chamber. Another 26 bills have had some sort of committee action (for example, a hearing, an amendment, or a committee vote). Since the 2020 election and as of September 2021, 19 states have passed 33 laws making it harder to vote. For example, Texas, Florida, Georgia, and Iowa bundled new voting restrictions into omnibus bills; Arkansas, Montana, Texas, and Arizona passed multiple laws to restrict voting; seven states imposed tougher voter identification requirements to cast ballots; and seven states shortened the time to apply for mail-in ballots. By contrast, however, 25 states enacted 62 laws expanding voting access during that same period (Brennan Center for Justice 2021).

The number of state-elected officials across the country is large, running into the thousands. For example, a study in 2012 found there were 7,382 state legislators, 10,036 statewide elected offices, and 1,331 state board or commission elected officials across the United States (Lawless 2012).

Elections at the Local Level

In the United States, there are more than 10,000 election jurisdictions, ranging from small towns of a few hundred voters to the County of Los Angeles, with more than 4.7 million voters—an election district with a population that is larger than the populations of 25 individual states. Throughout most of the nation, elections are run at the county level, and in New England and some midwestern states, elections are also administered by cities and townships. Local elections are typically run by a single individual, a board or commission of elections, or a combination to the two (see table 5.3).

Twenty-two states have local-level elections that are administered by a single election official, most often elected but varying within those states, usually by population size. For example, in Nebraska, counties with fewer than 20,000 in population elect their election official, while counties of 20,000 to 100,000 in population have an election official appointed by the county board, and counties with populations of more than 100,000 have an election official appointed by the governor (NCSL 2022). Other states have individual election administrators in most jurisdictions but maintain election boards for large cities. Most counties have an elected official to administer elections (frequently the county clerk). In large cities, the election administrator or supervisor bears sole responsibility for elections, but in smaller and medium-sized counties, the county clerk, recorder, registrar, assessor, or auditor (or controller) may serve as the election official in addition to fulfilling other county duties.

Ten states use a board of elections for the primary responsibilities of local election administration. Such boards of elections are most often bipartisan, and their members are either appointed at the state level, at the local level, or, in the case of Kentucky, by a combination of the two. Such boards have input from the two major political parties. In 18 states, the administration of elections is divided between two or more offices (see table 5.3). In Arkansas, for example, the county clerk runs the day-to-day operations for registration and voting, including both absentee and early voting, while a three-member county board (one each appointed by the two major parties and one by a state board of elections) deals with election-day procedures, appointment of election officials, delivering supplies to the various polling places, counting ballots, and canvassing the returns (Hale, Montjoy, and Brown 2015; NCSL 2022).

Chief executives at the local level, for example an elected county executive and elected mayors of large cities, are almost always elected through partisan ballots. These offices are frequently used as stepping-stones from which to campaign for state governor or another statewide elective office. In a few instances, mayors have even used their office as launching pads to seek their party's presidential nomination. For example, during their mayoral terms, both Bill de Blasio (New York City) and Pete Buttigieg (South Bend, Indiana) sought the Democratic Party's 2020 nomination for president.

The sheer number of local elected officials exceeded 500,000 in 2012. That total included 135,531 municipal government officials, 126,931 town or township officials, 58,818 county officials, 95,000 school district officials, and 84,089 special district officials (Lawless 2012). That comes to a staggering number of campaigns when one realizes that most of those offices have multiple candidates running in the elections.

Expansion of the Franchise by Law, Practice, and Court Decisions

Expansion of the Franchise in America's First 100 Years

What the above historical discussion illustrates is that in American politics, the right to vote has steadily expanded over time, but that progress has not occurred without setbacks. In fact, America's political parties have at various points in time during the history of the United States adopted a range of attitudes and positions on voting rights.

During the founding era, the franchise was constitutionally limited to free white men who were property-holders—probably less than 10 percent of the population. The total U.S. population in 1790 was just under four million, most of whom were descendants from 17th- and 18th-century arrivals or recent immigrants. Among them, about 75 percent were of British origin, with roughly 8 percent of German origin, a smattering of Dutch, French, and Spanish origin, and about a half-million Black slaves or Native Americans. The U.S. Congress passed the first naturalization law in 1790. The clause stating that only "free white men who were property owners" could vote was included to ensure that emancipation would not necessitate the naturalization of freed slaves.

Most leaders in the early decades of the republic thought that a multiracial society was not practical, and a good number of them were slave owners with deeply held racist beliefs about the intellectual and moral endowments of nonwhites. After the American Revolution, most states retained the power to establish standards for voting rights. As a result, white Anglo-Saxon Protestant male property owners over the age of 21 were the only Americans allowed to vote. In republican logic, especially among the Federalists, an economic stake in society—as represented by ownership of property—was necessary for a person to be trusted to vote wisely.

The election of Thomas Jefferson as president in 1800 resulted in a change in the naturalization law that had originally been enacted by the Federalists. Jefferson and his allies changed the immigrant waiting period for naturalization—and thereby the right to vote—from 14 years to 5 years. The Jefferson administration also negotiated the Louisiana Purchase in 1803. This acquisition from France more than doubled U.S. territory and added many new citizens to the young nation's voting rolls. Congress passed naturalization laws in 1804 and 1813 that dealt with widows and the children of immigrants. A separate bill passed in 1824 to naturalize minors who arrived in the United States unaccompanied by adults (often because their parents died during the passage to America).

Property requirements for voting were gradually abolished, and economic status disappeared as an obstacle to citizenship—but only for white men. For example, in 1807, New Jersey revised its state constitution to abolish property requirements for voting—but still prevented all women, even wealthy ones, as well as all free Blacks from voting. New York acted similarly in 1821. By 1840, more than 90 percent of adult white men possessed the right to vote.

In 1848, the Treaty of Guadalupe Hidalgo was signed, ending the Mexican-American War and greatly expanding U.S. territory again. Like the Louisiana Purchase, this treaty added Mexicans who had been living in Texas and other annexed territory to the rolls of American citizens. This action added to the expansion of the franchise in a significant way, as many of the native white Anglo-Saxon citizenry considered Mexicans to be nonwhite, inferior, and not worthy of citizenship and voting (LeMay and Barkan 1999, 25–26).

Between 1840 and 1850, many of the country's newer states experienced significant growth in their populations, as immigrants and native-born Americans from the already-settled East headed west in search of cheap land and new lives. For example, Arkansas's population more than doubled—from just over 87,000 in 1840 to more than 200,000 in 1850; Michigan grew from under 213,000 in 1840 to nearly 400,000 in 1850; Wisconsin expanded from less than 31,000 in 1840 to more than 300,000 in 1850; Iowa had 43,000 in 1840 and grew to more than 192,000 in 1850 (Zentner and LeMay 2020, 55).

In 1855, Congress passed a law granting citizenship to married women. While it did not expand the vote immediately, it added to those potentially able to vote after it passed the 19th Amendment (LeMay and Barkan 1999, 27–28). Another act that expanded the pool of eligible voters was the Homestead Act of 1862. It was an important inducement of immigrants to settle in the "frontier" states. Many if not most of those immigrants could naturalize after five years, thereby expanding America's ranks of voters. That same year Congress enacted a law granting naturalization—and thus voting rights—to honorably discharged soldiers from the Civil War. Literally tens of thousands of German-born and Irish-born immigrants who had not yet been naturalized served with distinction in the war, often in units such as the famed "Irish Brigade." Men who earned the right to vote in this manner were sometimes said to have gained "citizenship by fire." The 1862 law granting citizenship to honorably discharged immigrant soldiers set a precedent, and similar laws have been passed for U.S. military service in every war or military engagement since the Civil War.

Triumphs and Setbacks in Voting Rights since the Civil War

As stated before, following the Civil War, the 14th Amendment was ratified. In February 1870, the 15th Amendment was ratified, granting Congress the power to enforce it. The amendment effectively ended the "free white" clause in the Constitution. In decisions such as *Ozawa v. United States* (1922) and *U.S. v. Bhagat Singh Thind* (1923), however, the U.S. Supreme Court held the amendment's authority applied only to federal government actions and federal elections. Southern states subsequently enacted laws such Jim Crow laws as the poll tax, literacy tests, and grandfather clauses. When the Supreme Court issued its *Plessy v. Ferguson* (1896) decision establishing the judicial doctrine of "separate but equal" racial segregation, it effectively gave its blessing to Jim Crow laws designed to enforce segregation in the South and suppress Black voting. These laws were ruthlessly enforced in the South for many decades until the civil rights movement of the 1950s and 1960s finally tore them down.

In 1919, Congress enacted a law (H.R. 5007) that among its provisions granted citizenship to certain honorably discharged Native Americans who had served in World War I. In 1924, Congress passed the Indian Citizenship Act, which extended voting rights to Native Americans born in the United States. Despite its passage, however, some states continued to bar Native Americans from voting in state elections.

Another impactful extension of the franchise came with the August 18, 1920, ratification of the 19th Amendment granting American women the right to vote. For many years after this momentous law was passed, the turnout rates for women in elections were less than that of men, but that gradually changed. Today, the election turnout rate for women is higher than it is for men.

In the Act of December 17, 1943, and in recognition of China's alliance with the United States against the Japanese in World War II, Congress enacted the Magnuson Act. This law repealed the Chinese Exclusion Act, which had since 1882 barred Chinese immigrants from becoming naturalized citizens. Through this act, Chinese immigrants and their American-born families became the first Asian Americans eligible to naturalize and gain citizenship and, thereby, the right to vote.

In 1952, Congress passed, over the veto of President Harry Truman, the McCarran-Walter Act. It was significant for Asian American voter rights in that it eliminated the racial ban to citizenship of the Issei—Japanese immigrants to the United States. The Japanese American Citizens League (JACL) was instrumental in assuring passage of the act and Congress's override of Truman's veto. President Truman had vetoed the bill because it did not go far enough in revising immigration law. He had wanted Congress to end the quota system entirely.

In 1961, the 23rd Amendment was ratified, allowing American citizens living in the District of Columbia to vote for president and vice president. Prior to its passage, DC residents could only vote for those offices if they were registered to vote in another state. In 1964, the 24th Amendment was ratified, prohibiting the use of poll taxes in federal elections.

By far the most significant voting rights act was the Civil Rights Act of 1965 (79 Stat. 437). Signed into law in August 1965, it banned the use of literacy tests and expanded the reach of the 15th Amendment to state and local governments. It authorized federal examiners to register voters in certain jurisdictions that had demonstrated a pattern of discrimination against Black voters. The U.S. Supreme Court upheld the law against a flurry of legal challenges in 1965, 1969, and 1970.

In 1971, the 26th Amendment was ratified, granting the right to vote to U.S. citizens 18 or older (from 21) and prohibiting discrimination based on age. It was enacted in response to the fact that 18-, 19-, and 20-year-old American men were fighting and dying in Vietnam yet they would not even be able to vote in their country's elections.

The Voting Rights Act of 1975 (89 Stat. 400) was signed into law by President Gerald Ford. In addition to establishing a permanent ban on literacy tests and other discriminatory voting requirements used by some state and local governments, the law required districts with significant numbers of non-English-speaking voters to provide those voters with instructions in their native language or assistance in registering and voting.

In June 1982, President Ronald Reagan signed a law extending the Voting Rights Act for another 25 years. In September 1984, Congress passed the Voting Accessibility for the Elderly and Handicapped Act (42 U.S. C. 197), and President Ronald Reagan signed it into law. The act made it easier for people with disabilities and the elderly to register and to vote by providing that if no accessible location is available, an alternative way to vote on Election Day must be offered by states and localities administering elections. Six years later, the Americans with Disabilities Act (ADA) was passed into law, extending civil rights protections to people with disabilities that tens of millions of other Americans already enjoyed. Title II of the ADA specifically requires state and local governments to ensure that people with disabilities have a full and equal opportunity to vote. ADA protections apply to all aspects of voting, including voter registration, poll site selection, and the casting of ballots.

In May 1993, Congress passed the National Voter Registration Act, the aforementioned "motor voter" law (107 Stat. 77). It required state motor vehicle agencies to offer voter registration and for states to offer residents mail-in voter registration applications. It also included provisions mandating states to maintain current and accurate voter registration lists and give legal residents opportunities to register to vote at certain state and local offices. Its impact was significant and immediately apparent when, in the first year after its enactment, more than 30 million voters updated or completed their registration.

In October 2002, Congress passed the Help America Vote Act (HAVA) (116 Stat. 1666), signed into law by President George W. Bush. It mandated that the U.S. Election Assistance Commission improve and certify voting requirements, maintain a National Voter Registration form, and administer a national elections clearinghouse to share election "best practices" with the states. It also provided states with funds to meet the new standards and provisions of the law.

In 2010, the U.S. Supreme Court issued a 5–4 decision in *Citizens United v. FEC* that struck down numerous longstanding campaign finance restrictions in American law. The ruling from the Court's conservative majority gave a green light for rich corporations, trade associations, labor unions, and other outside interest groups to spend unlimited funds on American elections in the name of "free speech." According to the decision's many critics, *Citizens United v. FEC* further increased the influence of powerful corporations and other interest groups in American politics at the expense of ordinary voters. "In a time of historic wealth inequality," stated a report from the Brennan Center for Justice, "the decision has helped reinforce the growing sense that our democracy primarily serves the interests of the wealthy few, and that democratic participation for the vast majority of citizens is of relatively little value" (Weiner 2015).

Finally, in 2013, the Supreme Court struck down major provisions of the Voting Rights Act in *Shelby County v. Holder*. Decided in a 5–4 vote along partisan lines, the majority held that certain sections of the Voting Rights Act mandating that states with a well-documented history of discrimination toward voters of color receive federal approval before making changes to their voting procedures were unconstitutional. The conservative Court majority held that those "preclearance" provisions were outdated. The ruling affected nine states and several counties and townships. The ruling was bitterly criticized by voting rights activists, who predicted that the loss of these voting protections would bring a flood of new voting restrictions across the country that would disproportionately impact minority voters. As feared, Republican-led states across the country have enacted new voting laws that have closed polling places in communities of color, imposed new voter ID laws, limited early voting and mail-in voting, and imposed other measures that disproportionately impact minority voters (who are more likely to vote for Democratic candidates).

Types of Elections

General elections in the United States are held at all levels of government (local, county, state, and congressional district). They are held at set or regularly scheduled times (spring or fall; annually or in cycles every two or four years).

At the national level, general elections are held every two years for every seat in the U.S. House of Representatives and for one-third of the seats in the U.S. Senate (senators are elected for six-year terms, so only one out of three Senate seats are contested in any given election year). They are held in the fall on the first Tuesday in November. Every four years, also in the fall, a general election is held for the offices of president and vice president. These general elections are also referred to as presidential election years (as distinguished from midterm elections when the positions of president and vice president are not on the ballot).

In the United States, general elections use a plurality system in which the candidate who polls more votes than any other candidate is elected to that office. Plurality systems are distinguished from the majority system, in which to win, a candidate must receive more than half of all votes cast.

Primary elections in the United States are elections held by political parties to select candidates to run for public office in a subsequent general election. They are also held at regular intervals, typically several months before the upcoming general elections. Primary elections may be one of several types (see table 5.4). They may be closed (partisan), in which case only declared party members can vote. Other primaries are open (nonpartisan), which means that all voters, whether or not they formally belong to the party in question, may participate in the vote. For example, in a closed Democratic primary, only declared members of the Democratic Party can vote in the primary. But in an open primary, voters who are Republican or unaligned with either major party can also participate.

Primaries, which are administered by public officials at public expense, may be direct or indirect. A direct primary, now used in some form in all 50 states, functions as a preliminary election by which voters decide their party's candidates. They are the most common form of primary. The first direct primaries were used as early as the 1840s, but the primary system came into general use in the early 20th century. By 1917, all but four states had adopted the direct primary. Success in the early primaries, such as in New Hampshire, gives a candidate a significant advantage in garnering publicity and party campaign funding. Failure in the early primaries can doom a campaign.

In an indirect primary, the voters elect delegates who thereafter choose the party's candidates at a subsequent nominating convention. Primary elections have developed over time to replace the caucus/convention method for selecting a party's candidates for office. Indirect primaries for the presidency are used in many states. Voters select delegates who attend the national political convention of their party and are bound or pledged to cast their ballots based on the preferences expressed by the voters in their state. Such delegates are bound only for one convention ballot or until they are released by the candidate. In several states, the presidential preference vote is advisory only and does not bind the delegates.

The rules for selecting delegates are determined by the political parties and vary by state. Some delegates are selected by a winner-take-all process, as in many Republican Party state primaries. As the name implies, in winner-take-all primaries, the candidate who wins the most votes also wins all the delegates to the national nominating convention.

In proportional representation primaries, more commonly used in Democratic Party primaries, any candidate receiving a percentage of the votes above some predetermined threshold is entitled to at least one delegate. That process makes it harder for a candidate to build a landslide out of a series of narrow primary victories. Because of the difference in how the two parties award delegates, it usually takes longer for a clear front-runner to emerge in Democratic presidential contests. Prior to 2016, and often used since the 1980s, the Democratic Party designated and used "superdelegates," a group of unelected and unpledged delegates that typically included members of the Democratic National Committee, Democratic governors, and Democratic members of the U.S. House of Representatives and the U.S. Senate. Political criticism of that process led to rule changes in 2018 to limit the number and influence of superdelegates.

Caucuses were used in colonial times for local offices and for some time into the 19th century for state- and national-level offices. They declined in popularity in the 20th century, and since 2000, only a few states and territories continue to use the caucus system in selecting party candidates (see table 5.4).

The merits of the open versus the closed primary are debated. Proponents of open primaries argue that voters should be able to choose which primary they will vote in, for each election. They also assert that by allowing independents and even members of the opposing party to participate, open primaries can be useful tool in gradually expanding the party. Party organizations, however, often prefer the closed primary system, arguing it promotes party unity and keeps those with no allegiance to the party from having a voice in determining the party candidate. They claim that with closed primaries, they don't have to worry about members of a rival party (party X) "crossing over" to vote for the weakest general election candidate in party Y's primary. Some states have adopted variations (partially closed or partially open, as detailed in table 5.4). Washington, for example, used a blanket primary that enabled voters to select one candidate per office irrespective of party affiliation, with the top vote getter in each party then advancing to the general election. The Ninth Circuit Court of Appeals ruled, in 2003, that Washington's primary was unconstitutional in that it violated a political party's First Amendment right to freedom of association. The state responded with a modified blanket system in which voters could select one candidate per office, with the top two vote getters per office irrespective of party affiliation advancing to the general election. In 2010, California voters approved an initiative for the state to adopt a "top two" system like Washington's.

Special elections to the U.S. Congress are required in the event of vacancies (e.g., through death, resignation, or removal from office through impeachment). Depending on the specific state laws governing vacancies, a state can either hold an election for U.S. Senate within the same calendar year or wait until the next regularly scheduled election. Vacancies for the U.S. House of Representatives are filled through special elections.

Table 5.5 details congressional districts that changed parties because of special elections held between 2013 and 2022. Table 5.6 lists all the special elections held between 1986 and 2012.

Waning Parties and Rising Interest Groups in American Elections

In America's first years of existence, there were no nationally organized political parties operating in the country. Caucuses within Congress (and in many of the state legislatures at the time) were informal organizational efforts to recruit and promote candidates for national offices (Aldrich 2012; Epstein 2012; Wilentz 2005). With the rise of mass parties beginning in 1800 and developing particularly after 1828, political parties increasingly controlled the processes to select candidates for office. They shaped campaign messaging, marshaled campaign workers down to the grassroots level, and raised money for candidates. From the U.S. Civil War until the 1940s, political parties were the only game in town, so to speak, when it came to electoral politics.

Meanwhile, several political parties rose and fell in influence over the decades. By the early 20th century, however, the Republican and Democratic parties were firmly ensconced as the nation's two major parties. They have remained in those positions ever since, battling for control of the levers of government at the local, state, and federal levels (Aldrich 2012; Kleppner et al. 1983; Paulson 2007; Rosenof 2003). An apt analogy would be to compare the two major parties to the major television networks during the early years of broadcast television. Just as ABC, CBS, and NBC were the gatekeepers of the national airwaves, the Democratic and Republican Parties were the gatekeepers of American electoral campaigns at nearly every level of government (Wilentz 2005; Witcover 2003).

The major parties recruited candidates, groomed the more successful ones for higher office, organized campaign events, stirred enthusiasm among their followers, recruited and trained campaign volunteers and developed professional campaign staffers, raised money to finance campaigns, and often developed and produced campaign ads and flyers. To be successful as a career politician, any aspiring politician had to be affiliated with a political party.

Between 1800 and 1900, political parties also formed loose coalitions with affiliated or supportive interest-group organizations. The Democratic Party, for example, had the organizational support of labor unions such as the Knights of Labor, the American Federation of Labor, the Congress of Industrial Organizations (and later, the AFL-CIO); Irish ethnic organizations and, later, Italian and Eastern European immigrant groups; Jewish Americans; farmers associated with the Farmers Union; and Roman Catholics. The Republican Party attracted Protestants; farmers organized as the American Farm Bureau Federation, and the National Grange; business groups, such as the National Association of Manufacturers and the U.S.

Chamber of Commerce; and ethnic associations of German Americans and Scandinavians.

By the 1870s and 1880s, both the Democratic Party and the Republican Party developed urban political machines organized down to the precinct level. These machines became adept at running ethnically balanced slates of candidates to appeal especially to the increasingly numerous and diverse immigrant groups (LeMay 1987, 2017). By using tightly controlled caucuses and conventions, the parties dominated the selection of candidates. By using the spoils system, the parties cemented the loyalty of their respective coalitions of interest groups.

The grip on control of the electoral processes held by the two major parties began to slip with the structural reforms promoted by the progressive movement (roughly 1896 to 1920), such as primary elections, the direct election of senators, the initiative, referendum, and recall. These reforms were in some ways an effort to keep voters from casting their allegiance with the short-lived Progressive Party, but they also reflected the fact that both the Democrats and the Republicans had progressive wings active within their respective parties (Gould 1993, 2003; Witcover 2003).

As party control over the elective process loosened, political interest groups developed, spread, diversified, and began to influence party policies and priorities. They eventually formed electoral arms known as political action committees (PACs) to provide money and other support to preferred candidates. As of 2020, there are 1,959 PACs on file with the Federal Elections Commission (FEC). In the 2020 election cycle, those PACs raised collectively more than $1.1 billion and spent more than $292 million (FEC.gov/updates 2021-2022).

The funding of campaigns has always been a highly contested and a hotly controversial issue in U.S. elections (Ackerman 2002; Gierzynski 2011; Lessig 2019; Levinson and Balkin 2019). A PAC is any organization that raises money privately to influence elections (and thereby, public policy), especially at the federal level (FEC.gov 2021). Political action committees can take different forms, including separate segregated funds (SSFs), nonconnected committees, so-called super PACs, and so-called Leadership PACs. SSFs are political committees established and administered by corporations, labor unions, membership organizations, or trade associations. They can solicit contributions only from individuals associated with a connected or sponsoring organization. The money they raise is referred to as a form of "soft" money, which is money from an individual or organization not contributed to a campaign but spent in candidate-specific advertising, or other efforts that benefit that candidate by a group supporting the candidate, but not legally coordinated by the candidate's official campaign. It is less strictly regulated. "Hard money" is money contributed directly to a campaign by an individual or organization. Among the types of political contributions, it is the most strictly regulated.

Nonconnected committees are not sponsored by or connected to any of the SSF entities and are therefore free to solicit funds from the public. Super PACs are technically called independent-expenditure-only political committees. They may receive unlimited contributions from persons, corporations, labor unions, and other PACs for the purpose of campaign expenditures and other independent activity. Since the identities of contributors to super PACs are kept secret, they are unregulated.

A leadership PAC is a political committee that is directly or indirectly established by, financed, maintained, or controlled by a candidate or person holding federal office but is not affiliated with an official or authorized campaign. A leadership PAC may contribute up to $5,000 per election to any federal candidate committee. It is an important tool by which leading politicians in the major parties contribute money to other candidates in their party and thereby curry favor and influence with their beneficiaries.

The first attempt to regulate campaign finance by law was in 1867, but most major legislation to enforce campaign finance has been introduced into Congress, or enacted into law, since 1970. The Federal Election Campaign Act of 1971 (86 Stat. 3) required candidates to disclose the names of persons or organizations that contributed to their campaigns and to regularly file reports on campaign expenditures (Ballotpedia n.d.; Uscode.house.gov, 52 U.S. 301, 1972). The law was amended in 1974 to legally limit the contributions from individuals to $1,000 per campaign, and it banned direct contributions to political campaigns by corporations, trade associations, and labor unions. The law established a public funding plan for presidential primaries and elections and placed a limit of $5,000 per campaign on PACs. It spurred a significant increase in the number of PACs. In 1975, the law established the FEC to administer campaign finance law and banned contributions from foreign nationals.

In 1976, the U.S. Supreme Court heard challenges to the act in the case of *Buckley v. Valeo* (424 U.S. 1). While the decision upheld as constitutional most of the law's provisions, it did find that the mandatory spending limit imposed by the law was an unconstitutional infringement of free speech, as was the limit on campaign spending from an individual's personal funds and the provision that limited independent expenditures by persons and organizations that were supporting but not officially linked to a specific campaign. *Buckley v. Valeo* enabled very wealthy presidential candidates, such as Ross Perot and Steve Forbes, to spend enormous amounts of their own fortunes in support of their own campaigns. (These kinds of campaigns, in which candidates mostly spend their own money, are sometimes referred to as "self-financed" campaigns.) It allowed the use of "soft money" to expand greatly. Likewise, an amendment to the 1971 act passed in 1979 allowed political parties to spend unlimited amounts on "get-out-the-vote" and voter registration drives even if such efforts were done primarily to benefit a particular presidential candidate.

In March 2002, Congress enacted the Bipartisan Campaign Reform Act, better known as the McCain-Feingold Act (116

Stat. 81). It banned local and national political parties from spending soft money and banned national party committees from either accepting or spending soft money, and it increased the limit of contributions from individuals to $2,000. McCain-Feingold banned corporations and unions from directly funding advertisements and banned the use of corporate or union funds that mention a federal candidate within 30 days of a primary election or 60 days of a general election. The law was challenged, but the U.S. Supreme Court upheld most provisions of the law in *McConnell v. FEC* (2003).

Beginning with the 2004 presidential election, many "527 groups" became increasingly active in U.S. elections. A 527 group or organization is an Internal Revenue Service (IRS) designation for a type of political advocacy group such as, "a party, committee, association, fund, or other organization, whether or not incorporated, that is organized primarily for the purpose of directly or indirectly accepting contributions or making expenditures, or both, for an exempt function" (Ballotpedia n.d.). 527 groups receive contributions from individuals or groups and spend the money on issue advocacy. Generally, 527 groups have links to the major parties, although they may not be legally incorporated or coordinating their activities with the parties.

In March 2010, the U.S. Court of Appeals for Washington, DC, issued a ruling that upheld the establishment and constitutionality of super PACs in *SpeechNOW v. FEC.* SpeechNOW is a nonprofit organization formed by individuals to pool shared resources to make independent expenditures with express advocacy (that is, political advertisements uncoordinated with candidates or parties that contain explicit support for the election or defeat of a particular candidate). The ruling greatly accelerated the use of negative ads (FEC.gov 2010).

In April 2014, the Supreme Court ruled 5–4 in *McCutcheon v. FEC* that the aggregate limits for an individual's contributions to $48,600 in any one election cycle was unconstitutional under the First Amendment. The ruling was one in a string of contentious decisions striking down limits on campaign contributions (FEC.gov 2014).

Campaign finance reform remains highly controversial. Critics argue that our democracy is broken and that the corruption and excessive spending on campaigns have been spurred on by dark money allowed by the U.S. Supreme Court's 2010 decision in *Citizens United v. FEC* (Ackerman 2002; Lessig 2011, 2019; Levinson and Balkin 2019). Since that decision, the political reform group United for the People and other critics have called for the passage of a constitutional amendment that would finally place meaningful limits on political and campaign spending by powerful corporations, industry groups, individuals, and other organizations. That proposed solution, however, has been heavily criticized by observers such as the libertarian think tank Cato Institute, which argues that such an amendment would give Congress unchecked power over spending on political speech (Jayapal.house.gov. 2021; Cato Institute 2013).

Bibliography

Ackerman, Bruce. 2002. *Voting with Dollars*. New Haven, CT: Yale University Press.

Aldrich, John. 2012. *Why Parties? A Second Look*. Chicago: University of Chicago Press.

American Civil Liberties Union. n.d. *The Constitution of the United States of America*. Washington, DC: American Civil Liberties Union.

Annenberg Classroom. n.d. "Civil Rights Act of 1875 Declared Unconstitutional." Accessed April 22, 2021. https://www.annenbergclassroom.org/timeline_events/civil_rights_act_of_1875_declared_unconstitutional.

Ballotpedia. n.d. "Federal Elections Campaign Act of 1971." Accessed February 23, 2022. https://ballotpedia.org/Federal_Campaign_finance_laws_and_regulations#FederalCampaign_Act_of_1971.

Barone, Michael. 1990. *Our Country: The Shaping of America from Roosevelt to Reagan*. New York: The Free Press.

Bass, Harold. 2000. *Historical Dictionary of United States Political Parties*. New York: Scarecrow Press.

Bowen, Michael. 2011. *The Roots of Modern Conservatism*. Chapel Hill: University of North Carolina Press.

Brennan Center for Justice. 2021. "State Voting Bills Tracker 2021." Accessed April 25, 2021. https://www.brennancenter.org/our-work/research-reports/state-voting-bills-tracker-2021.

Brown, Mitchell, Kathleen Hale, and Bridget King, eds. 2019. *The Future of Election Administration: Cases and Conversations*. London and New York: Palgrave Macmillan.

Cato Institute. 2013, April 23. "Move to Defend: The Case Against the Constitutional Amendments Seeking to Overturn Citizens United." *Policy Analysis*, no. 724. Accessed May 12, 2021. https://www.cato.org/sites/cato.org/files/pubs/pdf/pa724_web.pdf.

Clubb, Jerome M., William Flanagan, and Nancy Zingale. 1990. *Partisan Realignment: Voters, Parties, and Government in American History*. Berkeley Hills, CA: Sage.

Congressional Quarterly Press. 2009. *National Party Conventions, 1831–2008*. Washington, DC: Congressional Quarterly Press.

Epstein, David. 2012. *Left, Right, Out: A History of Third Parties in America*. London: Arts and Imperium Press.

FEC.gov. 2010. Accessed May 3, 2022. https;//www.fec.gov/updates/speechnow.org-v-fec-appeals-court.

FEC.gov. 2014. Accessed May 3, 2022. https://www.fec.gov/legal-resources/court-cases.

FEC.gov. 2020–2021. Accessed May 3, 2022. https://www.fec.gov/resources/cms-content/documents_limits_chart_2019_2021.pdf?msclkid=9116764cc7261.

FEC.gov. 2021–2022. Accessed May 3, 2022. https://www.fec.gov/updates/contributions_limits_2021-2022.

Freidel, Frank. 1990. *Franklin Roosevelt: A Rendezvous with Destiny*. Boston: Little, Brown.

Gierzynski, Anthony. 2011. *Saving American Elections: A Diagnosis and Prescription for a Healthier Democracy*. Amherst, NY: Cambria Press.

Gould, Lewis. 1993. *Grand Old Party: A History of the Republicans*. New York: Random House.

Gould, Lewis. 2003. *Grand Old Party: A History of the Republicans*. New York: Random House.

Hale, Kathleen, and Mitchell Brown. 2020. *How We Vote: Innovation in American Elections*. Washington, DC: Georgetown University Press.

Hale, Kathleen, Robert Montjoy, and Mitchell Brown. 2015. *Administering Elections: How American Elections Work*. London and New York: Palgrave Macmillan.

James, Scott. 2000. *Presidents, Parties, and the State: A Party System Perspective on Democratic Regulatory Choice, 1884–1936*. Cambridge: Cambridge University Press.

Jayapal.house.gov. 2021. We the people amendment, Accessed May 3, 2022. https://jayapal.house.gov.2021/04/06/we-the-people-amendment.

Kleppner, Paul. 1979. *The Third Electoral System, 1853–1892: Parties, Voters, and Political Culture*. Chapel Hill: University of North Carolina Press.

Kleppner, Paul, Walter D. Burnham, Ronald P. Formis, Samuel P. Hays, Richard Jensen, and William G. Shade. 1983. *The Evolution of the American Electoral System*. Westport, CT: Greenwood Press.

Kurian, George T., ed. 2002a. *The Encyclopedia of the Democratic Party*. Armonk, NJ: M. E. Sharpe.

Kurian, George T., ed. 2002b. *The Encyclopedia of the Republican Party*. Armonk, NJ: M. E. Sharpe.

Lawless, Jennifer. 2012. *Becoming a Candidate*. Cambridge: Cambridge University Press.

LeMay, Michael C. 1987. *From Open Door to Dutch Door*. New York: Praeger.

LeMay, Michael C. 2009. *The Perennial Struggle*. 3rd ed. Upper Saddle River, NJ: Prentice-Hall.

LeMay, Michael C., ed. 2013. *Transforming America: Perspectives on U.S. Immigration, Vol. One: The Making of a Nation of Nations: The Founding to 1865*. Santa Barbara, CA: Praeger.

LeMay, Michael C. 2017. *The American Political Party System: A Reference Handbook*. Santa Barbara, CA: ABC-CLIO.

LeMay, Michael C., and Elliott Barkan, eds. 1999. *Immigration and Naturalization Laws and Issues: A Documentary History*. Westport, CT: Greenwood Press.

Lessig, Lawrence. 2011. *Republic Lost: How Money Corrupts Congress—and a Plan to Stop It*. New York: Twelve Books /Hachette.

Lessig, Lawrence. 2019. *They Don't Represent Us: Reclaiming Our Democracy*. New York: Dey Street Press.

Levinson, Sanford, and Jack M. Balkin. 2019. *Democracy and Dysfunction*. Chicago: University of Chicago Press.

Manza, Jeff, and Clem Brooks. 1999. *Social Cleavages and Political Change: Voter Realignment and U.S. Party Coalitions*. New York: Oxford University Press.

NCSL (National Conference of State Legislatures). 2022. "Election Administration at the State and Local Levels." Accessed April 22, 2022. https://www.ncsl.org/research /elections-and-campaigns/election-administration-at-state -and-local-levels.aspx?m/

NCSL (National Conference of State Legislatures). n.d. "Elections and Campaigns." Accessed March 15, 2021. https://www.ncsl.org/research/elections-and-campaigns /primary-type.

Ness, Immanuel, and James Clement, eds. 2000. *Encyclopedia of Third Parties in America*. 3 vols. Armonk, NJ: M. E. Sharpe.

Paulson, Arthur. 2007. *Electoral Realignments and the Outlook for American Democracy*. Boston: Northeastern University Press.

Rosenof, Theodore. 2003. *Realignment: The Theory That Changed the Way We Think about American Politics*. Lanham, MD: Rowman and Littlefield.

Safire, William. 1978. *Safire's Political Dictionary*. New York: Random House.

Sanders, Elizabeth. 1999. *Roots of Reform: Farmers, Workers, and the American State, 1877–1917*. Chicago: University of Chicago Press.

Sloan, John. 2008. *FDR and Reagan: Transformative Presidents and Clashing Visions*. Lawrence: University Press of Kansas.

Ueda, Reed. 1980. "Naturalization and Citizenship." In *Harvard Encyclopedia of American Ethnic Groups*, edited by Stephen Thernstrom. Cambridge, MA: Harvard University Press.

United for the People.org. 2013. Accessed May 12, 2021. http://www.united4thepeople.org.

USA.gov. Elected Officials. 2021. Accessed May 12, 2021. https://www.usa.gov/elected-officials/?msclkid=41e54ff2c72711ecb91ba251701718d3.

Weiner, Daniel I. 2015, January 15. *Citizens United Five Years Later*. Brennan Center for Justice. Accessed March 29, 2022. https://www.brennancenter.org/our-work/research-reports/citizens-united-five-years-later.

Wilentz, Sean. 2005. *The Rise of American Democracy: Jefferson to Lincoln*. New York: W. W. Norton.

Wilentz, Sean. 2007. *Andrew Jackson: The Seventh President, 1829–1837*. New York: Macmillan.

Witcover, Jules. 2003. *Party of the People: A History of the Democrats*. New York: Random House.

Zentner, Scot, and Michael C. LeMay. 2020. *Party and Nation: Immigration and Regime Politics in American History*. Lanham, MD: Lexington Books.

Zolberg, Aristide. 2006. *A Nation by Design: Immigration Policy and the Fashioning of America*. Cambridge, MA: Harvard University Press.

American
Democracy.
Going once…
Going twice…
SOLD!!!

2 Problems, Controversies, and Solutions

Introduction

This chapter focuses on some of the most pressing problems and controversies facing the conduct and control of elections in America.

Over the course of its nearly 250-year history, the United States has expanded from 13 original states huddled along the East Coast to 50 states and several territories spanning the entire North American continent and beyond. Meanwhile, the nation's population grew from fewer than 4 million people, most of whom were descendants from the British Isles, to more than 300 million in population. It became the most ethnically, racially, and religiously diverse population of any country on earth.

Its electoral politics likewise became ever more complex and diverse. As the American political party system evolved, a host of new problems and controversies developed, which, of course, had been largely unforeseen by the Founders. The role of political parties and assorted interest groups changed over time as well, resulting in new problems and challenges for the administration of government and elections. Varied and often conflicting solutions to those problems and challenges have

---

Although it is and was illegal to pay someone to vote, democracy has always been influenced by money. During the era of the big-city political machines especially, voters were often paid by party operatives, and the party's nomination for offices, particularly for state and local offices, was literally sold by the party bosses. (Redwood8/Dreamstime.com)

been suggested by the two major parties, by an assortment of third or minor parties, and by numerous interest groups active in U.S. electoral politics.

Several distinct issues and controversies related to elections in the United States are discussed herein. The first concerns arguments about who should be allowed to vote. Another concern focuses on the appropriate role for political parties in elections. Another problem area is the question of how electoral districts should be drawn or redrawn after each decennial census. The Constitution specified that a census be taken every 10 years of all persons residing in the United States—but it was silent as to how district composition should reflect census results, and it left the manner of redistricting to the individual states.

The chapter also devotes attention to the ever-growing cost of running for elected office and how it should be financed. Another area of study concerns recruitment and selection of candidates for office.

Another issue considered in this chapter is the internal tensions that have arisen due to the fracturing of America's political culture along geographic, religious, and educational lines. The impact of partisan and online social media in driving political polarization and diminishing public faith in the outcomes of elections is also examined.

Yet another significant area of debate concerns the complexity of elections in a federal system of government. Finally, political norms and rules governing elections and voting in America, such as the prevailing system of winner-take-all elections, are discussed.

Who Gets to Vote?

Who should be allowed to participate in elections and to legitimately exercise the right to vote? That question has been a central issue in American electoral politics since the inception of the nation and has been the focus of a large body of scholarly literature.

Voter eligibility has been a central issue to the concept of regime politics. In politics, a regime refers to the leaders of government and the associated set of rules, laws, and norms they use to regulate the operations of governmental institutions with society (Stone 1989; Zentner and LeMay 2020). With each major transformative presidential election and the regime change brought about by each new presidency (e.g., 1800, 1860, 1896, 1932, 1980, 2008, and 2016), electorates evolved and expanded, voting turnout increased, and the coalition of groups supporting the major political parties shifted and realigned.

One of the recurring threads woven through American history has been the struggle of disenfranchised people to secure U.S. citizenship and the corresponding right to vote. These efforts, however, have often been marked by struggle, disappointment, and heartache because of the implacable opposition of nativist-oriented political parties or white supremacist groups who saw expansion of the franchise as a threat to their political power and influence, such as the Federalist Party, the Know Nothing Party, the Whig Party, the American Party, and the Ku Klux Klan (Finley 2008; Hacker 2003). Prior to 1920, men generally opposed giving women the right to vote. In today's political environment, many voting rights advocates assert that the Trump wing of the Republican Party is engaging in vote-repression tactics for political advantage—a charge consistently denied by Trump and the GOP.

The first expansion of the franchise was to white males who were not property owners. That expansion was set in motion with the 1800 election of President Thomas Jefferson and was essentially completed by 1840. It took the bloody U.S. Civil War and the passage of the 14th and 15th Amendments to the Constitution to expand the right of citizenship and the vote to Black men (Budiansky 2018; Davis 2011). But this right was stamped out across the South with Jim Crow laws that withstood all legal, political, and cultural challenges until the 1950s–1970s civil rights movement (Alexander 2010; Bedell

2017; Berman 2015; Bullock, Gaddle, and Wert 2016; Finley 2008; Hacker 2003; Levinson 2003; Wolbrecht and Hero 2005).

It took a prolonged suffrage battle and the ratification of the 19th Amendment in 1920 to add women to the nation's electoral rolls (Baker 2004; Carroll and Fox 2018; Mead 2004; Keyssar 2009; Orozco 2009; Roydhouse 2016). In December 1943, Congress enacted the Magnuson Act, which repealed the Chinese Exclusion Act of 1882. The repeal enabled nonwhite, Chinese immigrants to naturalize and subsequently to vote. The McCarran-Walter Act of 1952 did the same for Japanese Americans. In 1961, the 23rd Amendment enabled citizens of the District of Columbia to vote. The 26th Amendment lowered the legal voting age from 21 to 18. Congress also acted to protect or expand voting rights with important civil rights laws enacted in 1965, 1968, 1975, and 1993.

The COVID-19 pandemic impacted voting behavior and practices in 2020 throughout that year's campaign and election. In response to the pandemic, numerous states eased their rules regarding early voting, expanded the number and location of voter drop boxes, and expanded vote-by-mail. Voter turnout reached all-time highs in many states. The voter turnout in the 2020 was the highest percentage of eligible voters in a century—66.7 percent. The typical turnout the previous two decades ranged from 58 to 61 percent.

In the 2020 presidential race, the Trump-Pence ticket received the greatest number of votes cast for any Republican candidate in history (more than 74 million votes). But that performance fell short of the support received by the Biden-Harris ticket, which received 81 million votes. Biden also was victorious in the Electoral College vote (ECV). He earned 306 ECV to Trump's 232, well over the 270 ECV needed to win the presidency. The Trump administration and many of its Republicans allies subsequently claimed the election was stolen but did not present any evidence. As an alleged solution to their unsubstantiated allegations of voter fraud, some 27 states with

Republican-controlled state legislatures submitted hundreds of bills promoting new limitations and rules on voting. Supporters said that these bills would restore voter trust in elections, while critics described them as transparent efforts to suppress the vote of Americans who were more likely to vote Democrat, such as African Americans. Some 50 such laws have been passed.

The Democratic Party's solution to this alleged threat to voter rights has been to enact or strengthen voting rights through federal legislation. As of the fall of 2021, however, neither the Biden administration nor Democrats in Congress have been able to push legislation past united opposition from Republicans, who argue the laws are unnecessary and interfere with state affairs.

Hyperpartisan Tribalism

Political observers warn that since the election of Ronald Reagan to the presidency in 1980, the United States has steadily fallen deeper into political polarization and intensifying tribalism. They warn that American voters increasingly see members of other political parties as enemies rather than just political opponents and that loyalty to party or political ideology sometimes seems stronger than loyalty to the country and the democratic institutions that are its foundation, enshrined in the Constitution (Cohen 2003; Staider 2018).

Political tribalism has been described as an attitude where loyalty to the political tribe is more important than loyalty to anything else. Tribalism means the tribe never concedes an inch to the other tribe. It is a total "us"-versus-"them" mentality. The "them" are seen as morally suspect and dangerous, while the "us" are seen as saints by comparison (Banner.org 2020). The tribe demands blind allegiance and promotes huge passions of partisan affiliation. The tribe is a badge of identity, not of thought. American politics today entrenches tribalism: in our winner-take-all elections, in the all-too-often dehumanizing commentary on cable news and on social media, and in the people whom we choose to talk to and live among (Packer 2018).

The prevalence of the hyper-partisan mentality is perhaps most evident in the U.S. Congress, where critics say that compromise has become a dirty word to many, party loyalty trumps loyalty to the Constitution, and our democratic political traditions and values are under siege (Hagedorn and LeMay 2019).

An example of the deleterious effect of such hyper-partisan mentality was the attempted insurrection of January 6, 2021, in which an angry and violent mob of Trump loyalists stormed and breached the Capitol in an effort to derail the certification of Electoral College votes formally acknowledging Joe Biden's victory over Trump in the 2020 election. The riot injured more than 100 Capitol police officers and many metropolitan police from Washington, DC, and rioters nearly reached members of Congress and Vice President Pence. The insurrection marked the first time in U.S. history that the transfer of power from one presidential administration to the next was stained by violence. Even immediately after the riot, more than 130 Republican members of Congress voted against certification of the 2020 presidential election results, citing false claims of voting irregularities and fraud made by Trump himself. Democrats in Congress voted unanimously to impeach President Trump for a second time, the only president in U.S. history to be impeached twice. But Trump avoided conviction when the 100-member Senate failed to garner the necessary two-thirds vote. In the end, only 7 out of 50 Republicans crossed the aisle to join all 50 Democrats in voting to convict.

The hyper-partisan nature of American electoral politics is reflected in the difference between "safe" states reliably controlled by one party versus the "swing" states, where power often swings back and forth from one party to the other. Going into the 2020 presidential election, only nine states were generally considered to be swing states: Arizona, Wisconsin, Minnesota, Nevada, Michigan, New Hampshire, North Carolina,

Pennsylvania, and Florida. As of the 2020 elections, 23 states were generally considered to be reliably Republican states (often mapped as red states): Ohio, West Virginia, Indiana, Kentucky, North Carolina, South Carolina, Tennessee, Georgia, Alabama, Missouri, Louisiana, Mississippi, Iowa, North Dakota, South Dakota, Nebraska, Kansas, Oklahoma, Texas, Montana, Wyoming, Idaho, and Utah. Eighteen states were generally rated as reliably Democratic states: Washington, Oregon, California, Colorado, New Mexico, Minnesota, Illinois, Virginia, Maryland, Delaware, New Jersey, Connecticut, Rhode Island, Massachusetts, Vermont, New York, Maine, and Washington, DC.

The rather stark geographic division into red and blue states affects where the two major parties' candidates tend to concentrate their campaign activities and which states tend to garner a lion's share of the media's attention. And when one or the other party dominates a state, the state's legislature tends to draw district lines to entrench its hold on political power (by gerrymandering; see discussion below).

Another aspect of the problems resulting from the attitude of hyper-partisanship relates to the polling of voters. The projections of voting behavior for the 2016 and 2020 presidential elections were notably off the mark. This growing inaccuracy may reflect partisan voters' increasing distrust of polling and perhaps even a willingness on the part of voters to purposely mislead pollsters. Even when voters are not misleading pollsters, a miniscule error in the sampling of voters' opinions and expressed intention to vote can result in a marked shift in the accuracy of projection of voters' behavior. A post-2020 study by the Pew organization noted the impact of a small shift in sampling: "Election polling in closely divided electorates like those in the U.S. right now demand a high degree of precision from polling. Sizable differences in the margin between the candidates can result from relatively small errors in the composition of the sample. Changing a small share of the sample can make a big difference in the margin between the two candidates. Changing the preference of 38 voters out of 1,000 respondents shifts the poll's margin from a 12-point Biden advantage to about four points, the actual 2020 election results, or about 4 percent of the total" (Keeter et al. 2021).

Meanwhile, the nation's two dominant parties have such dramatic differences in policy views and governing philosophies that when power in Congress or the White House changes hands from one to the other, these shifts can whipsaw the direction of the country back and forth. When President Trump replaced President Obama, for example, he quickly issued about a dozen executive orders reversing those issued by President Obama. Four years later, when President Biden replaced President Trump, Biden issued, during his first days in office, more than two dozen orders reversing orders of his predecessor.

The intensity of party or candidate loyalty can lead to another problem—confusing the enthusiasm evident at party election rallies with how the wider public is going to vote. The vastly larger turnout at Trump rallies during the 2020 campaign, especially given the fact that the Biden campaign eschewed holding such rallies during the COVID-19 pandemic, deceived Trump, his campaign staff, and many of his followers into believing that there was no way Trump could lose the election "except if it was stolen." That false assertion formed the basis for "the Big Lie" embraced by Trump and his supporters, that he would have won except for rampant voter fraud. In reality, the 2020 presidential election results were completely legitimate—a fact underscored by the fact that Trump and other critics could not cite any actual evidence of fraud and had some 50 cases thrown out of courts for lack of evidence.

Gerrymandering of Electoral Districts

Although the term was not coined until 1812, the practice of "gerrymandering" has been around since colonial times, when it was used in the colonies of Virginia and North and South Carolina. Simply put, gerrymandering can be defined as the manipulation of boundaries of an electoral district to favor one party or class of people. It has been described by many scholars and historians as a serious problem for democracy and one of the root causes of the decline in American democratic norms (Bullock 2021; Levinson 2003).

The term came into being in March 1812, when the *Boston Gazette* newspaper ran a cartoon depicting a strangely shaped electoral district in Massachusetts as a forked-tongue creature. The cartoon named the creature a "gerry-mander" because it had been drawn by the state's Jeffersonian Republican Party—and approved by Massachusetts governor Elbridge Gerry, also a Jeffersonian Republican—to increase the number of voters in the district that would likely support the party's candidate. The outline of the district reminded a Federalist newspaper reporter of a salamander, and the reporter combined "Gerry" and "salamander" to form a new word that has stuck ever since.

The term is now used whenever politicians redraw voting districts into odd shapes to benefit their political party or to weaken the election prospects of candidates of the opposition party. In many cases, gerrymandered districts also serve to dilute the voting power of ethnic or racial groups that are seen as key constituencies of the opposing party.

Use of gerrymandering has increased or declined depending on the intensity of the two-party competition at the time. After the U.S. Civil War, gerrymandering was used by white Southern Democrats to suppress the political power of the Republican Party. In this instance, they spread Black voters, who were strongly supportive of the Republican Party at the time, among electoral districts so that they would not account for a meaningful percentage of votes in most districts. Usage of the practice declined in the early 20th century, when the use of poll taxes, the threat of lynching and other racial violence, and various Jim Crow laws and practices made gerrymandering unnecessary to suppress Black political power and maintain disproportionate political power for white, rural, nonimmigrant citizens (Issacharoff et al. 2016; Levinson 2003; McGhee 2020; Medvic 2021; Whitby 2000).

The constitutionality of gerrymandering has been challenged on many occasions since the "redistricting revolution," mostly by a series of court decisions under Chief Justice Earl Warren. These decisions stipulated that courts could review redistricting plans, and they required districts to be drawn to keep the size of the populations in each district even. Two forms of gerrymandering have been distinguished legally: partisan and racial. The Supreme Court, citing provisions of the Voting Rights Act, has placed limits on the use of the practice more often when it was blatantly used in racially discriminatory ways (e.g., in *Thornburg v. Gingles*, 1986; *Shaw v. Reno*, 1993; *Miller v. Johnson*, 1995; *Bush v. Vera*, 1996, *Bartlett v. Strickland*, 2009; *Shelby v. Holder*, 2013; *Alabama Legislative Black Caucus v. Alabama*, 2015; *Cooper v. Harris*, 2017). It has been used successfully less often when used for strictly partisan reasons. Indeed, the U.S. Supreme Court has refused to outlaw partisan gerrymandering, giving the wide latitude granted to state legislatures in drawing such district lines (*Gaffney v. Cumings*, 1979; *Davis v. Bandemer*, 1986; *Vieth v. Jubelirer*, 2004; *Rucho v. Common Cause*, 2019) (NCSL.org 2019; RedistrictingOnline.org n.d.).

Two methods of gerrymandering may be distinguished: "packing" and "cracking." Packing and cracking do different things to voting districts to achieve similar results. Packing is when the district boundaries are modified in such a way that the opponent's voters are confined to a smaller number of districts. Cracking is when district boundaries are changed in a way that an opponent's base is spread out across so many different districts that the opponent's voting power in each district is greatly diluted. Both achieve the goal of weakening the opponent's power in elections.

Use of gerrymandering has been enhanced since 1990, when computer technology made it easier for political operatives to map districts with near-surgical precision to benefit their party, under Supreme Court rules that were issued to ensure that voters were more evenly represented in state legislatures and in the U.S. House of Representatives, broadly defined by the judicial principal of "one man, one vote" (Bullock 2021; Daley 2020; Levinson 2003; McGann et al. 2016; Kury 2018; McGhee 2020; Whitby 2000). In the past, gerrymandering was used to enhance the clout of certain ethnic groups, such as Irish Americans and the urban political machines, and, in the Northeast, against immigrants from Southern and Eastern Europe. More recently, especially in the South and Southwest, it has been used to undercut the voting power of Blacks, Asian Americans, and Hispanic Americans.

Gerrymandering enhances and entrenches the electoral power of politicians and of the dominant political party in a state. It confers a structural advantage that can last for several decades and has been widely criticized as an essentially antidemocratic structural feature of American politics. It gives a significant electoral advantage to the party in power in any given state, and it structurally disadvantages third or minor parties and ethnic and racial minorities. It gives politicians less incentive to broaden their message, compromise, or even have meaningful debates on issues, because voters in heavily gerrymandered districts are likely to be either very liberal or very conservative. Precisely because it creates "safe" seats, gerrymandering exacerbates the problem of hyper-partisan tribalism. It pushes electoral politics away from the middle and toward the political extremes at both ends of the political spectrum. This pressure even exists in districts that are solidly Republican or Democrat, because to win the right to represent their party, candidates need to win their party primaries—which often means appealing to the most extreme and uncompromising voters in their party. In 2014, only 39 out of 435 congressional seats in the U.S. House of Representatives were generally considered to be competitive in that year's midterm elections, and that number dropped to only 37 in 2016 (Bullock 2021; Daley 2020; Levinson 2003; McGann et al. 2016; McGhee 2020; Kury 2018; Whitby 2000).

Gerrymandering is a significant problem in the United States compared with other developed democracies (Handley and Grofman 2008). While a few court cases have condemned districts deemed to be designed to give an artificial advantage to the Republican Party in North Carolina, Texas, and Wisconsin, courts have generally shied away from intervention in what they consider to be an essentially political issue that should be resolved in the political process, such as through the passage of laws that restrain or eliminate the practice. But most Republicans, as well as some Democrats, have embraced gerrymandering as a political tactic, and there are not enough reform-minded members of Congress to pass legislation that would address the problem.

Meanwhile, the Supreme Court, in *Rucho v. Common Cause* (2019), for all practical purposes closed off the use of litigation to resolve the problem of partisan gerrymandering. A constitutional amendment is highly unlikely. Barring a profound political shift or cultural movement that would place redistricting responsibilities with either a nonpartisan or a bipartisan, independent commission, gerrymandering is likely to remain a troubling reality in the U.S. House of Representatives and many state legislatures.

As of 2021, a total of 10 states have established commissions with primary responsibility to draw district lines: Arizona. Colorado, California, Hawaii, Idaho, Montana, Michigan, New Jersey, Virginia, and Washington. In addition, nine states have advisory commissions that can assist the legislature in drawing district lines: Maine, New Mexico, New York, Rhode Island, Utah, Connecticut, Indiana, Ohio, and Iowa. Voters in Arizona and California passed initiative ballot measures to take away redistricting power from the legislature and establish nonpartisan redistricting commissions. The state of Iowa has a similar independent commission that draws a set of maps based on nonpartisan criteria from which the state legislature must choose.

Despite these efforts to depoliticize the drawing of voting districts, most states with Republican-dominated legislatures are moving in the opposite direction by enacting a host of voter suppression measures. Some are even taking administrative responsibility for monitoring and certifying elections out of the hands of statewide elected officers, such as secretaries of state, and giving that control back to legislatures that they control.

Campaign Costs and Election Finance Reform

One would think, given the high percentage of safe seats, generally around 95 percent, that the costs of campaigns and legislation to regulate campaign finance would not be highly controversial. In fact, however, the cost of funding campaigns has risen almost exponentially and to levels that reformers consider deeply problematic for American democracy (Ackerman 2004; Gierzynski 2011; Hartman 2004; Lessig 2011; Magleby and Monson 2004; Smith 2001). The cost of U.S. elections, for example, rose from just more than $1.6 billion in 1998 to more than $14.4 billion in 2020. The cost of the U.S. presidential race alone grew from $1.4 billion in 2000 to more than $5.7 billion in 2020 (OpenSecrets.org 2021).

There are several effects of the ever-rising costs of U.S. elections. Members of the U.S. House of Representatives, for example, spend more time on fundraising than on any other activity, including crafting and passing legislation (Ackerman 2004; Corrado, Magleby, and Patterson 2006; Hagedorn and LeMay 2019; Lessig 2011; Magleby and Monson 2004). Critics charge that the constant need to raise campaign funds corrupts politics and representative democracy. The exponential rise in the cost of elections has contributed significantly to the rise in the numbers and the growing political influence of PACs (Ackerman 2004; Gierzynski 2011; Hartman 2004; Lessig 2011; Magleby and Monson 2004; Smith 2001). The constant need to raise campaign contributions also pushes politicians to stay in the good graces of their base and their financial supporters, further exacerbating the problem of tribalism in American politics. Instead of seeking policy compromises and moving to the political middle, politicians face pressures to grandstand, using controversial issues as fundraising opportunities rather than problems to be solved.

Legislative efforts to regulate or reform campaign finance date back to the mid-1800s (see table 5.11). Often such efforts have pitted congressional legislators against the Supreme Court (see tables 5.10 and 5.11). Where congressional reformers have seen the need to regulate specific types or sources of abuse and potential corruption, the Supreme Court has generally seen such reform efforts as unconstitutional infringement on free speech. The Court has ruled that unlimited contributions by wealthy individuals, corporations, unions, and assorted PACs are forms of political free speech protected by the 1st and 14th Amendments.

On June 30, 1890, for example, Congress passed a naval appropriations act known as the Battleship Act. It approved construction of several battleships, but it also included provisions to protect naval yard workers from politicians running for federal office who were putting the bite on the workers by demanding campaign contributions in return for job security. Similarly, in 1907, congressional reformers passed the Tillman Act, which prohibited corporations and banks from directly contributing to federal election campaigns. In 1910 and 1911, Congress passed the Federal Corrupt Practices Act (FCPA). This legislation required candidates for Congress (whether in the House of Representatives or the Senate) to disclose their campaign spending and the sources of their funding.

Those campaign finance reform efforts were largely thwarted by the U.S. Supreme Court in 1921, when the Court's majority ruled in *Newberry v. the United States* that the spending limits regulations contained within the FCPA were unconstitutional. Congress amended the FCPA in 1925 to comply with the *Newberry* ruling.

In the 1930s, the financial resources of public-owned utilities (e.g., electricity, transit, and water) grew enormously, and they became major players in political campaign financing. Congress attempted to control and regulate such activity in

1935 by enacting the Public Utilities Holding Act (also known as the Wheeler-Rayburn Act). The law banned political campaign contributions from public utilities. During the reforms of the second New Deal, in 1939, Congress passed an Act to Prevent Pernicious Political Acts, better known as the Hatch Act, after its principal sponsor, Senator Carl Hatch (D-NM). The Hatch Act barred most federal employees from contributing to political campaigns and from participating in overt political campaign activities. The law was essentially designed to protect federal civil service employees from political pressure to contribute to campaigns. It also prevented politicians from using government workers as campaign volunteers when they were supposed to be working, and it barred high-level federal employees from using their public visibility and access to the media to make political endorsements.

In the 1940s, Congress enacted several campaign finance regulation laws. In 1943, it passed the War Labor Disputes Act, more commonly known as the Smith-Connelly Act, which bars labor unions from making direct contributions to federal campaigns. Largely in response to the War Labor Disputes Act of June 25, 1943, the Congress of Industrial Organizations (CIO), one of the nation's biggest and most powerful organized labor groups, created the first political action committee (PAC) in 1944. Virtually every PAC established since then has been modeled after it. In 1947, to control what was seen by union critics as the undue influence of organized labor, Congress passed the Taft-Hartley Act. The legislation imposed sweeping restrictions on labor unions in several areas, including barring them from making direct financial contributions to federal candidates.

In 1971, in response to the escalating costs of presidential campaigns, which were making candidates more dependent on PACs and wealthy donors, Congress enacted a law that supporters hailed as a step toward the public financing of presidential campaigns. Known as the Revenue Act of 1971, it allowed taxpayers to voluntarily contribute three dollars of their taxes to a presidential campaign fund. Any candidate for the presidency could use a set amount of funding from the account but had to use only those "public funds." Supporters hoped that it would give candidates another viable route for funding their campaigns, but candidates quickly realized they could raise and spend far more in nonpublic funds and avoid the law's numerous campaign restrictions.

After the political wrongdoing of President Richard Nixon's 1972 reelection campaign, uncovered in the Watergate scandal, Congress addressed the controversy by amending the Federal Elections Campaign Act, setting new contribution and spending caps. Those reform efforts were gutted by the U.S. Supreme Court's decision in the *Buckley v. Valeo* case, passed per curiam. Congress responded to the *Buckley* decision by further amending FECA in 1979.

The last major attempt by Congress to reform campaign finance was the Bipartisan Campaign Reform Act (BCRA), which was signed into law by President George W. Bush on March 27, 2002. It is more commonly known as the McCain-Feingold Act after its principal authors, Senators John McCain (R-AZ) and Russell Feingold (D-WI). The law bars certain amounts and types of "soft" money, offering PACs less opportunity to not report the source of their donations, and further defines "issue ads" funded by soft money. The U.S. Supreme Court upheld major provisions of the BCRA in 2003 in its 5–4 decision in *McConnell v. FEC*.

An increasingly conservative and Republican-oriented Court, however, has largely gutted congressional campaign finance reform efforts in three subsequent decisions on the matter, all of which were decided by 5–4 votes along party lines. In *FEC v. Wisconsin Right to Life* (2007), the Court held that regulations that banned political ads by corporations and unions in the weeks before an election were unconstitutional infringements of free speech. Even more devastating to campaign finance reform was the *Citizens United v. FEC* (2010), in which the Court declared that the government could not restrict unions and corporations from making political contributions. This decision dismantled the McCain-Feingold campaign finance law and unleashed a wave of so-called super PACs and nearly unlimited use of "dark money" (donations from unnamed donors) in political campaigns. Fresh torrents of money poured into campaigns, particularly at the federal level but also trickling down to state and local contests.

Finally, in terms of Court actions severely limiting congressional reforms, the Court struck down caps on total spending by individuals on federal campaigns and on political parties with its decision in *McCutcheon v. FEC* (2014). The *McCutcheon* decision put the final nail in the coffin of campaign finance reform (NCSL 2019; see table 5.11).

The impact of the COVID-19 pandemic also had an impact on campaign finance. It spurred the use of virtual fundraisers. Like many campaign activities undertaken since the pandemic struck, the two major parties diverged in reaction to the pandemic along party lines. Democrats raised funds using online events and automatic pooling of funds gathered with developments such as the super PAC known as ActBlue. Defying public health warnings, Republicans held more in-person events such as rallies and fundraisers, some of which became COVID-19 super-spreader events. WinRed, the Republican answer to ActBlue, developed a highly controversial and often criticized tactic with its online fundraisers. It used boxes in its donation appeals that automatically checked off making the donation an ongoing (usually monthly) contribution in the same amount unless the individual making the contribution, intending it to be a one-time contribution, actively "unchecked" the box. The practice generated numerous complaints, and the campaign by the Republican National Committee was forced to refund tens of millions of dollars. Critics of the tactic point to it as another sign of how desperately the country needs to pass comprehensive campaign finance reform.

As with the gerrymandering problem, the campaign finance problem has few solutions on the near horizon. There have been proposals for a constitutional amendment to overturn *Citizens United*. There have been calls for shortening the length of campaigns to something along the lines of those used in most European democracies and in such Asian countries as Japan and South Korea.

Barring a dramatic alteration in America's political culture, though, such reforms are highly unlikely. The U.S. Supreme Court, stacked in 2021 with a 6–3 conservative majority, is even less likely to change its position. It has clearly set precedent by such decisions as *FEC v. Wisconsin Right to Life* (2007), *Citizens United v. FEC* (2010), and *McCutcheon v. FEC* (2014). The Court deems that federal courts should stay out of the political thicket and let voters initiate reforms at the ballot box, a solution also unlikely given the current structural advantages Republicans have obtained through gerrymandering and voter suppression laws at the state level. Reformers hope that slim Democratic majorities in the 2021–2022 House and Senate might be able to pass new voting rights laws, but unless Democrats are also willing to strike down filibuster rules that the GOP is using to stop those reforms, those bills are doomed to fail.

In the longer-term perspective, however, a change in the American political culture will more likely follow the demographic trends now evident in the United States. U.S. Census Bureau projections have the United States becoming a majority-minority country by 2050. By 2050, 62 percent of the nation's children will be minorities, up from 44 percent today. The working-age population will become more than 50 percent minority by 2039, and by 2050, minorities will be about 55 percent of the working-age population. The working-age population is projected to become more than 30 percent Hispanic and 9.6 percent Asian by 2050 (Census.gov 2009).

The U.S. population is projected to reach 400 million in 2039 and by 2050 will likely reach 439 million, among whom an estimated 235.7 million will be minorities.

Although one cannot project what the political attitudes of that population will be in 2040 or 2050, it is safe to say that such profound demographic changes will impact the nation's dominant political culture. Inasmuch as non-Hispanic whites now constitute the conservative base of the population opposing campaign finance reform, these demographic shifts toward populations that are more supportive of reform portend a possible change in the prospects for campaign finance reform in future decades.

Recruitment of Candidates

Since the inception of political parties in 1800, and especially since the rise of the Jacksonian Democratic mass party since 1828, the recruitment and selection of candidates for elective office has been a basic function of political parties. The role of the parties organizationally and in relation to political pressure groups in the recruitment and selection of candidates has been examined in some of the classics of political science literature on the subject (Duverger 1954; Epstein 1980; Key 1942; Schattschneider 1942). The role of the political party vis-à-vis political interest groups in recruiting and selecting candidates to run for office in elections at all levels has been a source of controversy from the founding of the nation and has increased significantly since the 1990s.

In no small measure, the tension between the role of the political party and that of political interest groups in selecting and supporting preferred candidates can be traced to the Election Clause of the U.S. Constitution. Article I, Section 4 states that "the Times, Places and Manner of holding elections for Senators and Representatives, shall be prescribed in each State by the Legislature thereof," reflecting the Founders' wishes that the new nation would be one of a union of states that would regulate all its elections, even those of the U.S. Congress. Article I continues, however, to further provide that "Congress may at any time make or alter such regulations," thereby giving the federal government authority to override states and to enact laws that would apply equally to all states regarding federal elections. This basic aspect of federalism purposely builds in a tension between the states and the national government as an organizational form designed to limit the power of government. It is one of the aspects of the checks-and-balances system of government. That tension between levels of government has been the source of problems and controversy over the recruitment and selection of candidates for elective office.

Influential political scientist Lester Seligman distinguished two stages in the process of recruitment: (1) certification, which is the social screening and political channeling that results in eligibility for candidacy, and (2) selection, which is the actual choice of candidates to represent parties in the general election (Seligman 2014).

There are two institutional types of political selection: the convention system and the primary system. During the years when the political party machines dominated politics, the parties relied on the caucus/convention type of selection process. In the early years of the development of the mass political party in America, the party elite were white Anglo-Saxon Protestant (WASP) men. Until the 1870s, they recruited and selected fellow male WASPs (LeMay 2017; Zentner and LeMay 2020).

The political party elite chooses candidates typically based on five criteria, according to Seligman: (1) service in party positions, (2) strong acceptability to the party's base of electoral support, (3) loyalty to the party's organizational leadership, (4) conformity to an organizational code, and (5) representativeness of an important ethnic background, religious group, or geographic area (Seligman 2014).

When the urban political machines developed in America's rapidly growing cities in the 1870s and 1880s, they dominated the caucus/convention process. They recruited naturalized citizens of ethnic immigrant groups, offering slates of candidates to appeal to blocs of ethnic voters. These ethnic affiliations became tied to party loyalty. In the 1870s and 1880s, for example, to be Irish American was to be a loyal Democratic voter in most cases. Similarly, to be German American or Norwegian American after the U.S. Civil War meant that more than likely the voter identified as a Republican. That sorting process helped immigrant groups to assimilate into American society and incorporate into the political system.

Irish Americans were the first white ethnic group to use politics as their major route to assimilation in wider society. For decades, they were a loyal bloc for Democrats, and over time, they rose to increasingly prominent positions in the party at local, state, and national levels. It was not until 1960, however, when Democrat John F. Kennedy won the White House, that an Irish Catholic candidate became president.

During the 1890s and early 1900s, Italian Americans, Greek Americans, and Polish Americans followed the Irish American model of using the Democratic Party as a vehicle for accruing political influence (LeMay 1985). After the U.S. Civil War, German Americans and Scandinavian Americans used the same process to rise within Republican Party politics—and to eventually seek and win the same national-level offices that other ethnic groups were securing as Democrats. During the Reconstruction years, the Republican Party recruited Black Americans, former slaves, to run for and serve in statewide offices in several of the former Confederate states. A few African American Republican candidates even won election to the U.S. House of Representatives. After Reconstruction, however, white Democrats used poll taxes, literacy tests, and other Jim Crow laws to disenfranchise Blacks across the South. This systemic and often violent disenfranchisement of African Americans persisted until the 1950s and 1960s, when the hard-fought civil rights movement produced new laws and court decisions that finally tore down Jim Crow (LeMay 2021a).

The caucus/convention process could be easily corrupted, however; the urban machine's leadership sold nominations for office and used graft and the party spoils system to manipulate blocs of voters. As party corruption became more evident, a progressive reform movement proposed and popularized the primary selection model for determining a party's candidates. The primary model is characterized by four major principals: (1) the party electorate rather than the party elite chooses the candidates, (2) all candidates may freely enter the selection process, (3) no group or individual controls access to the party electorate, and (4) party officials are formally neutral in the selection process (Seligman 2014; NCSL.org 2021, January 5).

As the primary selection process became more popular and ubiquitous, however, new problems or issues became evident. In areas where one party dominated the politics of cities, counties, states, or even regions (e.g., the "solid South"), winning the party primary became tantamount to winning in the general election. Racial discrimination became rampant through use of the "white-only primary." Women and minority candidates were often excluded. The smaller base of the party had increasing influence in primary elections, where fewer voters generally participated. That skewed the party and its elected officials toward greater ideological loyalty and less willingness to compromise or support bipartisan proposals for public policy. It exacerbated the use of party purity as a litmus test to even run for an elective office (Ackerman 2004).

The ability to raise money early on to fund primary campaigns became an important factor in the selection process as well. The so-called money primary (or "invisible primary") refers to the period when potential presidential candidates test the waters for a possible run by raising campaign funds, introducing themselves to voters in states that conduct their primaries early in the nomination process, and seeking endorsements from political leaders and party donors. Fundraising totals (and early polling numbers) are used by the media to project who the front-runners for the nomination are. The money primary can be a crucial stage in the recruitment, selection, and nomination process, and disappointing results often force potential candidates to drop out of the race (Goff 2005).

With the growing use of the primary method of candidate recruitment and selection, political power shifted to interest groups and PACs, which by their very nature had a smaller or narrower base of appeal. In areas where the Democratic Party as an organization was weak, labor unions often became the de facto selector of the party's nominee. Women's interest groups, such as Emily's List and NOW, have become leaders of the women's movement, driving the Democratic Party to select record numbers of women candidates. Similarly, the Black Lives Matter movement has driven the recruitment and selection of a record number of Black candidates within the Democratic Party. Democrats have also been the primary drivers of recruitment and selection of a record number of Asian Americans for elective office.

In areas where the Republican Party as an organization is comparatively weak, conservative outside organizations that are generally supportive of the GOP sometimes step into the breach and dominate the recruitment and selection process. This process, too, has exacerbated the trend toward the use of ideological litmus tests to determine the strongest potential candidates.

Individual candidates possessing great personal wealth, or the ability to create a PAC to raise large campaign "war chests," are increasingly capable of bypassing party officials and committees and taking their message directly to voters—especially in this day of digital communication and social media. This weakens the party's ability to demand that its officeholders work to enact its party platform after winning office. To the extent that more members of the Republican Conference have been recruited, nominated, and elected based on that interest-group selection process rather than on a party-based selection process, the ability of the conference leadership to maintain control of its membership in working for common policy goals is weakened.

The shift away from political party domination of the recruitment and selection of candidates helped resolve some issues or controversies but exacerbated others. The recruitment, selection, and election of women and minority candidates have undoubtedly increased since the 1990s, with interest groups and PACs independent of the two major parties gaining an increased influence over the process. Political observers caution, though, that this growth in political representation for women, people of color, and members of the LGBTQ community probably has more to do with wider changes in American society, including broad demographic trends and increased recognition of the capabilities of these historically marginalized groups, than with the diminished stature of formal party organizations.

As the demographic trends discussed above take place, the political power of current minorities is widely expected to increase. That could ultimately translate in increased support for a more progressive public policy agenda in Congress. Those same demographic trends, however, will likely enhance the power of state and local levels of government. National control over elections will decrease. The U.S. Supreme Court's position, or judicial doctrine, of staying out of the "political party thicket," means that the courts are not likely to issue rulings that may help traditional political parties gain back control over the process for the recruitment and selection of candidates for elective office.

Facets of Political Culture

Political scientists have identified and discussed several variables that affect political participation, including socioeconomic status, education level, and ethnicity, gender, and race of the person. Political participation for members of the public who don't hold office themselves involves several possible behaviors: voting, contacting public officials to share perspectives on issues, taking part in political protests or rallies, volunteering in a campaign, contributing money to a candidate or party, and registering to vote or help others register. Voting is the most common and important form of participation.

Voter registration and voting are influenced by legal and structural factors, voter qualifications, the type and level of the election, voter enthusiasm, socioeconomic status, age, race, ethnicity, and gender, as well as the prevailing political culture in the community or region in which the voter lives. Political culture has been variously defined, but the influential political scientist Daniel Elazar defined it as the underlying semipermanent characteristics that can help explain how states and localities function (Elazar 1966).

Political scientists Gabriel Almond and Sidney Verba distinguished three types of political culture focusing on the relation of the individual to the central government: (1) parochial, in which citizens are only remotely aware of a central government; (2) subject, in which citizens are aware of a central government and occasionally participate in the political process; and (3) participant, in which citizens are able to influence government in various ways, including through robust participation in political activities and processes (Almond and Verba 1965), Samuel Huntington's view of political culture emphasizes geography and history and the potential for political and military conflict between different cultures. He distinguishes, for example, Western civilization, Japanese civilization, Islamic civilization, Hindu civilization, Slavic-Orthodox civilization, Latin American civilization, Chinese civilization, and African civilization (Huntington 2006).

Elazar's typology is perhaps the most relevant to understanding elections in America (Elazar 1966). His focus is on explaining the impact of federalism and how regional ethnic and religious factors shape political culture. Elazar argues that certain attributes are enshrined in a political culture as the consequences of ethnic and religious values of the settlers in specific regions of the country. As the groups migrated west, they took their unique political cultures with them and passed them down from generation to generation.

In Elazar's perspective, political culture explains state activities in the federal system and illuminates how states and localities interact with the national government. According to Elazar, political culture affects state government and intergovernmental relations in three important ways: (1) Political cultures help set perceptions of the purpose and range of government—what it can and should not do; (2) political cultures set the boundaries of who can participate and how much public involvement is encouraged in the policy-making process; (3) political culture affects the way that government is practiced, such as whether corruption is tolerated or innovative public policy reforms are welcomed.

In a way similar to Almond and Verba's system of distinguishing three primary political cultures, Elazar distinguishes three major political cultural types: the individualistic, the moralistic, and the traditionalistic. The individualistic political culture sees government as a marketplace of competing individual interests that use the levers of politics to better their own standing. The individualistic political culture focuses on private concerns and is not issue driven. It often results in strong political parties that are based on patronage and constituent service. In this culture, the goal of politics is to distribute payoffs to supporters. It has a high tolerance for corruption. Politics is seen as essentially a dirty business that is best left to professionals. Ordinary citizens are not encouraged to participate in government except to vote.

The moralistic political culture values collective action through politics. It holds that participation in politics and the betterment of the greater good should be primary objectives of government. In this culture, political activities revolve around the community's welfare as opposed to the individual's enrichment. Intervention by government into private activities is acceptable if it furthers a public good. Issues take on great importance in this culture. Politicians are supposed to search for solutions to policy problems even if there is no immediate electoral payoff.

In the moralistic political culture, political parties are viewed as secondary, and there is a proclivity toward finding nonpartisan or bipartisan solutions. The emphasis is on creating the "good society." It therefore tends to preclude patronage politics, and it eschews corruption. Participation is encouraged, is widespread, and is regarded as a civic duty. Citizens are offered a multiplicity of opportunities to participate. There are extensive government agencies, boards, and commissions.

In the traditionalistic political culture, governments are designed to preserve the status quo to benefit elites. Political and government positions are held or controlled by the wealthy elite, who rule in accordance with elitist conceptions of the common good. Political participation by nonelites is discouraged. Voter turnout is low. Only members of the privileged classes are welcomed into the political realm. Political party competition is rare, and rather than interparty competition, factions within the dominant party compete for power. Competition is rarely based on issues, and politicians are generally immune to electoral pressures. Elites tend to have a consensual position on public policy. Areas dominated by the traditionalist culture tend to be single-party-dominated political party systems.

Political Participation and Religion

According to Elazar's typology, each of the three political cultures is based on colonial geographic regions: the moralistic on New England, the individualistic on the mid-Atlantic states, and the traditionalistic on the South, with its agribusiness and plantation economy. Thus political culture is based on regionalism. The predominant religious affiliation of a state's settlers and residents has affected its political culture. In New England, the Puritans and the British establishment churches (Anglican, Episcopalian) dominated. In the mid-Atlantic states, Presbyterians, Lutherans, and Methodists set the culture. The traditionalistic political culture's values were shaped by fundamentalists (e.g., Southern Baptists) and Pentecostals. As these settlers and their descendants moved west, the states they moved to came to share those three political cultures. Elazar identified the dominant political culture in 48 states (absent Alaska and Hawaii).

To illustrate the impact of a state's political culture on voter participation, table 5.12 lists the state rankings of voter turnout among the voter-eligible population (VEP) for the 2020 elections (Ballotpedia.org 2020). While not a perfect correlation with Elazar's typology, the data in table 5.13 reflects the general trend one would expect from his typology. The states Elazar identifies as one with a moralistic political culture are generally those ranked within the top one-third of the states, those that Elazar categorizes as states with an individualistic political culture are generally ranked in the middle third of VEP percentage turnout, and those Elazar identifies as states with a predominantly traditionalistic political culture are clustered among the bottom third of the states on the turnout of voter-eligible citizens.

New Political Culture

Elazar's typology, which he developed in the 1960s, is not without its critics. More recently, scholars have suggested the emergence of a "new political culture" that is based on the postindustrial and highly mobile American society. Proponents of the new political culture note that more recent settlement patterns have not been random, that people locate in various metropolitan areas based on its political culture. A core principle of this perspective on political culture is that economic issues that used to dominate politics are no longer the only sources of political conflict in society. Fiscal and economic issues have declined in importance. Today's metropolitan areas are characterized by a more highly educated population that sees social issues (e.g., gay rights, or Black or women's equality) as more important than old class-based economic policies (Barzilai 2003; Diamond 1994; Kertzer 1996; Nichols Clark and Hoffman-Martinot 1998; Sharpe 1999, 2005).

The new political culture emphasizes that metropolitan areas have a multiplicity of civic clubs and more vibrant electoral politics. It also emphasizes that metropolitan populations are more ethnically and religiously diverse than cities were prior to the 1990s, full of people hailing from areas and regions of the world that have experienced political cultures more varied than the original three regions that formed the basis for Elazar's three regions. The new political culture does not value unqualified patriotism or the inherent virtues of the market economy. The more highly diverse populations of metropolitan America have lower levels of religious affiliation and are more tolerant of nontraditional lifestyles.

Media and Elections

Many critics of the media and the press, whether the critics are liberal or conservative, charge that media coverage contributes to or even causes divisiveness in American politics. Some critics contend that the level of vitriol—the extent of media bias and dishonesty—emanating from some influential news sources is an unsettling development in American politics (Acosta 2020; Attkisson 2020; Dershowitz 2020; Greenberg 2016; Halberstam 2012; Hemmer 2018; Holzer 2020; Kurtz 2018; McChesney 2004; O'Keefe 2018; Stelter 2021; Taibbi 2021).

The contentious relation of the media to government and politics, however, was evident even to the Founding Fathers, who saw an adversarial relationship between reporters and politicians as a good thing. The role of the media as the watchdog of democracy has been a consistent factor in electoral politics as far back as the colonial era (Kluger 2016; LeMay 2021b; Oates 2008; Schwartz 1992).

The first judicial case dealing with the subject of freedom of the press took place in colonial New York in 1735—the trial of John Peter Zenger. It has been called the birth of America's free press because it set a legal precedent allowing a free press to criticize politicians and influence electoral behavior (Kluger

2016; LeMay 2021b, 107–11; Schwartz 1992). Throughout U.S. history, American presidents have struggled with the press (Holzer 2020). Thomas Jefferson was a champion of freedom of the press during the Constitutional Convention, for example—yet during his presidency Jefferson attacked and tried to censor the New York press for its negative coverage of his administration.

In *Near v. Minnesota* (1931), the Court ruled 5–4 that "prior restraint on publication," that is, government acting to prevent the publication of information critical of the government, violated freedom of the press as guaranteed by the First Amendment. Chief Justice Charles Hughes wrote the majority opinion. The progressive Supreme Court under Chief Justice Earl Warren decided three landmark press freedom cases in the 1960s. In *New York Times v. Sullivan* (1964), the Court issued a unanimous decision that restricted public officials from suing news organizations for defamation based on First Amendment freedom. In *Garrison v. Louisiana* (1964), it issued another unanimous ruling, overturning the defamation conviction of Louisiana district attorney Jim Garrison. In the case of *Curtis Publishing Co. v. Butts* (1967), the Court ruled 5–4 in favor of Georgia football coach Wally Butts against the *Saturday Evening Post* (LeMay 2021b, 9–10). All three cases protected the freedom of the press over government restrictions and upheld the doctrine that a free press was essential to holding "free and fair" elections and holding governmental authority accountable.

Under Warren's successor, Chief Justice Warren Burger, who joined the Court in 1969, a conservative Supreme Court issued three landmark rulings involving freedom of the press. In the *New York Times v. U.S.* (1971), the Court ruled per curiam, 6–3, making it possible for the *New York Times* and the *Washington Post* to publish the classified Pentagon Papers without the threat of government punishment (Prado and Pratt 2004; Schwartz 1992; Sheehan, Smith, and Kenworthy 1971).

Nor is there really anything new about the press being very politically biased and partisan. Since the birth of political parties in U.S. electoral politics, news organizations have functioned as the propaganda arms of political parties (LeMay 2017; Zentner and LeMay 2020). In the early 1800s, the media format was the print media—newspapers, pamphlets, and flyers (which today would be called "screed sheets"). The viciousness of their personal attacks on opposing politicians was every bit as vitriolic as today's Twitter and other social media attacks. Today's "talk radio" political diatribes by the likes of Sean Hannity or the late Rush Limbaugh have been compared by some to the broadcasts hurled against Franklin D. Roosevelt by Father Charles Coughlin, the notorious Detroit "radio priest" of the 1930s and early 1940s.

American news media evolved over time, expanding from newspapers to broadcast media—first the radio and then television, when networks dominated the airwaves for political news and commentary. Telecommunications advances since then resulted in the advent of cable television, the internet, streaming services, and social media, all venues through which media consumers can get their news and political opinions rather than relying on political parties to provide same (Acosta 2020; Halberstam 2012; Hemmes 2018; Kurtz 2018; McChesney 2004; O'Keefe 2018; Stelter 2021; Taibbi 2021).

Politically Motivated News Source Preferences and Beliefs

A 2019 study found that the most popular platforms used by Americans to learn about government and politics issues are the following: news websites, 25 percent; social media, 18 percent; local television, 16 percent; cable television, 16 percent; national television networks, 13 percent; radio, 8 percent; and print newspapers and magazines, 3 percent (Statistica.com 2022).

Researchers have confirmed that media polarization is growing, with Americans of all political orientations increasingly basing their preferred information sources on whether the outlet in question slants liberal or conservative in its coverage. One 2021 Pew Research poll, for example, found that self-identified

Democrats and voters who "lean" Democratic expressed trust for their news from the following sources: CNN, 67 percent; NBC, 61 percent; ABC, 60 percent; CBS, 59 percent; and PBS, 56 percent, while only about 30 percent trusted Fox News. Meanwhile, 65 percent of respondents who self-identified as Republicans or who lean Republican expressed trust in Fox News, but only 33 percent agreed that ABC News was a trustworthy news source. Republicans also expressed low levels of trust in other "mainstream" news organizations such as CBS (30 percent), NBC news (30 percent), and CNN (30 percent) (Keeter et al. 2021). A similar partisan division is evident in the share of adults who believe "fake news" is a major problem in the United States; 62 percent of Republicans believed so, as opposed to 40 percent of those who self-identified as Democrats. Political observers ascribe these latter findings to the fact that Republican President Trump and many members of his administration routinely tried to neutralize any critical coverage of their actions or policies by identifying any such stories as "fake news." This political strategy was subsequently adopted by many other GOP lawmakers (from governors to members of Congress) as well.

Media scholars at the University of Oregon School of Journalism point out six ways that the media influences U.S. elections: (1) whether to cover or choose not to cover stories and events; (2) bias in presentation of news that contributes to the polarization of American electoral politics; (3) increased public reliance on social media outlets for news and political developments; (4) selection of images or videos that can be flattering or unflattering; (5) data journalism providing fact-checking and polling in a self-perpetuating cycle; and (6) serving as the watchdogs of democracy (Brichacek n.d.).

Similar results were found in a 2021 study on the impact of social media on politics. It documented increased spending on social media in the 2020 election, a notable increase in political ads on social media outlets, a sharp increase in the political content of social media posts; the political movement calling for content regulation of social media; a growing concern in Congress to regulate social media; the great impact of President Trump's use of Twitter "tweets," and a growing concern over the use and spread of the pejorative use of the term "fake news" (Statistica.com 2022).

Publicly owned and supported media outlets such as National Public Radio (NPR) and the Public Broadcasting Service (PBS) have an especially strong role in modern presidential campaigns and elections. The public media regularly provides more coverage of minor or third-party candidates and of minority candidates. The news organizations of public media have also examined mass media's influence, both negative and beneficial, on the electoral system, being especially critical, for instance, of the media's almost singular focus on the "horse race" aspect of elections. NPR and PBS instead try to inform the public through greater coverage of key issues, speeches, conferences, rallies, and live debates by candidates for office at all levels of government. It provides more in-depth, postelection analyses of voting results, particularly of state and local referenda and initiatives (Americanarchives.org n.d.).

Several solutions have been proposed for addressing problems of the media and elections. The major networks have all agreed to refrain from calling elections until all the relevant polls have closed. Congress is considering legislation to provide greater regulation of the content and operations of major social media platforms such as Facebook and Twitter, where falsehoods can and do spread like wildfire. Some social media companies have grudgingly introduced measures to clean up their platforms, hoping thereby to avoid national legislative restraints.

Interest Groups and Elections

An interest group can be defined as an organization or an organized group of persons that makes policy-related appeals to government. They are also commonly referred to as special-interest groups, advocacy groups, or pressure groups. The members (constituents) of the group share a common interest and seek to further that interest by applying pressure on government to influence public policy to enhance their shared interest or to avoid negative effects of policy on them. Interest groups focus more on policies and issues than do political parties, and less on determining government personnel. Where political parties are interested in policy as it affects their ability to succeed in elections, interest groups are interested in elections insofar as election results influence policies. Political parties strive to build broad bases, often by crafting coalitions of interest-group adherents. By contrast, interest groups are more narrowly based and focus exclusively on advancing policies that benefit their specific memberships.

Interest groups educate and mobilize their members and monitor government agencies and programs to protect their members from being adversely affected by relevant laws, policies, and regulations. They lobby Congress and state legislatures, governors' offices, and sometimes city councils or county commissions. Many such groups monitor the voting records of legislators with respect to issues pertinent to their memberships. Since the 1990s, there has been an explosion in the number of political interest groups, including PACs, which raise and distribute funds for use in elections. The rapid growth in the number and power of political interest groups followed several decisions of the U.S. Supreme Court (*McConnell v. FEC* in 2003; *FEC v. Wisconsin Right to Life* in 2007; *Citizens United v. FEC* in 2010; and *McCutcheon v. FEC* in 2014) that gave them a great deal of freedom to raise money for electoral politics.

Prior to 1940, political parties dominated the electoral process. Interest groups tended to be involved in elections as ancillaries to the parties. As mentioned, because the two major parties reached out to appeal to naturalized citizens of various (largely white European) nationality groups, they rose to majority party status (LeMay 2017; Zentner and LeMay 2020).

Some of the minor parties—for example, the Socialist Party—were heavily dependent on a few ethnic interest groups and foreign language societies. From the 1880s and 1890s to the 1930s, the mostly Democratic urban political machines began to involve in their local election campaigns Irish Americans, Italian Americans, Greek Americans, and Slavic Americans, when these groups began to concentrate in certain precincts, eventually running slates of candidates for local office with a balanced and diverse set of such ethnic groups represented. The Democratic Party also appealed to organized labor (first the Knights of Labor and then the American Miners Association, the American Federation of Labor (AFL), and the CIO until the latter two organizations merged as the AFL-CIO), whose members to this day tend to vote heavily Democratic. In some cities and even states, labor unions provide the campaign volunteers, help raise much of the party's campaign funding, and recruit candidates on behalf of the Democratic Party. Labor union interest groups even staff election phone banks to canvass voters and push get-out-the-vote efforts in the final stages of primary and general elections.

The modern Democratic Party also gets support from liberal, progressive, ethnic and minority advocacy groups, and PACs, including the American Civil Liberties Union, ActBlue, Black Lives Matter, Brennan Center for Justice, Center for American Progress, Common Cause, Emily's List, Government Accountability Project, MoveOn.org, the NAACP, NARAL-Pro-Choice America, National Organization of Women, OpenSecrets.org, People for the American Way, Progressive Majority, and Public Citizen.

Since its founding in 1854, the Republican Party has traditionally attracted support from pro-business groups ranging from the American Farm Bureau Federation to the National Association of Manufacturers and the U.S. Chamber of Commerce. The Republican Party also gets major PAC support from such groups as the Americans for Prosperity, American Medical Association, American Israel Public Affairs Committee

(AIPAC), Center for American Prosperity, National Rifle Association, and WinRed.

All political interest groups, by definition, are active in politics, although not all such groups participate in electoral politics. The strategies interest groups use in their efforts to shape public policy include: (1) lobbying, (2) rating the performance of lawmakers on pertinent issues and votes, (3) building alliances, (4) offering campaign assistance, (5) influencing public opinion, (6) using their constituents to act as lobbyists, (7) engaging in public protest demonstrations, and (8) forming PACs.

A number of types of interest groups are active in U.S. electoral politics: (1) economic groups, such as the U.S. Chamber of Commerce, National Association of Manufacturers, AFL-CIO, and Brotherhood of Teamsters; (2) trade associations (representing entire industries), such as the American Public Power Association; (3) professional groups, such as the American Medical Association; (4) public interest groups, such as Common Cause, the Environmental Defense Fund, and the League of Women Voters; (5) government interest groups, such as the National League of Cities, the National Conference of Mayors, and the National Conference of State Legislatures; (6) religious interest groups, such as the Christian Coalition, the Moral Majority, and the National Conference of Bishops; (7) civil rights groups, such as the National Association for the Advancement of Colored People, the Mexican American Legal Defense Education Fund, the National Organization of Women, and the National Gay, Lesbian, Transexual, and Queer Fund; (8) ideological groups, such as Americans for Democratic Action, and the American Conservative Union; (9) single-issue groups, such as the National Rifle Association, the Coalition to Stop Gun Violence, the National Right to Life Committee, the National Abortion Rights Action League, and Mothers Against Drunk Driving; and (10) ethnic group organizations, such as the America Israel Public Affairs Committee, the Asian American-Philippine Nurses Association, the Japanese American Citizens League, and the National Council of Asian Pacific Americans

(Barry and Wilcox 2018; Cigler, Loomis, and Nownes 2015; Crotty 2014; Holyoke 2014; Nownes 2012).

There are literally hundreds of interest groups that have been categorized into more than 40 types of special-interest groups active in elections in America, according to Project Vote Smart (2015). Prominent examples of some of these organization types are profiled in chapter three. Typically, in each category, there are groups that hold opposing views on the same problem or issue. Thus, for example, in the category of campaign finance and elections, the pro-Democrat group ActBlue is countered by the pro-Republican group WinRed. Other "good government" advocacy organizations include Common Cause, Public Citizens, Congress Watch, Term Limits America PAC; MoveOn.org PAC, Move to Amend, and the National Women's Political Caucus (USA Political Database 2015).

Are these interest groups a thorn in the side of U.S. elections or democracy in general? The answer to that question is, to a certain extent, in the eyes of the beholder. Some interest-group theorists argue that the competition among interest groups counterbalance one another, leading to better public policy whereby politicians seeking "electoral payoff" are attentive to the concerns of politically active citizens who are seen as representative of the wider population. Others contend that the proliferation of so many special-interest groups contribute to the divisiveness in American politics (Crotty 2014). Critics of the financial influence of interest groups on the political process argue that they drive up the total costs of elections, contribute to tribalism in electoral politics, and in some cases contribute to corruption in American politics. Rather than resulting in "competitive equilibrium," interest groups also are so often working against one another's policy priorities that they can become another contributor to policy-making gridlock.

The Impact of Federalism

The United States maintains a federal system of government. Federalism allows for experimentation and innovation among state governments but also intentionally limits the power and authority of the national government to set national standards or to impose national norms when it comes to election laws (Conlan and Posner 2008).

Intergovernmental problems and issues have been the focus of several scholars studying federalism (Conlan 1988; Conlan and Posner 2008; Doonan 2013; Nivola 2002; Rabe 2004; Sutton 2002). They have noted and debated the impact of such topics as: differing election systems, the importance of swing states in presidential elections, the growing partisan divide between voters living in the suburbs and cities and voters living in rural areas, the impact of regionalism on electoral behavior, and factors driving voter engagement and turnout.

Because the U.S. Constitution reserves the management of elections to the states, elections are complex and nuanced and vary in how they are conducted from state to state. The rotation of when the states hold their general elections for governor and statewide offices, for example, varies from state to state. And the day on which primary elections are held for national, state, and local offices also varies between states.

In 2020, for example, both the Republican and Democratic nominees for president were on the ballot in all 50 states. But variations from state to state in ballot access rules meant that some voters—depending on the state in which they were voting—had more "third party" candidate options than others did for the presidency.

In close swing states, being on the ballot in presidential years can make a difference as to which party's nominee wins the governorship. Swing states garner the most media attention and generally have higher election turnout rates as a result. Higher turnout for the presidential race in swing states can affect down-ticket races.

Federalism, in granting the regulation of elections to the states, has likely increased geographic polarization of the

United States, resulting in divisiveness between suburban and metropolitan areas versus rural areas as well as the U.S. regions. A map of the United States depicting states dominated by the Democratic Party (commonly known as blue states) versus those dominated by the Republican Party (red states) in recent years shows that the geographic regions of the country in which Democrats have the greatest strength are the Atlantic and Great Lake states and the West Coast, while Republican political power is concentrated in the South and the Great Plains. That division between blue and red states is increasingly evident in how they manage and regulate elections within their borders.

Blue states are more likely to allow the use of direct democracy devices, such as the initiative, referendum, and recall, that bring political questions directly to voters. Use of the initiative to essentially bypass the state legislature in policy making more often puts certain public policy issues on the ballot in blue states, such as local governments' attitudes toward the use of political protest, police reform, and LGBT rights protections. Blue states tend to be characterized as having more liberal (or progressive) social policy. Demographic data show that those states tend to have higher percentages of ethnic, racial, and religious minority populations, as well as higher percentages of women and minority elected officials at all levels of government. Finally, these states are characterized by having a moralistic political culture rather than a traditionalistic political culture.

Likewise, federalism affects how tolerant or intolerant the population within states are with respect to the use of political protest. Although in recent years virtually every state experienced some political protests, demonstrations over judicial and police reform, led by the Black Lives Matter movement, have occurred more often in blue states than in red states. Similarly, protests of the #Me Too movement demanding greater equality and justice for women are more visible and receive greater support in blue states, just like protests for gun safety reform measures. Conversely, red states are more likely to be hosts for large demonstrations in support of gun rights, protests over Trump's election defeat in November 2020, and demonstrations against statewide mask mandates to combat the spread of COVID-19 or mandates to require vaccination and other required public health measures.

By design, federalism is a structural arrangement designed to protect states' rights. But that means that when states seek to use those "rights" to give one party a political advantage over the other—such as by imposing new voter restrictions that disproportionately impact supporters of the other party—there are few legal remedies available. Many reformers believe that such partisan scheming over election and voting laws is accelerating and that federal legislation to establish national standards—at least for presidential and congressional elections—that would have to be followed in all states is essential to preserve American democracy. But to date, such bills have failed to gain enough support for passage in Washington's current hyper-partisan environment. National-level electoral reforms will ease electoral problems only if meaningful legislation is passed and signed into law. Otherwise, political observers believe that more Republican-run state legislatures will enact more of the "voting reform" measures that critics contend are tools to suppress turnout of African Americans and other traditionally Democratic constituencies.

Advocates of increased federal regulation of elections also assert that the courts have become unfriendly to such reforms. An increasingly conservative federal judiciary has vowed to stay out of the political thicket surrounding elections and political representation. In rulings such as *Gaffney v. Cummings* (1975), *Davis v. Bandemer* (1986), *Vieth v. Jubelirer* (2004), and *Rucho v. Common Cause* (2019), the Supreme Court has refused again and again to strike down partisan gerrymandering by state legislatures. And in cases like *McConnell v. FEC* (2003), *FEC v. Wisconsin Right to Life* (2007), *Citizens United v, FEC* (2010), and *McCutcheon v. FEC* (2014), the Supreme Court has repeatedly ruled in favor of states and private interest groups over the national Federal Election Commission with regard to campaign finance reform.

The Mechanics of Elections

Many issues and controversies have emerged over the last several elections concerning the mechanics of voting in America. Rules, procedures, and policies that for many years aroused only mild debate or comment have become infected by political polarization and in some cases become lightning rods for heated debate and disagreement. Examples include: (1) absentee voting and mail-in-voting, (2) election assistance for the disabled and elderly, (3) early voting, (4) long and short ballot forms, (5) usage and integrity of paper ballots and voting machines, (6) poll auditors and recounts, (7) poll judges and voting integrity, (8) poll watchers and voter intimidation, (9) polling places and drop boxes, and (10) U.S. Postal Service delays.

Rules regarding absentee voting and mail-in voting vary from state to state. The two terms are sometimes used interchangeably, but there are legal differences in their meaning and use. The COVID-19 pandemic raised concerns over public safety and led some states to relax their rules regarding absentee voting. Historically, most American voters cast their ballot in a polling booth located at a polling station. An absentee ballot is used to cast an absentee vote, which is then submitted, usually, by mail or deposited in an official ballot drop box. It is used by a voter who cannot be physically present at a polling station on Election Day. Use of absentee voting goes back to the U.S. Civil War. By federal law, every state must provide for some absentee ballots and requires states to provide ballots to be sent to military and overseas voters for federal elections.

Normally, states require voters to request an absentee ballot well in advance of Election Day. In 16 states, absentee voting is the only form of voting by mail allowed by state law, and the voter requesting an absentee ballot must provide a valid reason for not being able to go to the in-person voting location. The most commonly used valid reasons are: the person will be out of the county of registration on Election Day; the voter is a student living outside the county of registration; illness or disability; being on jury duty during voting hours; serving as an election worker or poll watcher; religious beliefs or practices that prevent the person from going to a voting center; and being incarcerated or confined to an institution but being eligible to vote. The 16 states that require reasons for absentee voting are Alabama, Arkansas, Connecticut, Delaware, Indiana, Kentucky, Louisiana, Massachusetts, Mississippi, Missouri, New Hampshire, New York, South Carolina, Tennessee, Texas, and West Virginia (Vote.org n.d.).

Twenty-eight states and the District of Columbia have what is called a "no-excuse" absentee ballot (also simply called a mail-in ballot in some states). The voter requests the absentee ballot but is not required to provide a specific reason for doing so in Alaska, Arizona, California, District of Columbia, Florida, Georgia, Idaho, Illinois, Iowa, Kansas, Maine, Maryland, Michigan, Minnesota, Montana, Nebraska, Nevada, New Jersey, New Mexico, North Carolina, North Dakota, Ohio, Pennsylvania, Rhode Island, South Dakota, Vermont, Virginia, and West Virginia. The use of "mail-in absentee voting" surged across the country in the November 2020 election due to the public health threat posed by the COVID-19 virus.

Finally, five states conduct their elections using all mail-in voting: Washington, Oregon, Colorado, Utah, and Hawaii. The experiences of those states in the use of all vote-by-mail shows it to be safe, secure, less costly, convenient, most popular with voters, and fraud free. In fact, voter fraud is extremely rare in general, despite the persistent claims of Trump and many of his supporters. Studies of voter fraud have found only 1,285 proven cases of fraud since 2000, during which 250 million votes were cast by mail. A study by Stanford University found that voting by mail does not usually favor voter share or turnout by voters of either major political party. In the 2020 presidential election, however, Democrats more often used mail-in voting than Republicans after Trump warned, without providing any evidence, that vote-by-mail could not be trusted.

Election assistance for the disabled (e.g., the vision-impaired) has long been legally provided for, as it has been more recently for the elderly. Such assistance has included federal requirements for states to provide alternative voting locations (polling stations) in instances when physical accessibility could be a problem at the main voting site (e.g., the lack of a wheelchair ramp at the main site). Election laws also permit a certified person to accompany the person with a disability into the voting booth, if necessary, to provide assistance. Such assistance may now be provided for the elderly as well (e.g., for a voter over 75 years of age requesting such assistance). Such assistance is typically provided by a relative of the voter but may be a nonrelative. Again, use of this practice increased because of the pandemic. Such assistance may be provided for mail-in voting as well. The federal government has established an election assistance commission to study and advocate for greater use of the practice, especially over safety concerns raised by the pandemic and the danger of spreading the virus among voters who may be at increased risk of contracting the virus due to compromised immunity systems (U.S. Election Assistance Commission 2021).

Another issue of concern with respect to the mechanics of voting has been the use of early voting as opposed to Election Day voting. As mentioned previously, a national Election Day was set by the U.S. Congress in 1848, but most states have provided for some days for early voting. Concern over the COVID-19 pandemic led some states to extend their early voting period for the 2020 election. Early voting always ends a few days before Election Day. The range in length of early voting is from 4 days to 45 days before an election; the average length is 22 days. Voting on Saturdays within the early voting period is allowed in 20 states and the District of Columbia. Five states (Alaska, Illinois, Maryland, New York, and Ohio) provide for Sunday voting, and 5 other states allow counties to open polls on Sunday (California, Georgia, Michigan, Nevada, and Massachusetts). Delaware will allow Sunday voting in 2022 (NCSL.org 2021c).

Early voting is popular with voters for several reasons. It reduces long lines on Election Day. With respect to COVID-19, it reduces risk, as it spreads out the days and times for voting in person, thereby reducing the size of the crowds voting on Election Day and making it easier to socially distance while voting. For persons being paid by the hour rather than by a fixed salary, early voting and weekend voting mean they will not have to suffer a loss of wages to vote. Black voters, especially in the South, have used the early voting option in great numbers. For example, some Black churches organize "souls to the polls" events, busing congregants from their Sunday church service to the polls to vote.

Precisely because early voting was used to a greater extent than ever before in 2020, and because it was used far more often by Democratic voters than by Republican voters, several Republican states have enacted or are considering bills designed to place new limitations on early voting and Sunday voting (notably, Texas, Georgia, and Florida). Georgia's voter suppression law even went so far as to make it a crime to provide food or water to voters waiting in line. Critics assert that this is a particularly outrageous provision, given that the legislation also reduced the number and location of polling stations in predominantly minority precincts—a move that will undoubtedly make voting lines even longer at polling stations that do remain open.

Problems arise from the states' use of the long ballot versus the short ballot form. As the name implies, the long ballot has many offices, candidates, and issues on the same ballot. Long ballots take voters a longer time to complete and thus contribute to long lines on Election Day. Voters are more prone to make mistakes when filling out long form ballots as well, and researchers have documented that the placement of a candidate's name on a long ballot can have a small influence on the number of votes the candidate receives. Long ballots tend to encourage "straight ticket" voting. A straight-ticket vote is one in which voters can just check a single Democrat or Republican box at the top of the ballot, thereby voting for the candidate of their preferred party for every office on the ballot. Conversely, short ballots have been shown to encourage "split ticket" voting, a practice whereby individual voters cast their ballots for candidates from more than one party.

Another point of contention in American elections concerns the choice of using paper ballots versus electronic voting machines. Paper ballots, like long ballots, generally take voters a longer time to complete, thereby contributing to longer lines. They are generally set up to be machine-readable for ease of tabulating, but even that process takes longer than electronic voting machines. Paper ballots usually use one of two methods to allow them to be read by machines: either squares or circles that voters blacken out with a pencil to indicate their choice or a punch-out process, in which voters make their choices by punching out perforated circles next to the names of their preferred candidates.

One problem with the blacken-out method is that stray marks or incomplete filling out of the circles can cause the machine to misread the vote. Critics also contend that during an audit or recount process, these ballots can be more easily tampered with by anyone with a pen. The punch-out type is also prone to errors if voters fail to completely punch out the space indicating their choice and leave behind what are called hanging chads, or if when being processed along conveyer-belts, a ballot accidentally picks up a fallen chad (the punched-out circle) that gets lodged in another spot, causing the machine to misread the vote—as famously happened during the critical recount of the Bush/Gore presidential vote in Florida in 2000 (LeMay 2006).

Poll judges, also called election judges, are officials who oversee voting at local precincts. The requirements to qualify as an election judge vary by state but usually require specialized training. In various states, they are also known as poll workers, election officers, election inspectors, or polling staff. No matter their title, they are primarily responsible for ensuring that everyone who is eligible to vote at a polling place can do so. They also dispense "provisional" ballots to people who are denied ballots because of record-keeping inconsistencies or problems with their voter registration. Provisional ballots allow these individuals to go ahead and vote—and allow for their vote to be counted once the record-keeping issue has been resolved.

Election judges are also responsible for setting up polling places; checking in voters; showing a voter how to use voting equipment if necessary; guarding against discrimination on ethnic, racial, or religious grounds; and protecting the integrity of polling places, ballots, and voting machines. They are supposed to be strictly nonpartisan in carrying out their duties. Election judges and poll workers of all types have traditionally been retired persons who have the time to work the polls at little to no pay, have long been involved in elections as volunteers, and who are interested in elections and view their work as community service.

By contrast, poll watchers, who are also known as partisan citizen observers or poll challengers, represent political parties, candidates, or groups such as ballot issue committees that often recruit them to work as poll watchers at polling locations. Supporters insist that their use is primarily aimed at guarding a party or group's chances at a "fair election." However, poll watchers typically receive minimal training, and they have been accused at some locations of intimidating voters who are seen as unlikely to support the poll watchers' preferred party or candidate.

Polling auditors or independent auditors are used in vote recount situations for close elections where the margin of victory was less than one-half a percentage point and when the election results are challenged by the apparent losing candidate or party. In many states and localities, a recount automatically takes place if the vote margin is below a certain level. Such recounts are paid for with public funds. If the margin of victory is above the automatic recount level but still close enough that a recount could change the results (e.g., above a half percentage point but less than 1 percent), a recount may be ordered if the results are formally challenged by the apparent losing candidate. In these cases, though, the campaign making the challenge is charged the cost of doing the recount or audit. Depending on the size of the recount, that expense can run into the millions of dollars. Typically, auditors are very experienced at conducting an audit and have a reputation for nonpartisan or bipartisan integrity. After the 2020 presidential election, however, the Trump campaign challenged election results in every swing state in which he lost. He lost all but one of these 60 challenges, and the one that Trump won, in Pennsylvania, had no impact on Biden's margin of victory in the state.

In Arizona, the Republican-controlled Senate ordered a highly controversial audit six months after the 2020 election, in which Arizona's electoral votes were certified to have been won by President Joe Biden, even after several recounts. Republican lawmakers nonetheless gave auditing responsibilities to an unaccredited firm, Cyber Ninjas, led by people who had already issued public statements of support for Trump's false claims of fraud. Critics of the Arizona audit, such as David Becker, executive director of the Center for Election Innovation Research, see such politically motivated "fake audits" as an ominous new development in American elections Indeed, the Arizona audit inspired GOP calls for similar audits in other states where Trump lost (such as Wisconsin, Michigan, Pennsylvania, Georgia, and Florida). Critics note there is zero chance that those partisan-sponsored and funded audits can legally overturn the 2020 election results and reinstate Trump as president, as some audit proponents claim.

Another issue of voting mechanics that has attracted attention, especially in Republican-dominated states with significant minority populations, concerns cuts to the number of available polling stations and ballot drop boxes. Several states reduced the number of polling stations for the 2020 election due to the COVID-19 pandemic and the difficulty in recruiting poll workers of all types who, because of their age, felt at greater risk to the virus. The cut in the number and location of polling stations caused long lines at polling stations on Election Day—some lasting for as long as eight hours. Some critics, noting that reductions in polling stations tended to hit minority communities the hardest, claimed that the closures amounted to voter suppression. State officials who approved the closures rejected the charge and said that numerous factors played into their polling place closure decisions.

Several states responded to the pandemic by increasing mail-in voting, implementing additional early voting days or longer hours for early voting, and increasing the number of drop boxes and curbside collections for ballots.

Since the 2020 election, however, hundreds of bills have been introduced that if passed, would reduce the number of polling places, reduce the number of drop boxes, and reduce the number of days for early voting. Many require new provisions for voter identification, and some expand the use of automatic purges of voter registration rolls. A few deny ex-felons from being reinstated as eligible voters.

Voting rights advocates contend that these bills are proposed solutions for election fraud problems that simply do not exist. Instead, the bills perpetuate "the Big Lie" that voter fraud was widespread in the 2020 election. These GOP-crafted bills have also been criticized for undermining public trust and confidence in U.S. elections and the democratic norms necessary for free and fair elections. In June 2021, the Department of Justice announced it was doubling the staff of its Civil Rights Division to deal with increased voter suppression and discrimination cases as well as rising numbers of "menacing and violent threats" against state- and local-level election officials.

A final controversial issue related to U.S. elections is the performance of the U.S. Postal Service, which until the 2020 election had a notably nonpartisan reputation. When the COVID-19 pandemic prompted a surge in interest in mail-in voting, however, Postal Service policies and reforms taken under the direction of postmaster general Louis DeJoy, a Trump appointee, came under intense scrutiny.

Immediately after his May 2020 appointment, DeJoy implemented a series of controversial "cost-cutting" policies that slowed mail delivery across the nation and raised alarms by postal workers, rural election officials, and election advocates. DeJoy reassigned 23 postal executives and removed 2 top postal officials who oversaw day-to-day operations. He also ordered the dismantling of hundreds of mail-sorting machines at a time when mail-in voting was at historically high levels.

In the meantime, Trump's conviction that increased voting by mail would increase Democratic voting in 2020 led him to hold up $10 billion in aid to the United States Postal Service that was approved by Congress as part of its first pandemic relief effort.

More than 30 states have laws against accepting any mail-in ballots that do not arrive by Election Day. Those rules were challenged in court by organizations like the Lawyers' Committee for Civil Rights under Law. They won some of these challenges and increased awareness of and concern over the politicizing of the U.S. Postal Service. Meanwhile, DeJoy's postal service cutbacks resulted in longer delays in mail delivery service—including delivery of completed ballots. As public and congressional anger about the delays increased, DeJoy was forced to announce an end to his cutback measures until after the election. In June 2021, a new Biden appointee to the USPS governing board was finally confirmed, prompting increased speculation that the administration might seek to remove DeJoy from the position of postmaster.

Bibliography

Ackerman, Bruce. 2004. *Voting with Dollars*. New Haven, CT: Yale University Press.

Acosta, Jim. 2020. *The Enemy of the People: A Dangerous Time to Tell the Truth in America*. New York: Harper Collins.

Alexander, Michelle. 2010. *The New Jim Crow*. New York: New Press.

Almond, Gabriel, and Sidney Verba. 1965. *The Civic Culture*. Boston: Little, Brown.

Americanarchives.org. n.d. Accessed June 1, 2021. https://www.archives.gov/new/topics/presidential-elections-and-inaugurations.

Anderson, Carol. 2019. *One Person, No Vote: How Voter Suppression Is Destroying Our Democracy*. New York: Bloomsbury/Macmillan.

Attkisson, Sharyl. 2020. *Slanted*. New York: Harper.

Baker, Jean. 2004. *Women and the U.S. Constitution, 1776–1920*. Washington, DC: American Historical Association.

Ballotpedia.org. n.d.-a. "History of Campaign Finance Regulation." Accessed May 27, 2021. https://ballotpedia.org/History_of_campaign_finance_regulation.

Ballotpedia.org. n.d.-b. "What Are Poll Watchers? (2020)." Accessed June 6, 2021. https://ballotpedia.org/What_are_poll_watchers%3F_(2020).

Ballotpedia.org. 2020. "Election Results 2020 Analysis of Voter Turnout." Accessed May 5, 2022. https://ballotpedia.org/Election_results_2020_analysis_of_voter_turnout.

Banner.org. 2020, February 17. "Political Tribalism." Accessed May 21, 2020. https://www.thebanner.org/columns/2020/02/political-tribalism.

Barry, Jeffrey, and Clyde Wilcox. 2018. *The Interest Group Society*. 6th ed. New York: Routledge.

Barzilai, Gad. 2003. *Communities and Law: Politics and Cultures of Legal Identities*. Ann Arbor: University of Michigan Press.

Bedell, Kenneth. 2017. *Realizing the American Dream: Diagnosing and Treating American Racism*. Santa Barbara, CA: ABC-CLIO.

Berman, Ari. 2015. *Give Us the Ballot*. New York: Farrar, Straus and Giroux.

Boschma, Janie, Fredreka Schouten, and Priya Krisnakumar. 2021, April 3. "Lawmakers in 47 States Have Introduced Bills That Would Make It Harder to Vote. See Them All Here." CNN. Accessed March 30, 2022. https://www.cnn.com/2021/04/03/politics/state-legislation-voter-suppression/index.html.

Bowen, Michael. 2011. *The Roots of Modern Conservatism*. Chapel Hill: University of North Carolina Press.

Brichacek, Andra. n.d. "Six Ways the Media Influence Elections." University of Oregon School of Journalism and Communication. Accessed March 16, 2022. https://journalism.uoregon.edu/news/six-ways-media-influences-elections.

Brown, Donathan, and Michael Clemons. 2015. *Voting Rights under Fire: The Continuing Struggle for People of Color*. Santa Barbara, CA: Praeger Press.

Brown, Nadia, and Sarah Gershon. 2016. *Distinct Identities: Minority Women in U.S. Politics*. New York: Routledge.

Budiansky, Stephen. 2018. *The Bloody Shirt*. New York: Penguin Press.

Bullock, Charles, III. 2021. *Redistricting: The Most Political Activity in America*. 2nd ed. Lanham, MD: Rowman and Littlefield.

Bullock, Charles, Ronald Gaddle, and Justin Wert, eds. 2016. *The Rise and Fall of the Voting Rights Act*. Norman: University of Oklahoma Press.

Burden, Barry, and David Kimball. 2004. *Why Americans Split Their Tickets: Campaigns, Competition, and Divided Government*. Ann Arbor: University of Michigan Press.

Carroll, Susan, and Richard Fox, eds. 2018. *Gender and Elections*. 4th ed. New York: Cambridge University Press.

Census.gov. 2009. "United States Population Projections: 2000 to 2050." Accessed March 30, 2022. https://www.census.gov/library/working-papers/2009/demo/us-pop-proj-2000-2050.html.

Cigler, Allan, Burdett Loomis, and Anthony Nownes, eds. 2015. *Interest Group Politics*. 9th ed. Washington, DC: Congressional Quarterly Press.

Clubb, Jerome, William Flanigan, and Nancy Zingale. 1990. *Partisan Realignment*. Beverly Hills, CA: Sage.

Cohen, Geoffrey. 2003. "Party over Policy: The Dominating Impact of Group Influence on Political Beliefs." *Journal of Personality and Social Psychology* 85:808–22.

Conlan, Timothy. 1988. *The New Federalism: Intergovernmental Reform from Nixon to Reagan*. Washington, DC: Brookings Institution Press.

Conlan, Timothy, and Paul Posner, eds. 2008. *Intergovernmental Management for the 21st Century*. Washington, DC: Brookings Institution Press.

Corrado, Anthony, David Magleby, and Kelly Patterson, eds. 2006. *Financing the 2004 Election*. Washington, DC: Brookings Institution Press.

Crotty, William. 2014. *Polarization Politics: The Impact of Divisiveness in the U.S. Political System*. Boulder, CO: Lynne Rienner Publishing.

Dahl, Robert. 2005. *Who Governs? Democracy and Power in an American City*. 2nd ed. New Haven, CT: Yale University Press.

Daley, David. 2020. *Unrigged: How Americans are Battling Back to Save Democracy*. New York: Liveright Press/W. W. Norton.

Daniels, David D., III. 2020, October 30. "The Black Church Has Been Getting 'Souls to the Polls' for More Than 60 Years." Rice/Kinder Institute. Accessed March 30, 2022. https://kinder.rice.edu/urbanedge/2020/10/30/elections-2020-black-churches-get-voters-to-polls.

Davis, Hugh. 2011. *We Will Be Satisfied with Nothing Less: The African American Struggle for Equal Rights in the North During Reconstruction*. Ithaca, NY: Cornell University Press.

Dershowitz, Alan. 2020. *Cancel Culture: The Latest Attack on Free Speech and Due Process*. Pittsburgh, PA: Hot Books.

Diamond, Larry, ed. 1994. *Political Culture in Developing Countries*. Boulder, CO: Lynne Rienner Publishing.

Dictionary.com. 2020, July 28. "Absentee Ballot vs. Mail-In Ballot: Is There a Difference?" Accessed June 7, 2021. https://www.dictionary.com/e/absentee-ballot-vs.=mail-in-ballot.

Doonan, Michael. 2013. *American Federalism in Practice: The Formulation and Implementation of Contemporary Health Policy*. Washington, DC: Brookings Institution Press.

Duverger, Maurice. 1954. *Political Parties: Their Organization and Activity in the Modern State*. New York: Wiley and Sons.

Elazar, Daniel. 1966. *American Federalism: A View from the States*. New York: Thomas Crowell.

Epstein, Leon. 1980. *Political Parties in Western Democracies*. 2nd ed. New Brunswick, NJ: Transaction.

Finley, Keith. 2008. *Delaying the Dream: Southern Senators and the Fight against Civil Rights, 1936–1965*. Baton Rouge: Louisiana State University Press.

Fiorillo, Steve. 2020. "Gerrymandering: Definition, History and Legality." TheStreet. Accessed March 30, 2022. https://www.thestreet.com/politics/what-is-gerrymandering-14796491.

Gierzynski, Anthony. 2011. *Saving American Elections: A Diagnosis and Prescription for a Healthier Democracy*. Amherst, NY: Cambria Press.

Giles, Ben. 2021, May 29. "As Controversial Maricopa County Audit Continues, Calls for Election Reviews Grow." NPR. Accessed March 30, 2022. https://www.npr.org/2021/05/29/1001603698/as-controversial-maricopa-county-audit-continues-calls-for-election-reviews-grow.

Goff, Michael. 2005. *The Money Primary: The New Politics of the Early Presidential Nomination Process*. Lanham, MD: Rowman and Littlefield.

Greenberg, David. 2016. *Republic of Spin: An Inside History of the American Presidency*. New York: W. W. Norton.

Grofman, Bernard, Andre Blais, and Shaun Bowler, eds. 2009. *Duverger's Law of Plurality Voting*. New York: Springer Publishing.

Hacker, Andrew. 2003. *Two Nations, Black and White, Separate, Hostile, Unequal*. New York: Scribner.

Hagedorn, Sara, and Michael LeMay. 2019. *The American Congress: A Reference Handbook*. Santa Barbara, CA: ABC-CLIO.

Halberstam, David. 2012. *The Powers That Be*. New York: Open Roads Media.

Handley, Lisa, and Bernard Grofman, eds. 2008. *Redistricting in Comparative Perspective*. New York: Oxford University Press.

Hartman, Thom. 2004. *Unequal Protection: The Rise of Corporate Dominance and the Theft of Human Rights.* Emmaus, PA: Rodale Books.

Hemmer, Nicole. 2018. *Messengers of the Right: Conservative Media and the Transformation of American Politics.* Philadelphia: University of Pennsylvania Press.

Holyoke, Thomas. 2014. *Interest Groups and Lobbying: Pursuing Political Interests in America.* Boulder, CO: Westview Press.

Holzer, Harold. 2020. *The President and the Press.* New York: Penguin Publishing.

Huntington, Samuel. 2006. *Political Order in Changing Societies.* New Haven, CT: Yale University Press.

Issacharoff, Samuel, Pamela Karlan, Richard Pilides, and Nathaniel Persily. 2016. *The Law of Democracy: Legal Structure of the Political Process.* 5th ed. New York: Foundation Press.

Jurkowitz, Mark, Amy Mitchell, Elisa Shearer, and Mason Walker. 2020, January 24. "U.S. Media Polarization and the 2020 Election: A Nation Divided." Pew Research. Accessed March 30, 2022. https://www.pewresearch.org/journalism/2020/01/24/u-s-media-polarization-and-the-2020-election-a-nation-divided.

Keeter, Scott, Nick Hatley, Arnold Lau, and Courtney Kennedy. 2021, March 2. "What 2020's Election Poll Errors Tell Us about the Accuracy of Issue Polling." Pew Research Center. Accessed March 30, 2022. https://www.pewresearch.org/methods/2021/03/02/what-2020's-election-poll-errors-tell-us-about-the-accuracy-of-issue-polling.

Kertzer, David. 1988. *Ritual, Politics, and Power.* New Haven, CT: Yale University Press.

Kertzer, David. 1996. *Politics and Symbols.* New Haven, CT: Yale University Press.

Key, V. O., Jr. 1942. *Political Parties and Pressure Groups*. New York: Thomas Crowell.

Key, V. O. 1955. "A Theory of Critical Elections." *Journal of Politics* 17 (1): 3–18.

Keyssar, Alexander. 2009. *The Right to Vote: The Contested History of Democracy in the United States*. 2nd ed. New York: Basic Books.

Kleppner, Paul, Walter Dean Burnham, Ronald P. Formisano, Samuel P. Hays, Richard Jensen, and William G. Shade. 1983. *The Evolution of the American Electoral System*. Westport, CT: Greenwood Press.

Kluger, Richard. 2016. *Indelible Ink: The Trial of John Peter Zenger and the Birth of America's Free Press*. New York: W. W. Norton.

Kurtz, Howard. 2018. *Media Madness: Donald Trump, the Press, and the War over Truth*. Washington, DC: Regnery Publishing.

Kury, Franklin. 2018. *Gerrymandering: A Guide to Congressional Redistricting, Dark Money, and the Supreme Court*. New York: Cambridge University Press.

LeMay, Michael C. 1985. *The Struggle for Influence: The Impact of Minority Groups on Politics and Policy in the United States*. Lanham, MD: University Press of America /Rowman and Littlefield Group.

LeMay, Michael C. 1987. *From Open Door to Dutch Door*. New York: Praeger Press.

LeMay, Michael C. 2006. *Public Administration: Clashing Values in the Administration of Public Policy*. Boston: Wadsworth/Cengage Learning.

LeMay, Michael C. 2009. *The Perennial Struggle*. 3rd ed. Upper Saddle River, NJ: Prentice-Hall.

LeMay Michael C., ed. 2013. *Transforming America: Perspectives on Immigration*. 3 vols. Santa Barbara, CA: Praeger Press.

LeMay, Michael C. 2017. *The American Political Party System*. Santa Barbara, CA: ABC-CLIO.

LeMay, Michael. 2021a. *Civil Rights and Civil Liberties in America: A Reference Handbook*. Santa Barbara, CA: ABC-CLIO.

LeMay, Michael. 2021b. *First Amendment Freedoms: A Reference Handbook*. Santa Barbara, CA: ABC-CLIO.

LeMay, Michael C., and Elliott Barkan, eds. 1999. *U.S. Immigration and Naturalization Laws and Issues: A Documentary History*. Westport, CT: Greenwood Press.

Lessig, Lawrence. 2011. *Republic Lost: How Money Corrupts Congress and a Plan to Stop It*. New York: Twelve/Hachette Groups.

Lessig, Lawrence. 2019. *They Don't Represent Us: Reclaiming Our Democracy*. New York: Dey Street.

Levinson, Sanford. 2003. *Wrestling with Diversity*. Durham, NC: Duke University Press.

Levinson, Sanford, and Jack M. Balkin. 2019. *Democracy and Dysfunction*. Chicago: University of Chicago Press.

Little, Becky. 2021, April 20. "How Gerrymandering Began in the US." History. Accessed March 30, 2022. https://www.history.com/news/gerrymandering-origins-voting.

Magleby, David, and Quin Monson, eds. 2004. *The Last Hurrah? Soft Money and Issue Advocacy in the 2002 Congressional Elections*. Washington, DC: Brookings Institution Press.

Maisel, L. Sandy, Jeffrey Berry, and George Edwards III, eds. 2010. *The Oxford Handbook of American Political Parties and Interest Groups*. New York: Oxford University Press.

Manza, Jeff, and Clem Brooks. 1999. *Social Cleavages and Political Change*. New York: Oxford University Press.

McChesney, Robert. 2004. *The Problem of the Media: U.S. Communication Politics in the Twenty-First Century*. New York: Monthly Review Press.

McGann, Anthony, Charles Smith, Michael Latner, and Alex Keena. 2016. *Gerrymandering in America: The House of Representatives, the Supreme Court, and the Future of Popular Sovereignty*. New York: Cambridge University Press.

McGhee, Eric. 2020. "Partisan Gerrymandering and Political Science." *Annual Review of Political Science* 23:171–85.

McGillivray, Alice, and Richard Scammon. 2005. *A Handbook of American Election Statistics*. 2 vols. Washington, DC: CQ Press.

McGillivray, Alice, Richard Scammon, and Rhodes Cook, eds. 2010. *America Votes: A Handbook of Contemporary American Election Statistics*. Washington, DC: CQ Press.

McMahon, Mary. 2021. "What Is an Election Judge?" MyLawQuestions. https://www.mylawquestions.com/what-is-an-election-judge.htm.

Mead, Rebecca. 2004. *How the Vote Was Won: Woman Suffrage in the Western United States, 1868–1914*. New York: New York University Press.

Medvic, Stephen. 2021. *Gerrymandering: The Politics of Redistricting in the United States*. New York: Polity Books.

Morgenstern, Scott, and Peter Siavelis. 2019. "Recruitment and Selection for Elected Office." Oxford Bibliographies. Accessed March 30, 2022. https://www.oxfordbibliographies.com/view/document/recruitment-and-selection-for-elected-office.

NCSL.org. 2019, September 14. "Redistricting and the Supreme Court: The Most Significant Cases." Accessed May 24, 2021. https://www.ncsl.org/research/redistricting/redistricting-and-the-Supreme-Court-the-most-significant-cases.

NCSL.org. 2021a, January 5. "State Primary Election Types." Accessed May 29, 2021. https://www.ncsl.org/research/elections-and-campaigns/primary-types.

NCSL.org. 2021b, December 10. "Redistricting Commissions: Congressional Plans." Accessed April 30, 2021. https://www.ncsl.org/research/redistricting/redistricting-commissions-congressional-plans.aspx.

NCSL.org. 2021c. "2021 Election Enactments." Accessed May 24, 2021. https://www.ncsl.org/research/elections-and-campaigns/2021-election-enactments.

NCSL.org. 2022, January 17. "Early In-Person Voting." Accessed June 7, 2021. https://www.ncsl.org/research/elections-and-campaigns/early-voting-in-state-elections.aspx.

Nice, David. 1986. *Federalism: The Politics of Intergovernmental Relations*. New York: St. Martin's Press.

Nichols Clark, Terry, and Vincent Hoffman-Martinot, eds. 1998. *The New Political Culture*. Boulder, CO: Westview Press.

Nivola, Pietri. 2002. *Tense Commandments: Federal Prescription and City Problems*. Washington, DC: Brookings Institution Press.

Nownes, Anthony. 2012. *Interest Groups in American Politics: Pressure and Power*. New York: Routledge.

Oates, Sarah. 2008. *Introduction to Media and Politics*. Newberry Park, CA: Sage.

O'Keefe, James. 2018. *American Pravda: My Fight for Truth in the Era of Fake News*. New York: St. Martin's Press.

O'Mara, Margaret. 2017. *Pivotal Tuesdays: Four Elections that Shaped the Twentieth Century*. Philadelphia: University of Pennsylvania Press.

OpenSecrets.org. 2021. "Elections Overview." Accessed May 27, 2021. https://www.opensecrets.org/elections-overview.

Orozco, Cynthia. 2009. *No Mexicans, Women, or Dogs Allowed: The Rise of the Mexican Civil Rights Movement*. Austin: University of Texas.

Packer, George. 2018, October 12. "A New Report Offers Insights into Tribalism in the Age of Trump." *New Yorker*. Accessed May 21, 2021. https://www.newyorker.com/news/daily-comment/a-new-report-offers-insight-into-tribalism-in-the-age-of-trump.

Paulson, Arthur. 2007. *Electoral Realignments and the Outlook for American Democracy*. Boston: Northeastern University Press.

Pérez, Myrna. 2013, May 15. "U.S. Supreme Court Examines Voting Rights in Two Cases." Brennan Center for Justice. Accessed April 1, 2022. https://www.brennancenter.org/our-work/research-reports/us-supreme-court-examines-voting-rights-two-cases.

Polyas.com. n.d. "Split-Ticket Voting." Accessed March 17, 2022. https://www.polyas.com/election-glossary/split-ticket-voting.

Prados, John, and Margaret Pratt, eds. 2004. *Inside the Pentagon Papers*. Lawrence: University Press of Kansas.

Project Vote Smart. 2015. Accessed May 3, 2022. https://justfacts.votesmart.org/interest-groups.

Rabe, Barry. 2004. *Statehouse and Greenhouse: The Emerging Politics of American Climate Change Policy*. Washington, DC: Brookings Institution Press.

Redistricting Online.org. n.d. "Gerrymandering." Accessed June 1, 2021. https://redistrictingonline.org/basics-gerrymandering.

Rosenof, Theodore. 2003. *Realignment: The Theory that Changed the Way We Think about American Politics*. Lanham, MD: Rowman and Littlefield.

Rowen, Beth. 2017, February 28. "Campaign-Finance Reform: History and Timeline." Infoplease. Accessed June 1, 2021. https://www.infoplease.com/history/us/campaign-finance-reform-history-and-timeline.

Roydhouse, Marion. 2016. *Votes for Women! The American Woman Suffrage Movement and the Nineteenth Amendment: A Reference Guide*. Santa Barbara, CA: ABC-CLIO.

Schattschneider, E. E. 1942. *Party Government*. New York: Holt, Rinehart and Winston.

Schwartz, Bernard. 1992. *Freedom of the Press*. New York: Facts on File.

Seligman, Lester. (1961) 2014. "Political Recruitment and Party Structure: A Case Study." *American Political Science Review* 55 (1). Reprint online, Cambridge University Press. Accessed May 29, 2021. https://www.cambridge.org/core/journals/american-political-science-review/article/abs/political-recruitment-and-party-structure-a-case-study/BA8ED85164EB9D6DDECE8801C75EC54D. Citations refer to the online edition.

Sharpe, Elaine. 1999. *Culture Wars and Local Politics*. Lawrence: University Press of Kansas.

Sharpe, Elaine. 2005. *Morality Politics in American Cities*. Lawrence: University Press of Kansas.

Sheehan, Neil, Hedrick Smith, and E. W. Kenworthy, eds. 1971. *The Pentagon Papers*. New York: New York Times Press.

Sloan, John. 2008. *FDR and Reagan*. Lawrence: University Press of Kansas.

Smith, Bradley. 2001. *Unfree Speech: The Folly of Campaign Finance Reform*. Princeton, NJ: Princeton University Press.

Staider, Daniel. 2018. *The Power of Context: How to Manage Our Bias and Improve Our Understanding of Others*. Amherst, NY: Prometheus Books.

Statista.com. 2022, February 8. "Social Media and Politics in the United States: Statistics & Facts." Accessed June 1, 2021. https://www.statista.com/topics/3723/social-media-and-politics-in-the-united-states.

Stelter, Brian. 2021. *Hoax: Donald Trump, Fox News, and the Dangerous Distortion of Truth*. New York: Atria/One Signal Publisher, Simon & Schuster.

Stone, Clarence. 1989. *Regime Politics*. Lawrence: University Press of Kansas.

Sutton, Robert P. 2002. *Federalism: Major Issues in American History*. Westport, CT: Greenwood Press.

Taibbi, Matt. 2021. *Hate, Inc.: Why Today's Media Makes Us Despise One Another*. New York: OR Books.

Tarr, David, and Bob Benson. 2012. *Elections A to Z: A Ready Reference Encyclopedia*. Washington, DC: Congressional Quarterly Press.

Ueda, Reed. 2001. "Historical Patterns of Immigrant Status and Incorporation in the United States." In *E Pluribus Unum? Contemporary and Historical Perspectives on Immigrant Political Incorporation*, edited by Gary Gerstle and John Wollenkopp. New York: Russell Sage Foundation.

U.S. Elections Assistance Commission. 2021, February 16. *Disability and Voting Accessibility in the 2020 Elections: Final Report on Survey Results Submitted to the Election Assistance Commission*. Accessed March 26, 2022. https://www.eac.gov/sites/default/files/voters/Disability_and_voting_accessibility_in_the_2020_elections_final_report_on_survey_results.pdf.

USA Political Database. 2015. Accessed May 3, 2022. https://usapoliticaldatabase.weebly.com/obergefell-v-hodges-2015.html.

USelections.com. n.d. "What Is the Difference between a Primary, a Caucus and a Convention?" Accessed May 29, 2021. https://uselections.com/QandA/primary-caucus-convention.shtml.

Vote.org. n.d. Accessed June 7, 2021. https://www.vote.org.

Whitby, Kenny. 2000. *The Color of Representation: Congressional Behavior and Black Interests*. Ann Arbor: University of Michigan Press.

Wilentz, Sean. 2005. *The Rise of American Democracy*. New York: W. W. Norton.

Williams, R. Hal. 2010. *Realigning America: McKinley, Bryan, and the Remarkable Election of 1896*. Lawrence: University Press of Kansas.

Winger, Richard, ed. 2020, October 24. "Nationwide Voter Registration Data by Party." Ballot Access News. Accessed May 21, 2021. https://ballot-access.org/2020/10/24/nationwide-voter-registration-data-by-party.

Wise, Alana, and Deirdre Walsh. 2021, March 3. "House Approves Major Election Reform and Voting Rights Bill." NPR. Accessed May 26, 2021. https://www.npr.org/2021/03/03/972568115.

Wolbrecht, Christina, Karen Beckwith, and Lisa Baldez, eds. 2008. *Political Women and American Democracy*. New York: Cambridge University Press.

Wolbrecht, Christina, and Rodney Hero. 2005. *The Politics of Democratic Inclusion*. Philadelphia: Temple University Press.

Zentner, Scot, and Michael LeMay. 2020. *Party and Nation: Immigration and Regime Politics in American History*. Lanham, MD: Lexington.

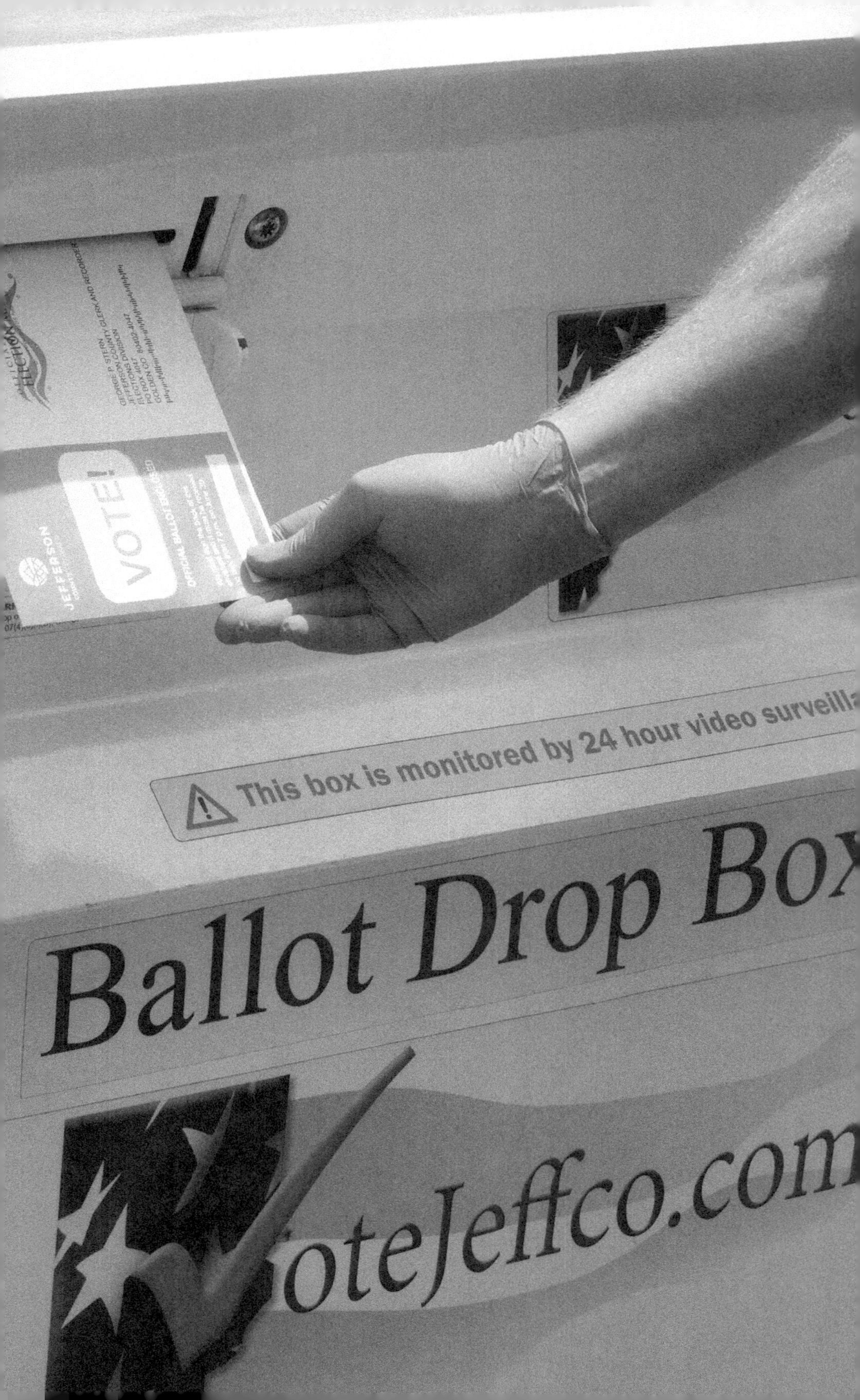
JEFFERSON
VOTE!
This box is monitored by 24 hour video
Ballot Drop Box

3 Perspectives

Introduction

This chapter presents nine original essays on the topic of elections in the United States written by activists, scholars, and stakeholders working on the frontlines of electoral politics at the state and national levels. Collectively, these essays provide insights, perspectives, and bold proposals regarding some of the most pressing and troubling challenges facing the American election system as the nation moves deeper into the 21st century.

Equality and Constitutional Electoral Reform: Problems and Prospects

Ken Bedell

Voter suppression comes in many flavors, but the goal is always the same: one political party or another wants to gain an advantage to win an election. The purpose of voter suppression is never to empower the will of the people but to assist a

---

The extensive spread of the corona virus during the COVID-19 pandemic impacted elections and voting in numerous ways in the 2020 elections. The use of mail-in voting was significantly expanded as well as the use of drop-off boxes. Citizens voting in person on Election Day often wore masks and protective gloves and were asked to maintain safe social distancing (six feet or more) from other voters waiting in line to cast their ballot. (Dorothy Merrimon Crawford/Dreamstime.com)

particular political party or special interest in gaining possession of the power of the government.

A desire to manipulate the rules to control the election process is a strategy used by both Democrats and Republicans. Republicans attempt to repress votes by African Americans and other minority groups. Democrats attempt to keep minority parties such as the Green Party off the ballot so that progressive movement supporters do not have choices. These and other attempts to ensure electoral success are a serious problem, but the largest and most consequential disenfranchisement of American voters results from the design of the Constitution itself.

The authors of the Constitution worried that the governmental structure they invented might be controlled by a special interest and fail to meet the needs of all the people. George Washington chaired the deliberations at the Constitutional Convention of 1787. In his Farewell Address at the end of his presidency in 1796, he pointed to the danger of the organized faction, which "in the place of the delegated will of the nation the will of a party . . . make[s] the public administration the mirror of the ill-concerted and incongruous projects of faction, rather than the organ of consistent and wholesome plans digested by common counsels and modified by mutual interests."

Today we are experiencing the nightmare that Washington and other Founders feared. Many popular legislative proposals, such as the Equal Rights Amendment or commonsense gun laws, are held up by factions that do not represent the will of the American people. At the same time, progress on economic equity has stalled for decades. It is time to look at the government's structure with an open mind, as the Founders did.

When the Founding Fathers decided to establish geographic regions as the basis for representation in the Senate and House of Representatives, they did not see any alternatives. For one thing, the delegates to the Constitutional Convention represented states. Notes and letters from the convention that were recently made available describe the proceedings. They make it clear that protecting their home states' economic interests was a top priority for all the delegates.

To be fair to the authors of the Constitution, the context in which they were operating was different from today. They could not imagine that America would become a multicultural nation in which nonwhite people would constitute a majority of the population by 2030. They were writing a constitution under which white people would govern. They did not think about how the government could benefit from the experiences and insights of many different racial, ethnic, and other identity groups.

While there has been progress in recent years to increase diversity in Congress, it remains more white, more male, and older than the population. The 116th Congress, elected in 2018, continued a trend of increasing diversity in elected Democrats and decreasing diversity in elected Republicans. The 116th House of Representatives had only 13 Republican women, which is down from 23 in the previous Congress. And the 116th Congress had only one nonwhite Republican. Today, congressional districts that elect Republicans are doing very little to contribute minority voices to the legislative process. For the 117th Congress, whites made up 77 percent of the House and 89 percent of the Senate, Blacks 13 percent of the House and 3 percent of the Senate, Hispanics 8 percent of the House and 6 percent of the Senate, and Asians 3 percent of the House and 2 percent of the Senate. By party, 83 percent of Democrats and 17 percent of Republicans were of racial/ethnic minority backgrounds. As to gender, there were 46 Democratic women in the House and 43 in the Senate, versus 5 Republican women in the House and 5 Republican women in the Senate. At 120 total, women comprised 27 percent of the Congress (144 seats out of 539). Among Democrats,

38 percent were female, versus 14 percent among Republicans (AmericanBar.org 2022; Pew Research.org 2021).

One 2018 MIT Survey found 28 House members, with more than 85 percent of the voters in their district supporting them. This included four districts where a candidate had no or only symbolic opposition. Thirteen members were elected with fewer than 50 percent of the voters supporting them. In all, there were 41,599,772 voters represented in Congress by someone who was not their first choice. This is 36.6 percent of all 2018 voters (MIT Election Data 2020). Across the country, more than one-third of all voters did not have their right to vote suppressed; instead, they had their opinion ignored. A consequence of ignoring these voters is that the country is not fully benefiting from the gifts of all racial and cultural groups.

Is there a way to solve this problem? I propose that a possible solution is for the United States to elect members to a single legislative body through a national voting registry. Members would be chosen by every citizen signing up with a candidate of their choice. In this way, every citizen is represented in the legislature by a person that they choose. And legislators know exactly who they are representing. Once a candidate has a certain number of followers—maybe 300,000—the candidate would join the legislature. Members would serve for four years. Then citizens would either reaffirm their choice or make a new choice.

This system addresses many of the problems with the existing constitutional process of determining who serves in Congress. The problem of gerrymandering would disappear because geographical boundaries would no longer determine districts. Also, attempts by state legislatures to make it more difficult for specific groups of citizens to vote would no longer be a problem, because a federal registry would certify citizens. The disproportionate influence of states with small populations in the Senate would disappear. Of course, accommodations would need to be made to ensure that people without phone or internet access could vote.

When George Washington led the Founders in their quest to design a government to serve the needs of the colonists, the group took bold steps and created something that had never been tried before. Today, Americans need leaders who will again boldly design a government that will benefit from the contributions of all racial and identity groups. America needs a government that does not acknowledge the representational desires of more than one-third of the voting citizens when elections are held.

References

AmericanBar.org. 2021. "Demographics and Composition of the 117th Congress." Accessed January 10, 2022. https://www.americanbar.org/advocacy/governmental_legislative_work/publications/washingtonletter/january-2021-wl/demographics-117thcongress.

MIT Election Data and Science Lab. 2020. "U.S. House 1976–2020." Harvard Dataverse. Accessed December 2, 2020. https://dataverse.harvard.edu/dataset.xhtml?persistentId=doi:10.7910/DVN/IG0UN2.

Pew Research.org. 2021. "Racial-Ethnic Diversity Increases Yet Again With the 117th Congress. Accessed January 10, 2022. https://www.pewresearch.org/fact-tank/2021/01/28/racial-ethnic-diversity-increases-yet-again-with-the-117th-Congress.

Ken Bedell is a longtime civil rights activist and was senior advisor of the Faith Based and Neighborhood Partnership Center, U.S. Department of Education. An ordained Methodist minister, Bedell is the author of Civil Rights Dream: Diagnosing and Treating American Racism *(2017)* and Different Ships—Same Boat *(2000).*

Is Colorado a One-Party State?

Tom Cronin and Bob Loevy

Colorado went blue in the 2020 elections, with Democratic presidential candidate Joe Biden and Democratic U.S. senator candidate John Hickenlooper scoring impressive victories over their Republican opponents. This, of course, built on the blue wave in 2018. Four of Colorado's metropolitan areas (Colorado Springs, Fort Collins, Boulder, and Denver) were among the leading areas in America swinging more Democratic in 2020 than in 2016. Those 2020 election results beg the question: Is Colorado now a one-party state?

One factor to weigh when considering that question is that Democrats are exceeding Republicans in political party registration across Colorado. As of November 2021, there were 1,129,733 active registered Democrats in Colorado, about 100,000 more than the 1,028,239 active registered Republicans. Of course, the largest number of active voters in Colorado registered as unaffiliated (1,541,199). Democrats, however, have a solid lead among those who choose to register in one major political party or the other, and we expect the Democratic Party lead in registered voters to grow. Growth in registered Democrats will be driven in part by the fact that most of the statewide officials in Colorado are Democrats. This makes registration as Republican less attractive, because non-Democrats are unable to vote in the Democratic primary: in Colorado, you must be registered as either Democratic or unaffiliated to vote in the Democratic primary.

Colorado's transition into a more reliably blue state means that Democratic Party primaries increasingly determine who will hold the contested seat after the general election. Indeed, precisely this scenario unfolded in the 2020 U.S. Senate race in Colorado. Winning the Democratic primary over former Colorado Speaker of the House Andrew Romanoff proved to be a tougher fight for John Hickenlooper than was defeating his Republican opponent, incumbent senator Cory Gardner, in the general election.

Polls taken in fall 2020 showed that Gardner had little chance of winning reelection, mainly because he was a Republican in a year when the Republican nominee for president, Donald Trump, was deeply unpopular in the state. That he was a Republican, however, hurt him less than that he was seemingly running on a Trump-Gardner ticket, defending the president at every turn.

As the Democratic primary election becomes the main event in statewide election to office, voter turnout in the Democratic primary will go up. In the meantime, voter turnout in the general election will stay steady or go down, because the Democrats may regularly win most elections. News media may increasingly give top billing to the Democratic primaries for statewide office and take a ho-hum attitude toward the "one party always wins" general election.

As Republicans fall further behind the Democrats in Colorado, the party will become limited geographically to rural agricultural counties and outlying suburbs of major metropolitan areas, where Republican voters still predominate. The Republican Party's last remaining area of real political strength will be in electing county commissioners and other county officials in the underpopulated regions of the state. The same will be true of those Republicans who succeed in getting elected to the state legislature. They may become a permanent minority with little power to stop the Democratic majority in the state senate and the state house of representatives from carrying out their policy priorities.

In this scenario, debate over bills in the state legislature will often pit moderate Democrats against progressive Democrats rather than Democrats against Republicans. Were the Democrats to split on a controversial bill, the Republicans could cast deciding votes on a few bills. Obviously, when the Democrats are united, the Republicans will be outvoted and lose.

It is possible a "problem-solving" caucus will emerge in the legislature, such as what has happened in the U.S. House of Representatives. Moderate Democrats hoping to weaken the position of Far Left members will reach out to moderate Republicans to seek more centrist legislation. This will probably be inevitable in Colorado, at least on some policy issues, such as water management, criminal justice reform, and infrastructure investment.

For a while at least, the Republicans should continue to dominate in sizable metropolitan areas outside the Denver-Boulder metropolitan area: El Paso County (county seat, Colorado Springs), Weld County (Castle Rock), and Mesa County (Grand Junction). But even these GOP stalwarts are not as Republican as they once were, and their downtown urban areas are increasingly turning Democratic.

As the Democrats take more control of government policy and practice in a one-party Democratic Colorado, the Republicans main chance at winning statewide political office will come when the Democrats make mistakes, push the state's politics too far to the left, or otherwise antagonize large numbers of moderate voters, all of which can happen. Statewide elections are the place where disenchantment with the dominant Democrats would likely first appear. An occasional charismatic Republican candidate for governor, one who pledges to clean up the Democratic mess in Denver, will win the governorship, temporarily clip the wings of the dominant Democrats, and perhaps even win reelection. That is what happened in states such as Massachusetts, Maryland, and Vermont. In otherwise strongly Democratic Massachusetts, Republican Charlie Baker is a popular two-term Republican governor. In largely Democratic Maryland, Republican Larry Hogan has been elected and reelected by pledging to correct the faults of Maryland Democrats. Note that these are relatively progressive Republicans, as is Vermont governor Phil Scott.

Many independents in Colorado and elsewhere seem to like the "checks and balances" of having the governorship and the state legislature divided between the two parties. That is probably why there are Democratic governors in several Republican states right now, as in Kentucky, Louisiana, and North Carolina. For the present, however, the Democratic Party has outorganized the Republican Party in Colorado. With all major statewide offices occupied by Democrats, including two U.S. senators, the GOP in Colorado has fewer places to go to groom candidates for statewide offices in future elections.

Republicans do, however, run a handful of the state's bigger cities, with Mayor John Suthers in Colorado Springs and Mayor Mike Coffman in Aurora as perhaps the most visible examples. Things will likely be politically and governmentally different in Colorado if the state remains a one-party Democratic state.

Tom Cronin and Bob Loevy are retired professors of political science at Colorado College and regularly write on Colorado and national politics.

Thoughts on the 2020 Election

Sara Hagedorn

The first question in my senior U.S. elections course during the spring 2021 semester was "What are your thoughts about what happened at the Capitol on January 6?" It is a good question, and frankly, I am glad students are thinking about it. One student, knowing the Capitol was my office for seven years when I worked as a U.S. Senate staffer, asked it. I often talk with my students in reverent tones about the shining white dome and the feeling of awe that overcame me every time I went onto the Senate floor during a debate. I impart to them how it was an honor to go to work, every single day, for the American people.

To see the Capitol building and the institution it represents breached and trashed the way it was on January 6, 2020, took my breath away. I try not to be emotional and subjective when

I discuss politics, because that is not what good scholarship is about, but this event hit a bit different. I was sad, angry, and confused that day, so when my student asked, I was honest about my feelings. I described it as an almost inevitable end to a tumultuous election cycle. But I was clear about my belief that it does not have to be this way—and that as Americans, we can and should do better.

During that first class, I stressed the fact that despite the horror we witnessed on January 6, we were able to view the normal, peaceful transition of executive power two weeks later. That peaceful transfer of power has been a hallmark of American democracy for much of our 230-year history. By all accounts, the inaugural festivities were average and without much excitement, which for most people was a welcome change from January 6. It seems impossible that these two events took place in the same year, let alone month, but occur they did, and they seemed to put a cap on the already turbulent 2020 political year.

Throughout 2019 and early 2020, the reelection of President Trump sometimes seemed an inevitability and at other times an impossibility. The economy was booming; unemployment was at record lows; interest rates were practically nonexistent. Political scientists like myself look to these economic factors, among other indicators, to help us predict election results. They all looked like positives for Trump that could lift him to reelection despite his low personal approval ratings.

Then the COVID-19 pandemic arrived in the United States in early 2020, and the deck was shuffled. The summer saw protest events and civil unrest in countless cities across the country after the murder of George Floyd, an African American man, at the hands of a white police officer. Some pundits and analysts, including me, thought the unrest could trigger a backlash that might mean more votes for the incumbent president in some of these states, but we also recognized that the effects of the pandemic on the nation's politics were harder to model. The Democrats ended up nominating a moderate, long-term political fixture in Joe Biden, who did not engage in typical campaigning because of concerns about the spread of COVID-19 at political rallies.

Election Day finally arrived on November 3, 2020, and Biden was elected. But a few surprises were in store, courtesy of America's voters. We did not see a typical election. Instead, national unrest, the soaring COVID-19 death toll, the crippling economic effects of the pandemic, and the strong feelings (both positive and negative) that Trump elicited from the American public all worked together to produce astronomical turnout numbers in every state, with more people voting in the 2020 election than ever before.

We saw most American voters reject the sitting president, even though President Trump received more votes than any previous presidential candidate in history—except for former vice president Biden, of course. Over 74 million people still preferred President Trump's policies and brand of politics to the potential Biden administration. Several states' results were close, not the previously speculated blowout. This was not a lopsided victory for Biden by any means, and any effort to categorize it as such would be folly, just as it would be folly to dismiss the more than 80 million people who supported him. But any effort to dismiss the 74 million voters who cast their ballots for Trump should not be dismissed either. The losing side voters should never be ignored in American politics.

Some election observers may look at the 2020 results and think it was a clear repudiation of conservative or even Republican policies and politics. They would be wrong. Yes, President Trump lost states and voters from 2016. His bombastic rhetoric was voted out of the White House. However, many of the policies and priorities of his administration could not be considered conservative or even traditionally Republican. The 2020 presidential election was a rejection of Trump himself, not of the ideas of conservatism or even the Republican platform. In many cases those ideas were embraced. Let me explain.

In the 2020 election, instead of Democratic congressional candidates catching and riding Biden's coattails to victory and expanding Speaker Nancy Pelosi's majority in the House of Representatives, the opposite occurred. President-elect Biden outperformed Democratic House and Senate candidates around the country. Republican challengers beat Democratic congressional incumbents in numerous districts. In fact, the Republicans had a net gain of more than 10 seats in 2020, greatly diminishing the Democrat majority in the House. Voters may not have agreed with President Trump, but they were not necessarily buying what the Democratic candidates were selling either.

Senate races were even more interesting and show us that voters were separating their thoughts about the top of the ticket from down-ballot races. The Democrats had a net gain of three seats in the Senate, but many had speculated that number would be greater. Many incumbent Republican senators were seen to be in danger of losing. Few pundits thought Senators Susan Collins (ME), Thom Tillis (NC), Joni Ernst (IA), Steve Daines (MT), and Lindsey Graham (SC) would all win new six-year terms. As we know, they were all reelected. This tells us voters across the country were ready to take their chances on a new president, someone whose personality and polices were a known commodity, but also wanted to keep a relatively conservative and Republican Congress.

What later happened in the Georgia runoff races should not be conflated with the November races, as according to the *Washington Post*, half a million voters stayed home in the January runoff after being told for two months their votes probably were not counted anyway. We should not take what happened in Georgia as a signal against Republicans or conservative policies. It was voters listening to conspiracy theories about voter fraud from Trump, his campaign, and the GOP.

Elections have consequences, and one major consequence is coming together to govern in the aftermath. The Democrat majority in the House is razor-thin, with many Democrats representing moderate districts, making the Speaker's job difficult on a good day. House Democrat leadership must work with moderate members of their own party and members of the minority to get their priorities, and those of the new administration, passed. This means more moderate legislation may be coming out of the House. The Senate is split evenly at 50–50 and will look like the Senate of 2001, when Senators Tom Daschle (D-SD) and Trent Lott (R-MS) worked out a power-sharing agreement for much of that year.

What all of this means is Congress needs to return to actual cross-aisle legislating and negotiating. This means compromise can no longer be the dirty word of politics and that nobody gets everything they want. It means moderates play a larger than normal role in legislative politics, a role they have not enjoyed for several years. It also opens the door to real negotiation and policy outcomes that benefit a larger swath of Americans. Now is not the time to inflict retribution or punishment upon the minority party. It is not the time to eliminate the filibuster, to silence the voice of the minority. It is a time to heal the wounds of 2020 and the events of January 6. It is time to call those events what they were: domestic terrorism by a radical fringe who do not represent all 74 million Americans who voted for the minority party. It is a time to be more tolerant and civil toward those with whom we disagree. It is time to be American.

Sara Hagedorn is an assistant professor of political science at the University of Colorado–Colorado Springs. She is coauthor of The American Congress *(ABC-CLIO, 2019), her area of expertise.*

Colorado's Election System: A National Model

Beth Hendrix

In the 2020 election, held during the COVID-19 pandemic, more than three million Coloradans cast their ballots from the comfort, convenience, and safety of their own homes by using a secure drop box or by mailing their ballots. They were also able to cast their ballots in person at Voter Service and Polling Centers. The county clerks and the secretary of state are to be commended for a safe, secure, and seamless election.

For mail-in ballots to work, accurate voting rolls must be maintained, and Colorado works hard to do so. The Colorado secretary of state works with the U.S. Postal Service and Colorado's Driver's License Bureau to receive changes of address; lists of those who have died are received from the Colorado Department of Public Health and the Environment, and the Social Security Death Index. Citizenship status is checked. The state is a member of the Electronic Registration Information Center, a nonprofit consortium of states that compares voter registration among states; membership in the consortium allows election officials to see if a voter voted in another state as well as Colorado. There are nine additional security features built into Colorado's mail ballot system that allow voters to be assured of the integrity of the election system:

1. Each county in Colorado in each election uses a bipartisan board to test its voting systems prior to using them.
2. Ballot vendors use special paper that the scanning and tabulating machines can accommodate. This paper is difficult to duplicate by any person attempting to submit a fraudulent or counterfeit ballot.
3. A barcode on the ballot envelope is specific to each voter, allowing signatures on the ballot return envelope to be checked against the signature on record by a bipartisan team of election workers. If there is a discrepancy with the signature during the verification process, the voter is notified and requested to "cure" (fix) the signature in person or by electronic means. The signature database is updated each election by county election offices.

4. First-time voters who registered online are required to send identification and proof of citizenship along with their returned ballot.
5. Bipartisan election judges oversee the entire process.
6. Colorado's county clerks use two-factor authentication to access voter registration databases.
7. Ballot tracing is available to let voters know that their ballot has been mailed to them and, when returned, that it has been received by election officials for processing. This feature gives voters the confidence that their ballot is, in fact, being counted. It also indicates that the ballot is ready to be processed.
8. The availability of Voter Service and Polling Centers allows a voter experiencing coercion to safely vote in person in a pristine environment. The centers open three weeks ahead of Election Day, allowing voters to choose their vote date.
9. Postelection, a risk-limiting audit is conducted to ensure results match voter intent. In 2017, Colorado became the first state in the nation to complete a statewide risk-limiting audit.

Only five cases of voter fraud have led to criminal convictions in Colorado since 2006, according to a database maintained by the Heritage Foundation. Colorado refers potential voter fraud to the district attorney to maintain voter confidence.

Indeed, Colorado's election systems are truly a national model. Colorado's election systems ensure that voting is easier and more accessible for voters, all the while maintaining vital security. As elections around the country are being scrutinized, Coloradans can trust that their state's certified election results match voter intent because of the layered security systems in place that have been repeatedly tested. In fact, former secretary of state Wayne Williams recently reported that Colorado's voting systems have been tested more than 800 times since 2016 and that they have successfully passed every test. It is no wonder, then, that Colorado has been declared to be the safest state in which to cast a vote. The state and county elected officials are to be thanked for their dedicated service to establish and implement a safe, secure, and efficient election system that may justifiably be considered a model for the entire nation to follow.

Beth Hendrix is the executive director of the League of Women Voters of Colorado, a nonpartisan nonprofit providing services to empower voters and defend democracy for all.

Voter Suppression and the Exclusion of American Citizenship

Adam Le

The national election of 2020 brought back to light conversations about voter suppression in the United States. For example, as Georgia and Texas opened early voting in early October 2020, it wasn't long before reports arose of extremely long waiting times, with American citizens waiting in lines to vote for upwards of 11 hours (Tsioulcas 2020). These reports echoed similar accounts of long wait times disproportionately impacting Black, Indigenous, and other People of Color (BIPOC) voters in states such as Georgia and Florida during the 2016 election. For many voting rights advocates and other observers, these events sparked heightened fears of voter suppression as the 2020 election got closer.

Voter suppression in the United States, however, is not new. It has long historical ties to racism and exclusion in American politics. The Founders agonized over the relationship between voting and citizenship. Americans fought over the franchise during the Reconstruction period, debated it in Congress during both the women's suffrage and civil rights eras, and still discuss it today, especially given rising fears that the right to vote, earned over decades of struggle and violence, is under attack again. In each of these scenarios, racism plays a role in shaping the debate over who can participate in electoral politics. While all debates have tied the franchise to a practice of citizenship, Black people in the United States have been denied the right to vote for much of the nation's history, and their experiences need to be considered when thinking about voter suppression.

The Founders relied on a system of strict voter eligibility to stabilize American government. Their form of voting and citizenship in general was premised on exclusion of most groups besides wealthy white landowners. The Constitution left voting eligibility to the states, and in the early years of American history, this meant "most states limited the right to vote to propertied white males" (Karch 2016, 370).

The Founders were concerned about the influence of "factions" vis-à-vis minority groups such as landowners (Hamilton, Madison, and Jay 1987). Systems of chattel slavery in the United States upheld the dichotomy of citizens versus noncitizens and the dichotomy between those with political rights and citizenship versus those who faced the "social death" of exclusion from political participation (Patterson 1982; Alexander 2012; Du Bois 1935). The Constitution framers and Founders' exclusion of most Americans from the ballot box was executed through state-level restrictions and other methods of voter suppression that gave more power to those who could vote (Shklar 1991; Young 1990).

This exclusion continued into the 19th century, interrupted only briefly by the passage of the 13th, 14th, and 15th Amendments and the Reconstruction era. As French diplomat Alexis de Tocqueville observed in his classic 1835 text *Democracy in America*, everyone in the United States had a vote "except for slaves, servants, and paupers fed by the township . . . and, hence, [everyone had] an indirect share in lawmaking" (de Tocqueville 1969, 240). Tocqueville's observations of popular sovereignty in America, then, were heavily constrained by voter suppression, as large numbers of people were restricted access to legislative institutions and customs. After the Civil War, when voting rights were given to African American men and slavery was declared illegal, it briefly appeared that marginalized ethnic and racial groups might become full participants in American political life. Instead, across the Jim Crow South by the late 1800s, African Americans who technically had the legal right to vote were still stripped of the franchise through poll taxes, grandfather clauses, and literacy tests. This remained the status quo until the civil rights protests of the 1950s and 1960s.

Today, though, voting rights advocates contend that equal access to the ballot box, regardless of race, creed, gender, or income, has become imperiled once again. One of the clearest ways contemporary voter suppression is expressed itself is through incarceration. Incarceration upholds the dichotomy between citizens and noncitizens by legally disenfranchising citizens in most states and by making it more difficult for re-enfranchised citizens to vote (Alexander 2012). Academics have underscored the extent to which incarcerated people participate in politics. Studies have found that incarceration and contact with the criminal justice system (i.e., "custodial contact") have a demobilizing effect on individuals' likelihood to formally participate in politics by voting, donating to campaigns, or contacting representatives (Lerman and Weaver 2014; Walker 2020). Even when incarcerated citizens complete their sentences and regain the right to vote, they are disillusioned and wary of drawing attention toward themselves (Lerman and Weaver 2014; Weaver and Lerman 2010).

With racialized voter identification laws and people being questioned about their citizenship on a day-to-day basis, citizens may disengage from formal politics for their own personal safety. This reality highlights the need to look beyond formal voting restrictions and examine how voter suppression affects peoples' likelihood to engage in politics. Disenfranchisement efforts continue to reflect a societal belief in "the ideal citizen as white, male, innocent, worthy, and mentally independent"

(Dilts 2014, 159). American incarceration excludes millions of Americans with few mentions of the disproportionate number of Black people who are incarcerated and are thus excluded from political participation. Voter suppression continues to be a problem, and it is necessary to address its origins in racism to understand how voter suppression navigates through politics, voting, and representation today.

References

Alexander, M. 2012. *The New Jim Crow: Mass Incarceration in the Age of Colorblindness.* New York: New Press.

De Tocqueville, Alexis. 1969. *Democracy in America.* Trans. George Lawrence. Ed. J. P. Mayer. New York: Harper Perennial Modern Classics.

Dilts, A. 2014. *Punishment and Inclusion: Race, Membership, and the Limits of American Liberalism.* New York: Fordham University Press.

Du Bois, W. E. B. 1935. *Black Reconstruction in America, 1860–1880.* New York: Free Press.

Hamilton, A., J. Madison, and J. Jay. 1987. *The Federalist Papers.* New York: Penguin Books.

Karch, A. 2016. "The States and American Political Development." In *The Oxford Handbook of American Political Development,* edited by Richard Valelly, Suzanne Mettler, and Robert Lieberman. New York: Oxford University Press.

Lerman, A. E., and V. M. Weaver. 2014. *Arresting Citizenship: The Democratic Consequences of American Crime Control.* Chicago: University of Chicago Press.

Patterson, O. 1982. *Slavery and Social Death: A Comparative Study.* Cambridge, MA: Harvard University Press.

Shklar, J. N. 1991. *American Citizenship: The Quest for Inclusion.* Cambridge, MA: Harvard University Press.

Tsioulcas, A. 2020, October 12. "Georgia Voters Face Hours-Long Lines at Polls on First Day of Early Voting." NPR KQED.

Walker, H. L. 2020. *Mobilized by Injustice: Criminal Justice Contact, Political Participation, and Race*. New York: Oxford University Press.

Weaver, V. M., and A. E. Lerman. 2010. "Political Consequences of the Carceral State." *American Political Science Review* 104 (1): 817–33.

Young, I. M. 1990. *Justice and the Politics of Difference*. Princeton, NJ: Princeton University Press.

Adam Le is a PhD candidate at the University of Minnesota studying American politics, political theory, and sociology. His research focuses on how citizens interact with government in the United States.

The Kornacki Effect: Vote Count Framing in a Pandemic Year

Kimberly Nalder

In this era of concern about disinformation and conspiracy theories, it's easy to overlook subtler ways in which we may be misled. In the case of election night (November 3) 2020, the frenzied rush on the part of many news media outlets to report who was "winning" is the culprit and has ended up setting the table for some serious policy and political outcomes.

Election night is a time when Americans gather around the glow of their television, laptop, and cell phone screens to see what is in store for the country but also, let's face it, to cheer for their "team," hoping the blue team or the red team emerges victorious.

The TV networks, financially pressured to attract eyeballs, serve up what the people seem to want: sports-like reporting, complete with live scoreboards and cheesy pictures of the "players" popping up on screen. The mass media has long been criticized for "horse-race" coverage of politics that focuses on candidates' prospects for victory or defeat instead of focusing on policy plans or stories about candidates' backgrounds. On election night (and these days, more like election week), this is "turned up to 11." You hear constant present-tense, sport-style phrasing: "The president has to continue winning precincts"; "the president is playing defense"; "things have to change quickly for Biden to pull this one out."

But sporting events are live and happening as we view them. As much as it appears otherwise, postelection coverage is not covering events in real time. The votes have already been cast. We're just counting them. Nobody is "winning" or "losing" or "pulling ahead." They have already won or lost. We are just catching up with the results.

Election night serves as a huge draw for cable TV news, which assigns dedicated journalists to keep us up on the very latest reported counts. John King, of CNN, frantically reports changes or imagines potential scenarios on the "magic board," circling counties, adding up numbers, and reporting extremely preliminary results ("with 3 percent of precincts reporting . . ."). Fox News deploys "map guy" Bill Hemmer to walk the audience through the "action." And MSNBC features Gap khaki–clad Steve Kornacki, whose mathematical theatrics with election result maps on election night 2020 became a pop sensation of sorts. Most famously, comedian Leslie Jones tweeted out videos of herself watching his map mastery while shouting out encouragement. She's such a fan that she exclaimed on the *Tonight Show* that "Steve Kornacki is my snacky."

This type of election coverage is fun, but is it good for us?

In 2020, the circumstances under which the election was held were unprecedented. A global pandemic was ravaging the nation, schools were closed, many people (the lucky ones) were working remotely, and mask mandates were being enforced in most of the country. Under these conditions, many states made allowances to let more people than ever vote by mail (also called "absentee" ballots) or submit their ballots in other, less traditional ways, such as drop boxes, to avoid potentially dangerous in-person contact due to COVID-19.

A second factor was also at play. Responses to the COVID-19 pandemic had become politicized, largely due to messaging from then president Trump, who told journalist Bob Woodward in March 2020 that he "wanted to always play it [the virus] down." He did so, appearing maskless, denigrating mask wearers, calling for schools and businesses to reopen despite escalating COVID-19 caseloads and deaths, and generally defying recommendations from public health officials. So, taking cues from the president, Republicans were much less concerned about the virus and much less likely to take precautions. This ended up creating a dynamic in which voters from America's two major parties cast their ballots in different ways. Republicans were more likely to vote in the traditional way, in person at the precinct, while Democrats were more likely to vote by mail or deposit their ballots in drop boxes. Such a partisan disparity in voting method had not existed in previous elections.

But why would vote method matter? It matters because in most states, including some key swing states, precinct votes are counted and reported first, while mail-in ballots are counted after polls close. Only 32 states allowed some sort of "precanvassing" of mail-in ballots in 2020 (verifying voter eligibility, taking the ballots out of the envelopes to be ready to be scanned, or even starting to count the early ballots). Even those that started the process early often did not plan to finish until after the precinct votes had been reported. Key swing states such as Michigan, Wisconsin, and Pennsylvania had laws on their books that did not allow much or any of this processing of ballots prior to Election Day. As a result, election officials in these and other states were only able to begin the labor-intensive process of counting mail ballots on Election Day, even though many had been received days or weeks earlier.

This set up a situation in which, in the early horse-race coverage of vote counting, more Republican (in-person) votes were tallied early, while proportionately more Democratic mail-in votes were added in later. It artificially made it look like Republicans were "ahead" and then suddenly blue votes flooded in, altering the outcome. The Trump campaign turned this predictable sequence of events into an opportunity to claim that something was amiss with the election tallies in states that Trump ultimately lost.

In Wisconsin, for example, there was a sudden surge of mostly Democratic votes added to the tally at 4:00 a.m. on November 4. What occurred is that the absentee ballot count from Milwaukee was added at that time, and Milwaukee is a heavily Democratic city. That's pretty normal stuff and expected by anyone paying attention to demographics and vote tally rules in the state.

But to anyone wishing to confuse and mislead, this was a perfect opportunity to create doubt about the legitimacy of the vote count. President Trump tweeted around 9:00 a.m. that his lead in vital states "started to magically disappear as surprise ballot dumps were counted." Popular right-wing website Gateway Pundit posted an article titled "Voter Fraud in Wisconsin—Massive Dump of Over 100,000 Ballots for Biden All of a Sudden Appear Overnight." Unsurprisingly, many Americans were persuaded that this and other examples of "late ballots" were nefarious.

In fact, the election was free and fair. In mid-November 2020, as the disinformation spread, the Trump administration's Cybersecurity and Infrastructure Security Agency, which oversees election security, joined with the National Association of State Election Directors and the National Association of Secretaries of State, which run elections at the state level, to release a statement to counteract the false narrative. The statement featured unequivocal language declaring that "the November 3rd election was the most secure in American history" and that "[t]**here is no evidence that any voting system deleted or**

lost votes, changed votes, or was in any way compromised" (bold in original).

Nevertheless, the waters had been muddied, and the idea of a "stolen election" took hold with many on the Right. The false narrative was so pervasive that members of Congress were able to argue essentially that even if this was all untrue, many people believed it, so members should act on that deeply absorbed lie and vote against certification of the true Electoral College results. Just before the start of the January 6 insurrection, Republican senator Ted Cruz made this case: "Recent polling shows that 39% of Americans believe the election that just occurred, 'was rigged.' You may not agree with that assessment. But it is nonetheless a reality for nearly half the country. . . . Even if you do not share that conviction, it is the responsibility, I believe, of this office to acknowledge that as a profound threat to this country and to the legitimacy of any administrations that will come in the future."

This false idea that the election had been stolen motivated one of the greatest threats to American democracy to date. On January 6, 2021, a mob of Trump supporters, convinced that votes for an illegitimate president were about to be certified by Congress, stormed the Capitol as the vote certification was proceeding. They broke windows and doors, injured Capitol police, ransacked members' offices, and erected gallows on the grounds outside the Capitol building. They shouted, "Hang Mike Pence"—Trump's vice president—for doing his constitutional duty that day.

The momentum for action justified by the false claims did not slow after the horror of the January 6 insurrection though. Republican-controlled state legislatures across the country began passing laws restricting voting, using the nonexistent election fraud as justification to make voting more difficult. Since typically, Republicans are more likely to vote than Democrats are, increases in voter turnout tend to mean more of those reticent Democrats are voting. So making it harder to vote, especially for traditionally Democratic constituencies, is more likely to benefit Republican candidates.

By mid-2021, 17 Republican-led states had enacted a total of 28 new laws making it harder for Americans to vote, with many others in process. The laws do things such as shortening the window of time for requesting a ballot, making it harder to automatically get a ballot, imposing stricter ID requirements, and reducing the number of polling places and the hours that are open, among other measures. Some proposals even make it easier for partisan officials to overturn election results at the state level.

All of this is spectacularly dangerous for our democracy. Although the election was free and fair, and that President Biden was duly elected, a large proportion of citizens have been told the opposite by conservative news outlets, social media posts, and GOP party leadership. No wonder many Americans have lost their trust in the electoral system. Rank-and-file members of both parties have come to believe that the other party is corrupt and getting away with stealing an election. It's understandable that Republican voters feel hostile toward the new president and vice president, who they have been repeatedly told are not legitimate officeholders. Will they obey laws signed by the new president? Will more violence occur among the more extreme factions? How will they feel about future elections? Will they ever trust true electoral outcomes that they don't like?

Though not its intent, breathless, Kornacki-style play-by-play coverage of the vote count during the days surrounding the election toppled over some of the first few dominoes leading to this democracy-threatening reality. Reporting as if the voting itself were occurring live created this perfect storm to form the semi-plausible (yet false) appearance of vote fraud. Those repeated claims, coming from trusted public officials and partisan media outlets on the right, convinced millions of Americans that the vote was tainted. Falsely manufactured mass suspicion was used as justification for Republican members of Congress to refuse to support certification of the vote on January 6 and for subsequent state legislatures to create laws to restrict voting and even to possibly allow some officials to overturn election results they find displeasing.

So, what can be done? This chain of events may have been prevented or at least minimized if media outlets had framed election coverage more responsibly. In a perfect world, they would only report results once they were fully counted and certified by the states. Or perhaps it is up to election officials to only reveal results once they are complete, or even after recounts and reviews have taken place, so that there isn't a misleading appearance of "changing" vote totals. If results were reported out by the news media only once they were completed, we'd miss out on the live Kornacki-style math wizardry. However, seeing complete results come in from states would still generate some electric moments. Given the 2020 example, we now realize the reality of a fuller range of negative outcomes that branch off from this style of reporting. This should give pause to us all, news directors included. And let's not forget the role of each American in all of this. Perhaps in this government "of the people, by the people, and for the people," it's up to us to be more skeptical of claims and accusations that are unsupported by any evidence. Next election, American voters need to support media outlets that report results responsibly and exercise critical thinking about claims by partisans.

Kimberly Nalder is a full professor of political science at California State University-Sacramento. She is executive director of Cal Speaks Opinion Research and director of the Project for an Informed Electorate.

Social Justice Protests and the 2020 Presidential Election

August H. Nimtz

On Monday, May 25, 2020, a white Minneapolis police officer named Derek Chauvin buried his knee into the neck of George Floyd, a 49-year-old African American male lying handcuffed and prone on the ground. After nine minutes of this treatment by Chauvin, Floyd was dead. Minneapolis thus became ground zero for the largest social protest in U.S. history. An estimated 15 million to 26 million Americans took to the streets, and the protests of police violence in African American communities extended from major cities to small towns. The protest that began in Minneapolis factored significantly into the presidential election. I had the privilege to attend and to report on the first protest. Having come of age politically in the 1950s and 1960s, I was able to bring both political and historical perspective to the events that took place that day.

An estimated 5,000 persons participated in the Minneapolis-St. Paul protests—most wearing masks but not able to social distance. The police were conspicuously absent. It was the first progressive mass action anywhere in the United States during the pandemic lockdown. The crowd was overwhelmingly youthful and white.

For anyone who has been involved in anti–police brutality protests in Minneapolis and St. Paul since at least 2014, that was not surprising. But for an African American of my generation, the racial composition of the crowd spoke volumes about what is so different today from the civil rights protests of the 1960s. Anti–police brutality protests in that era were almost exclusively African American affairs, and it could be dangerous for whites to be around when the protests took place. As late as 1992, a white truck driver, Reginald Denny, was nearly beaten to death by rioters in Los Angeles in the wake of the Rodney King beating.

Back in 1920, three Black men were lynched in Duluth, Minnesota, for allegedly raping a white woman. Ten thousand white people came out to celebrate their murder. A century later, on May 30, 2020, more than 1,000 mostly white people in Duluth came out to denounce what happened to George Floyd. Clearly, something had happened between 1920 and 2020 to explain that attitudinal change. That "something" was the Freedom Now movement, known today as the civil rights movement. Mass disciplined and nonviolent marches were decisive in the attitudinal change that took place between 1920 and 2020.

As noted by the *New York Times*, three-quarters of Americans supported the protests in June 2020. A large majority, including an estimated 60 percent of whites, also expressed support for the Black Lives Matter movement. These numbers declined over the summer, yet even as of September 2020, 55 percent of Americans—and 45 percent of white Americans—continued to express support for Black Lives Matter and its social justice agenda (Levitsky and Ziblatt 2020).

The most important voting, I argue, is with our feet. I am living testimony to that political truth. The first time that I tried to vote was in 1964, in Jim Crow New Orleans, when I was denied the right to vote because of the color of my skin. Four years later, it was possible for me to vote. Why? Because between 1964 and 1968, civil rights protestors took to the streets.

Some observers have speculated that the Black protests of the 1960s resulted in white backlash and, thus, in the election of Republican Richard Nixon over Democrat Hubert Humphrey in the 1968 presidential election. It has been suggested that the violence and looting carried out by a relatively small number of people during some of the George Floyd protests may similarly work to benefit Trump's reelection. Tucker Carlson, on Fox News, led Trump's cheerleaders hoping exactly for that outcome. I could not count how many times the burning liquor store on Lake Street in Minneapolis was shown on nightly news coverage, with the clear intent to stoke backlash and a "law and order" response to the protests. Carlson never showed footage, which was often replayed by other news outlets, of Chauvin burying his knee in George Floyd's neck. Trump embraced the opportunity to cast his reelection efforts around "law and order" issues, just as Republican Richard Nixon did in 1968.

I am convinced that the law-and-order/white backlash appeal did not work as well for Trump as it did for Nixon for four reasons. First, the COVID-19 pandemic—and Trump's response to that crisis—was the single most important issue of the 2020 election. Second, the sporadic violence that followed a few of the George Floyd protests in Minneapolis and a few other cities paled in comparison to those that took place between 1964 and 1968. The protests in 2020 were overwhelmingly peaceful and were framed by the media as such, despite the effort to paint them otherwise at Fox News and other conservative media outlets.

For the 1968 election, anecdotal evidence suggests that the "law and order" appeal got a hearing in the mostly white suburbs following isolated rioting, looting, and vandalism that took place in North Minneapolis in 1966 and 1967 during otherwise peaceful protests. Nixon, however, only got 40 percent of the vote in Minnesota, and the third-party campaign of segregationist George Wallace garnered only 4 percent of the statewide vote. In 2020, the arrests of right-wing, white nationalist Boogaloo Bois members who were involved in the looting and vandalism in Minneapolis may have factored into the local vote. Front-page coverage of the Boogaloo Bois story in the *Star Tribune*, the most widely circulated newspaper in the state, may have given pause to some who are susceptible to the law-and-order appeal, particularly when painted in black skin.

The third difference between 1968 and 2020 was the racial composition of the protestors. Anti–police brutality protestors in the 1960s were almost exclusively African Americans. Today, the situation in quite different, not only in Minneapolis but elsewhere. That fact made it difficult for the Fox crowd "to other" the protestors as the media did in the 1960s. Too many people of all skin colors participated in nonviolent protests in all kinds of communities.

Lastly, another key difference between 1968 and 2020 is that the Floyd protests took place in a United States where the American dream is a fading hope for an increasing number of white workers. In 1968, they were more likely to be true believers in the status quo and in defending it, because they were its beneficiaries. Those born after 1980 have a less than even chance of having the same life opportunities as someone born before then.

Let me end with what was also unique about the George Floyd protests in comparison to the earlier protest movement and relative to presidential elections. With the 1964 election, all the major civil rights leaders, including Dr. Martin Luther King Jr., called for a moratorium on protests beginning in the summer of that year. Everything, they argued, had to be subordinated to the November election to ensure Lyndon Johnson's election and Barry Goldwater's defeat. Their call was successful. In 2020, despite calls by Democratic Party leaders such as Stacey Abrams to end the protests and channel that energy into the electoral process, George Floyd protestors did not heed the siren call: "Wait until November."

References

Abrams, Stacey. 2020. "I Know Voting Feels Inadequate Right Now." *New York Times*. Accessed March 30, 2022. https://www.nytimes.com/2020/06/04/opinion/stacey-abrams-voting-floyd-protests.html.

Levitsky, Steven, and Daniel Ziblatt. 2020, October 23. "End Minority Rule." *New York Times*. Accessed March 30, 2022. https://nytimes.com/2020/10/23/opinion/sunday/disenfranchisement-democracy-minority-rule.html.

Wasow, Omar. 2020. "Agenda Seeding: How 1960s Black Protests Moved Elites, Public Opinion and Voting." *American Political Science Review* 114 (3): 638–59.

August H. Nimtz is professor of political science and African American and African studies, Distinguished Teaching Professor, University of Minnesota.

Indigenous Voters Helped Swing the 2020 Election

Anna V. Smith

The 2020 presidential election was a close race in a handful of states, including Arizona, where Native turnout made the difference in Joe Biden's slim but winning margin. Indigenous people in Arizona constitute nearly 6 percent of the population, some 425,000 people, and eligible voters in the Navajo Nation alone number around 67,000. Democratic candidate Joe Biden, who released a robust policy plan for Indian Country, beat Republican candidate Donald Trump in Arizona by a margin of about 41,000 total votes in the 2020 presidential election.

Precinct-level data shows that outside of heavily blue metropolitan areas such as Phoenix and Tucson, which also have high numbers of Indigenous voters, many of the rural Arizonans who voted for Biden and Mark Kelley, the successful Democratic candidate for the U.S. Senate, lived on tribal lands. In some Tohono O'odham Nation precincts, Biden and Kamala Harris won about 98 percent of the Native vote. According to the *Navajo Times*, the three counties that overlap with the Hopi Tribe and the Navajo Nation gave Biden 73,954 votes, to just 2,010 for Trump. In these counties, Biden won 97 percent of the vote, as opposed to 51 percent statewide.

That pattern is consistent with the 2016 election results, when the rest of the state went for Trump. Jordan James Harvill, a Cherokee and the chief of staff of the nonpartisan group VoteAmerica, an organization that worked directly with the Navajo Nation and community partners to get out the vote, noted that partisan groups long ignored Native voters in states such as Arizona, New Mexico, North Dakota, and Montana. Harvill, however, sees them as some of the highest-potential voters, and VoteAmerica is expected to continue to invest in voters in Indian Country for years to come.

Indigenous people in Arizona were especially hard-hit by the COVID-19 pandemic, which was exacerbated by Republican state officials who refused to support public-safety measures to limit the spread of COVID-19, such as mask mandates, business closures, or adequate allotment of pandemic resources. This was compounded by an inadequate federal response that delayed financial relief to tribal governments. In May 2020, the Navajo Nation had the highest per capita ratio of pandemic cases in the United States, surpassing even New York City. Navajo Nation president Jonathan Nez criticized the Trump administration for botching the federal pandemic response. Navajo Nation joined other tribal nations in a lawsuit over the dispersal of the pandemic-relief funds to tribal governments.

Exit polls after the 2020 election showed that the pandemic was the most important issue on the minds of Arizona's Indigenous voters in favoring Biden.

In the weeks before the 2020 election, several Navajo citizens filed suit against the state of Arizona over the state's deadline for mail-in ballots, pointing to the myriad challenges that Indigenous communities faced with vote-by-mail. They asked the court to allow ballots to be postmarked, instead of received, by 7:00 p.m. on Election Day. Although they lost the case, efforts by groups such as VoteAmerica, Four Directions, Rural Utah Project, and the Nez administration in counties like Apache County, which overlaps the Navajo Nation and Hopi Tribe, saw a 116 percent voter turnout compared to the 2016 election.

On the Tohono O'odham Nation, which spans Pima, Maricopa, and Pinal counties, most precincts were above 90 percent for Biden. Throughout the Trump administration, O'odham citizens and the tribal government had been vocal in their opposition to construction of a wall along the U.S.-Mexico border, which President Trump had forced through without tribal consultation. Indigenous critics said that the wall severs the natural landscape and destroys ancestral O'odham sites. Similar levels of support for Biden were repeated throughout precincts covering the lands of the Haulapai, Havasupai, White Mountain Apache, Gila River, San Carlos Apache, Pascua

Yaqui, Cocopah, and Colorado River tribes; 70 to 90 percent of voters in these areas checked their ballots for Biden.

Indigenous voters are by no means a monolith, and most Indigenous people live in urban areas. This reality makes it likely that most Indigenous Arizona voters cast their ballots in metro areas and therefore don't appear in voting data from tribal lands. A survey by a coalition of Indigenous organizations called Building Indigenous Power found that Indigenous voters on reservations were less likely to vote compared to those in cities or small towns. Nonetheless, clear voting patterns can be seen across Indian Country—including states other than Arizona.

In Montana, where the state voted for Trump overall, counties overlapping the reservations of the Blackfeet Nation, Fort Belknap Tribes, the Crow Tribe, and the Northern Cheyenne Tribe went blue. The Blackfeet Nation went 64 percent for Biden, the highest in the entire state, while the neighboring county went for Trump by 75 percent. The Native vote in Montana made the difference when Indigenous voters helped U.S. senator Jon Tester, a Democrat who has advocated for Indian Country in legislation regarding water settlements, missing and murdered Indigenous women, and tribal recognition, win a third Senate term in 2020.

Wisconsin, a closely watched swing state, went narrowly for Biden, who won by fewer than 21,000 votes. In Wisconsin, the Indigenous population is 90,189 (as of 2018). Wisconsin counties overlapping the lands of the Bad River Band of Lake Superior Chippewa, the Menominee Tribe, and the Stockbridge-Munsee Band of Mohicans voted heavily Democratic and helped tip the count to the party. Menominee County, which overlaps the Menominee Tribe's reservation, voted for Biden 82 percent, compared to the statewide average of 49.4 percent.

South Dakota went for Trump by 61 percent—except on tribal lands. Counties overlapping the lands of the Standing Rock Sioux, Cheyenne River Sioux, Oglala Sioux, Rosebud

Sioux, and Crow Creek tribes went solidly for Biden. In Oglala Lakota County, which overlaps the Oglala Sioux Tribe's Pine Ridge reservation, Biden won 88 percent of the vote. In Todd County, which overlaps the Rosebud Sioux reservation, Biden won 77 percent.

Additionally, Indigenous candidates did well. Six Native candidates, a historic high, were elected to the U.S. Congress in 2020. New Mexico made history by becoming the second state after Hawaii whose delegation to the U.S. Congress was made up entirely of women of color, two of whom were Native. That success is in addition to dozens of state and local offices to which Native candidates were elected, 11 of whom were elected to state office in Arizona.

As Harvill stated, the 2020 elections illuminated the importance of the Native vote. That vote is only likely to grow as an increasingly young Native population enters the electorate. Harvill maintains that Native American voters will likely become one of the defining groups of the American electorate, much like Latinx and Black voters.

Anna V. Smith is an assistant editor for High Country News.

Latinx Voting Behavior: Key Insights from Recent Presidential Elections

José D. Villalobos

Since the time of the Chicano civil rights movement, the Latinx community has emerged as an influential and politically active constituency and done so in a resolute, expanding, and multifaceted manner (e.g., see Affigne, Hu-DeHart, and Orr 2014; Bedolla 2014). What scholars refer to as the "Latinx" (or Hispanic) community is a very richly diverse population made up of many generations of people from different countries of origin, cultures, ideologies, and dialects. Media coverage of Latinos often oversimplifies the population as immigrants from

Mexico now living in the United States. However, Latinx immigrants hail from all corners of Latin America and beyond and have assorted political backgrounds, while many other Latinos today are native-born Americans thoroughly acculturated in American principles and politics. And yet despite the many differences, Latinos of all backgrounds experience shared commonalities, often referred to as pan-ethnic connections. As the U.S. Latinx population has grown substantially in size, Latinos of various Latin American origins have grown closer in residential proximity to one another, have experienced a growth in shared interests as they have worked to assimilate into U.S. society, and have become more socially and politically active, often uniting behind key issues (Monforti 2014).

Over the last half century, the Latinx vote was often referred to as a "sleeping giant," denoting a significantly growing population that had yet to realize its full potential as a powerful voting bloc. More recently, however, that perception has been replaced with the sense that Latinos are a political constituency to be reckoned with. The Latinx vote has increasingly affected and helped determine major election outcomes, including for critical presidential elections. Outreach to Latinos in an election cycle can pay dividends, while any time a candidate takes Latinos for granted, it usually results in a loss of political prospects and electoral support. Just as importantly, the rich diversity of the Latinx community provides ample opportunity for political officials and candidates of all stripes to compete for and earn the Latinx vote. This essay focuses on a few key insights from some of the most recent presidential elections to illustrate just how critical and influential the Latinx vote—and competing for that vote—has become.

In modern U.S. history, particularly since the civil rights movements during the presidencies of John F. Kennedy and Lyndon B. Johnson, the Democratic Party has sought to expand its voting base by more actively courting Latinos and other minority constituencies, both symbolically and substantively. Consequently, Democratic candidates have typically fared much better than Republicans in pursuing the Latinx vote. In recent presidential elections, Democrats have garnered up to as much as two-thirds of the overall Latinx vote, while Republicans have often struggled to keep above a 30 percent threshold to remain competitive overall. However, President George W. Bush's 2004 reelection campaign managed to buck the Latinx voting trend to a significant degree, aided in part by the relatively timid Latinx outreach of his opponent, Senator John Kerry. While Kerry took the Latinx vote for granted vis-à-vis a relatively nominal effort to directly engage the Latinx community, the campaign of President Bush, who had served as governor of Texas prior to his presidency, actively promoted his Spanish "Viva Bush" slogan, ran numerous bilingual television and radio ads, and touted a "compassionate conservative" policy agenda that catered to both traditional religious moral values and social programs (such as Bush's "No Child Left Behind" educational policy), which connected with many segments of the Latinx population.

As election night unfolded in 2004, news outlets took note that Bush had clearly overperformed among Latinos compared to past Republican nominees, earning as much as 44 percent of their vote (although the exact Latinx vote percentage was difficult to confirm due to some limitations with the exit polling data employed; see Leal et al. 2005; Suro, Fry, and Passel 2005). Thanks in part to that achievement, Bush went on to a clear reelection victory. Despite falling short of a majority of Latinx support, Bush's success in courting a much higher than typical percentage of Latinx voters proved a critical factor in aiding his reelection.

The impact of the Latinx vote became even more evident in 2012. The presidential election that year between Democratic incumbent Barack Obama and Republican challenger Mitt Romney became an historical "watershed moment," when the Latinx vote was most plausibly the decisive factor in the final vote outcome (Segura and Barreto 2012). In terms of the popular vote, Obama won the final vote margin by 2.8 percent, but it would not have turned out that way without the net 5.4 percent Latinx vote contribution that boosted Obama's overall vote advantage in the popular vote. Still, presidential elections are won by Electoral College votes, not the popular vote, and Obama benefited most critically across key swing state victories that fashioned his 332–206 Electoral College triumph. Across five key swing states—Colorado (9 electoral votes), Nevada (6), New Mexico (5), Florida (29), and Ohio (20)—Obama's net Latinx vote contributions were vital in determining the final results (Segura and Barreto 2012). In Colorado, Obama's +4.7 percent final margin of victory was made possible by the +10.9 percent net vote contribution from Latinx voters, who made up 14.1 percent of the total state vote. Overall, Obama received 87 percent of the Latinx vote in Colorado, compared to Romney's dismal 10 percent. Obama's Nevada and New Mexico Electoral College victories were similarly impressive, with Obama garnering a +10.5 percent net Latinx contribution amid an overall 6.6 percent margin of victory in Nevada, while the New Mexico victory was doubly impressive, with a +22.2 percent net Latinx contribution to his 9.9 percent overall margin of victory. Meanwhile, Florida proved to be a nail-biter as usual, with Obama barely edging out Romney 50 percent to 49.1 percent (a slim +0.9 percent victory margin!) on the strength of a critical +3.1 percent net Latinx vote contribution. Florida Latinos, who made up 17.4 percent of the state's voters, favored Obama 58 percent to 40 percent. Finally, one must also note that in Ohio, which Obama narrowly won by a +1.9 percent margin, the president was victorious because of a +1.4 percent Latinx vote contribution and strong support from other key constituencies, including African Americans. In total, these states represented 69 critical Electoral College votes that helped put Obama over the top. Without the Latinx vote in those key states, it would have been a much tighter race, and Obama's total might have fallen to 263 Electoral College votes—just below the 270 threshold needed to win.

Aside from the vote margins of Obama's victory, what was it that helped the incumbent garner another four years in the White House? To put things in perspective, one can consider a few key survey results among Latinx voters. With respect to Latinx outreach and responsiveness to community needs, 66 percent of Latinos viewed Obama as someone who cared about the Latinx community, whereas only 14 percent of Latinos saw Romney that way (see Segura and Barreto 2012). In fact, 56 percent of Latinos thought Romney did not care that much about the Latinx community, and another 18 percent even viewed Romney as hostile toward Latinos—compared to only 23 percent and 3 percent, respectively, for Obama. Another driving factor underlying Obama's strong Latinx support may have been Obama's deferred action policy on behalf of Latinx immigrant "Dreamers." After Obama undertook this policy the summer before the election, pollsters found an overall +52 percent net increase in enthusiastic feelings across the Latinx community toward Obama. By contrast, Romney's embrace of "self-deportation" for undocumented immigrants in America (as an alternative to outright deportation roundups) was widely criticized as a poorly conceived policy position based on the questionable belief that economic woes in the United States would entice them back to their home countries, presumably Mexico and other parts of Latin America (Madison 2012).

In the aftermath of the 2012 election, the Republican National Committee prepared and released a comprehensive "autopsy" that called for a more inclusive party, with more robust outreach efforts to Latinos (Walshe 2013). Despite its calls for internal reform to make the GOP more minority- and Latinx-friendly, the party went in another direction when Donald Trump entered the fray of presidential politics in the summer of 2015. Trump took the Republican Party by storm with his presidential announcement speech, in which he falsely mischaracterized Mexican immigrants by claiming, "When Mexico sends its people, they're not sending their best. . . . They're bringing drugs. They're bringing crime. They're rapists.

And some, I assume, are good people" (Lee 2015). But rather than draw ire and widespread criticism from Republican voters, Trump's fiery populist and nativist campaign strategy (often fueled by racial resentment) was enthusiastically embraced. Trump subsequently dominated all primary campaign coverage and beat out 16 other, more mainstream, Republican candidates for the GOP presidential nomination. He went on to defeat Democratic nominee Hillary Clinton in stunning fashion with a narrow Electoral College victory in 2016. Trump secured the White House despite losing the popular vote and garnering merely 28 percent of the Latinx vote (Krogstad and Lopez 2016). Thereafter, during his term in office, Trump's xenophobic and racist rhetoric extended and often blurred the lines between immigrants and native racial/ethnic minorities, while his most controversial policies—including family separation, pushbacks against refugees and Deferred Action for Childhood Arrivals recipients, various travel bans, defense of racial profiling tactics, and a project to build a massive border wall between Mexico and the United States—garnered widespread criticism. They were blamed by critics for deepening racial tensions and imposing hardships on immigrants, Latinos, and various other minorities (see Sirin, Valentino, and Villalobos 2021).

Trump's subsequent tumultuous term in office was marked by immigration policies that critics called inhumane, divisive politics, and a mismanaged COVID-19 pandemic response leaving hundreds of thousands dead, which set the stage for his own electoral defeat in the 2020 election. Trump once again lost the Latino vote (32 percent) in 2020, but he still managed to slightly improve from his first run in that respect and pulled a few better-than-expected outcomes at the state level, including a margin of 56 percent to 41 percent over Biden among Cuban Americans voters in Florida (Sonneland 2020).

Much like his overall base of support that remained firm throughout his term, Trump's base of Latinx support also remained loyal despite his many controversial actions, demonstrating that partisan and ideological loyalty also dwell firmly among Latinos who generally identify as Republican or pro-Trump. On the flipside, Joe Biden ran a successful campaign with extensive, positive outreach to Latinos through an "empathy offensive" that sought to stimulate political unity across racial/ethnic lines. Biden ultimately garnered 66 percent of the Latinx vote amid a record turnout for which he reaped an all-time high 81 million votes and essentially flipped the Electoral College map results of 2016, thereby making him the 46th president of the United States. These election results also made his running mate, Kamala Harris, the country's first female and first African American and South Asian descendent elected vice president. Biden's victory was underscored by his explicit and intentional use of empathy as a foundational principle and rhetorical tool to connect with and unify public support, including among Latinos (see Sirin, Valentino, and Villalobos 2021). However, it was complicated by Trump's relentless efforts to delegitimize the election outcome itself. Trump's false claims of voter fraud culminated with the horrific January 6, 2021, insurrection at the U.S. Capitol. This riot delayed but did not derail Congress's official certification of Biden's Electoral College victory.

As with the other electoral presidential victories of George W. Bush and Barack Obama highlighted above, Biden's 2020 election victory lent additional credence to the notion that candidates who make greater efforts to reach out and respond to Latinos are more likely to fare well at the end of their campaigns. Looking forward more broadly, political observers emphasize that American political parties and their flagship candidates will need to put in the work to earn and sustain Latinx votes if they wish to survive politically in the long term.

References

Affigne, Tony, Evelyn Hu-DeHart, and Marion Orr. 2014. *Latino Politics en Ciencia Política: The Search for Latino*

Identity and Racial Consciousness. New York: New York University Press.

Bedolla, Lisa García. 2014. *Latino Politics*. 2nd ed. Cambridge, UK: Polity Press.

Krogstad, Jens Manuel, and Mark Hugo Lopez. 2016. "Hillary Clinton Won Latino Vote but Fell Below 2012 Support for Obama." Pew Research Center. Accessed March 30, 2022. https://www.pewresearch.org/fact-tank/2016/11/29/hillary-clinton-wins-latino-vote-but-falls-below-2012-support-for-obama.

Leal, David L., Matt A. Barreto, Jongho Lee, and Rodolfo O. de la Garza. 2005. "The Latino Vote in the 2004 Election." *PS: Political Science and Politics* 38:41–49.

Lee, Michelle Ye Hee. 2015. "Donald Trump's False Comments Connecting Mexican Immigrants and Crime." *Washington Post*. Accessed March 30, 2022. https://www.washingtonpost.com/news/fact-checker/wp/2015/07/08/donald-trumps-false-comments-connecting-mexican-immigrants-and-crime.

Madison, Lucy. 2012. "Romney on Immigration: I'm for 'Self-Deportation.'" CBS News. Accessed March 30, 2022. https://www.cbsnews.com/news/romney-on-immigration-im-for-self-deportation.

Monforti, Jessica Lavariega. 2014. "Identity Revisited: Latinos(as) and Panethnicity." In *Latino Politics en Ciencia Política: The Search for Latino Identity and Racial Consciousness*, edited by Tony Affigne, Evelyn Hu-DeHart, and Marion Orr. New York: New York University Press.

Segura, Gary M., and Matt A. Barreto. 2012. "Obama Wins 75% of Latino Vote, Marks Historic Latino Influence in Presidential Election." *Latino Decisions* (blog). Accessed March 30, 2022. https://latinodecisions.com/blog/obama-wins-75-of-latino-vote-marks-historic-latino-influence-in-presidential-election.

Sirin, Cigdem V., Nicholas A. Valentino, and José D. Villalobos. 2021. *Seeing Us in Them: Social Divisions and the Politics of Group Empathy*. New York: Cambridge University Press.

Sonneland, Holly K. 2020. "Chart: How U.S. Latinos Voted in the 2020 Presidential Election." Americas Society/Council of the Americas (AS/COA). Accessed March 30, 2022. https://www.as-coa.org/articles/chart-how-us-latinos-voted-2020-presidential-election.

Suro, Roberto, Richard Fry, and Jeffrey S. Passel. 2005. "How Latinos Voted in 2004." Pew Research Center. Accessed March 30, 2022. https://www.pewresearch.org/hispanic/2005/06/27/iv-how-latinos-voted-in-2004.

Walshe, Shushannah. 2013. "RNC Completes 'Autopsy' on 2012, Calls for Inclusion Not Policy Change." ABC News. Accessed March 30, 2022. https://abcnews.go.com/Politics/OTUS/rnc-completes-autopsy-2012-loss-calls-inclusion-policy/story?id=18755809.

José D. Villalobos is professor of political science at the University of Texas at El Paso. He is coauthor of Seeing Us in Them: Social Divisions and the Politics of Group Empathy *(2021), which examines outgroup empathy as a powerful predisposition in politics that pushes individuals to see past social divisions and work together in complex, multicultural societies.*

VOTE
TUESDAY
LWV
LEAGUE OF WOMEN VOTERS®

4 Profiles

Introduction

This chapter presents profiles of some important organizations and activists involved in shaping and overseeing elections in the United States. These stakeholder organizations and people have influenced Congress and state legislatures, political parties, and the federal judiciary by advocating for or against enactment of laws affecting or reforming the highly complex American electoral system. They did so in the courts of the United States through landmark judicial decisions that affected and set precedents influencing courts at all levels. They did and continue to do so by engaging in electoral politics at the federal, state, and local government levels. There are literally hundreds of organizations and persons that could justifiably be profiled here, but space constraints limit the chapter to first briefly describe 28 key stakeholder organizations by type of organizational and ideological activism in electoral politics.

This chapter also profiles 26 individual actors in the arena of electoral politics and processes. These include government officials and leading activists from nongovernmental groups who impact electoral systems and represent a spectrum of ideological perspectives, advocacy groups, and think tanks. A few are

A nonpartisan interest group, the League of Women Voters performs many voter services during elections. They conduct issue forums for voters, volunteer to help voters on Election Day, and often serve as election judges. They also strenuously campaign against enactment of voter suppression laws by state and local governments. (Ken Wolter/Dreamstime.com)

profiled because of their historically important contribution to elections in America. The profiles are presented in alphabetical order in each category.

Organizations

ACLU (American Civil Liberties Union)

The ACLU is a nonpartisan, nonprofit organization formed to defend the individual rights and liberties of every person in America as guaranteed by the Constitution and laws of the United States. It was founded in 1920 in reaction to then attorney general Mitchell Palmer's "Red Scare" raids that rounded up thousands of radicals and deported hundreds. Many Americans targeted in these raids were arrested without warrants and without regard for constitutional protections against unlawful search and seizure. Among the group's founders were Helen Keller, Roger Nash Baldwin, Jane Addams, Walter Nelles, Elizabeth Gurley Flynn, Felix Frankfurter, Norman Thomas, and Crystal Eastman. As of 2021, ACLU is headquartered in New York City and is led by Executive Director Anthony Romero, Deputy Executive Director Dorothy Ehrlich, and National Legal Director David Cole. ACLU claims a membership of over 1.5 million. Its annual budget exceeds $234 million. It is staffed by 300 attorneys and several thousand volunteer attorneys in offices across the United States.

The ACLU lobbies for a variety of policy positions affecting elections: (1) opposition to "election reform" bills in more than 40 state legislatures that ACLU considers racial voter suppression and violations of the 14th Amendment; (2) support for voting rights and equal access to polling stations for the elderly and physically handicapped, including through such means as mail-in voting and early voting; (3) elimination of discrimination against former felons, including reinstatement of former felons' franchise rights; (4) opposition to government preference of religion over nonreligion as shown by laws closing elections on Saturdays and Sundays; and (5) support for equal access to the ballot box for all voters (LeMay 2018, 162–63).

ACLU has two separate but closely affiliated nonprofits: the ACLU, a 501(c)(4) social welfare group; and the ACLU Foundation, a 501(c)(3) public charity. Both engage in civil rights litigation, advocacy, and education, but only donations to the 501(c)(3) ACLU Foundation are tax deductible, and only the 501(c)(4) group can engage in unlimited political lobbying and electoral politics. ACLU has supported countless suits by filing amicus curiae briefs, including several landmark cases on elections and campaign finance reform. It has lobbied as a champion to end Sunday closing laws (a.k.a. blue laws).

ACLU's more famous battles include defense of Japanese American citizens incarcerated in the internment camps and supporting the naturalization and voting rights of Chinese and Japanese immigrants; opposition to the USA Patriot Act; defending immigrant rights; supporting enactment of the Americans with Disabilities Act; and protecting free speech both in person and on the internet.

ActBlue

ActBlue is a political action committee (PAC) that funds Democratic and progressive candidates, campaigns, and organizations with an online platform. It began in 2004 and by the 2020 election had raised $4.8 billion. It is the most important fundraising platform for progressive Democrats. Funds distributed through ActBlue are individual donations, not PAC donations. It exemplifies a nonprofit that empowers small-dollar donors. Through its powerful online funding tool, ActBlue enables grassroots supporters to amplify their voices and help build people-powered movements. Prior to ActBlue, traditional Democratic fundraising platforms were decidedly *not* user-friendly. ActBlue is a platform that is easy to use and highly efficient. Its easy payment software and its ability to tailor fundraising to the core message of a particular candidate's campaign is the key to its high rate of success. Those characteristics make ActBlue attractive to candidates, causes, and donors. By the 2016 presidential race, its donor list topped 2.7 million. In 2018, with Erin Hill at the helm, the platform raised more than $1.5 billion. That gave the Democratic National Committee (DNC) and Democratic congressional candidates a massive fundraising edge. It was so successful, in fact, that in 2019 Republicans decided to create a GOP counterpart with WinRed. ActBlue is used by the DNC, the Democratic Senate Campaign Committee (DSCC), the Democratic Congressional Campaign Committee (DCCC), and the Democratic Governors Association (DGA). ActBlue is located in Somerville, Massachusetts.

AFL-CIO Workers' Voices PAC

When the American Federation of Labor (AFL) and the Congress of Industrial Organizations (CIO) merged in 1955 to form the AFL-CIO, it became the nation's largest federation of unions. It was among the earliest lobbying organizations to use ratings of members of Congress to influence their reelection campaigns, and to form a political action committee (PAC) for electioneering. AFL-CIO is officially nonpartisan; historically, however, its support for liberal and progressive economic policies often aligns it with Democratic Party efforts. Its Workers' Voices PAC is a new initiative designed to expand the AFL-CIO network of 14,000 work sites for outreach to working-class and middle-class nonunion members, their families, and their communities. The PAC also focuses on voter registration and voter protection for communities of color, seniors, and student groups affected by voter suppression laws and measures enacted or being considered in nearly every state under Republican control. Its website attracts workers by email and social media platforms such as Facebook and Twitter. It lobbies congressional and state legislators and utilizes relational voter data tools to merge online networks into phone banks to canvass persuasion efforts at the grassroots level. Its political director is Mike Podhozer.

American Bridge 21st Century

American Bridge exemplifies the liberal super political action committee (PAC) approach to electioneering by conducting opposition research for Democratic candidates and organizations. It was founded in 2010 by conservative-turned-liberal activist David Brock. Brock started Media Matters in 2004 as a liberal website to monitor and fact-check conservative media misinformation. A super PAC, it accepts unlimited donations from Democratic donors and labor unions. It spends a half-million dollars each year on independent electioneering communications. It specializes in negative "attack ads" against Republicans. It shares research with major Democratic super PACs such as Priorities USA Action, Senate Majority PAC, and House Majority PAC.

Americans for Prosperity

Americans for Prosperity began in 2004 as a leading 501(c)(4) PAC. It is a conservative political advocacy group begun by David and Charles Koch and Karl Rove. It is a leading political action committee (PAC) in raising and utilizing "dark money" to fund negative ads against Democratic candidates and officeholders. It promotes conservative economic and fiscal policies such as lower taxes and less regulation. It is a model for a host of similar conservative groups that since the 2020 election cycle have consistently outraised and outspent all other PAC organizations combined.

American Heritage Society

Founded in 1973 as the Heritage Foundation, it is one of America's most influential conservative think tanks. As an advocacy group, it supports research and education on the conservative Right that directly impacts electoral politics. It claims a half-million dues-paying members supporting libertarian-based policies on freedom, property rights, and conservative civil society. It is a 501 (c)(3) public policy advocacy organization promoting limited government, individual liberty, traditional social values, and national defense. It describes itself as a defender of the principles and values of the Founding Fathers. It is an important lobbying organization for "originialist" judges at all levels of courts and a source of conservative policy proposals to Congress, the executive branch, the media, and the American public. It is governed by a 22-member board of trustees.

Brennan Center for Justice

The Brennan Center for Justice at the New York University School of Law began in 1995 by former law clerks to Justice William Brennan (1906–1997) in memory of and to promote the ideas of Justice Brennan. The Center describes itself as committed to a fair and inclusive democracy, support for the disadvantaged, and respect for individual rights and liberties. It views "human dignity" as the core value of the law.

Justice Brennan is regarded as one of the most influential justices on the Supreme Court during the Warren Court, with its civil rights and liberties emphasis. Brennan was appointed by President Dwight D. Eisenhower in 1956. He wrote landmark decisions like *Baker v. Carr* (1962), which established "one man, one vote," and *New York Times Co. v. Sullivan* (1964), which expanded press freedoms.

The Center has grown to become one of the nation's leading legal and policy think tanks. It is staffed by 130 attorneys, scholars, and legal journalists. It has an annual budget of $27 million and maintains offices in New York and Washington, DC. Since 2006, it expanded from litigation to a focus on research, public policy, and communication. It combines the elements of a think tank and legal advocacy group and has formed a new agenda for legal reform at both the state and federal levels. A more recent emphasis of the Center has been tracking, publicizing, and fighting state government efforts to suppress voting rights.

Center for American Progress (CAP)

Founded in 2003 by former Clinton administration chief of staff John Podesta, who also chaired the 2016 Hillary Clinton presidential campaign, CAP is a prominent progressive think tank in Washington, DC. Its president is Neera Tanden, and its board of directors is chaired by former U.S. Senate minority leader Tom Daschle. It describes itself as an independent, nonpartisan policy institute dedicated to improving the lives of all Americans. Liberal in its orientation on a host of economic and social issues, it promotes progressive ideas, leadership, and concerted policy advocacy. It advocates for opportunity to encourage people to upward economic mobility. It promotes environmental policy, peace, and more equally shared prosperity and asserts that government can earn the trust of the American people by championing the common good over narrow self-interest. It challenges the media to cover issues that matter, as opposed to covering the horse-race aspect of electoral politics. CAP also supports policy teams concerning the major issue areas and employs extensive outreach efforts to adapt to a rapidly changing media landscape and introduce ideas into the national debate.

In 2003, CAP launched Generation Progress, a youth-engagement organization. For advocacy work, it has the Center for American Progress Action Fund as a counterbalance to the Heritage Foundation. From 2005 to 2019, CAP hosted a progressive news website, ThinkProgress. CAP is a 501(c)(3) nonprofit. CAP Action is a 501(c)(4) organization that allows it to fund lobbying. CAP plays an important role in many aspects of Democratic Party electoral politics, but especially presidential politics. Its annual budget is about $50 million. Among its individual donors are George Soros and Bill and Melinda Gates. CAP receives dark money from corporate donors such as Walmart, Citicorp, Wells Fargo, Northrop Grumman, America's

Health Insurance Plans, the Eli Lilly Company, Goldman Sachs, Bank of America, Google, Time Warner, and Pharmaceutical Research and Manufacturers of America.

Club for Growth

The Club for Growth is a super political action committee (PAC) 501(c)(4) organization. It is headquartered in Washington, DC, and uses two political arms: Club for Growth Action and Club for Growth PAC. Donations to Club for Growth Action have limits, and its donors are reported. Donations to the PAC are unlimited and are not publicly disclosed. It claims 250,000 Americans who, as donors, favor growth and limited government.

Club for Growth describes itself as dedicated to free market and limited government ideals. It lobbies on the federal budget and spending, education, free trade, regulation, taxes, term limits, and tax reform. Its founders are Stephen Moore, Richard Gilder, Harlan Crow, and Thomas Rhodes. It regularly issues KEY VOTE alerts and congressional scorecards (ranking U.S. House and Senate members on the purity of their conservative votes on bills before Congress) and often endorses Republican candidates for Congress who pledge support for economically conservative policies. In 2020, it reportedly raised over $55 million and spent more than $22 million on U.S. House and Senate races. Its donors include notable GOP donors like PayPal cofounder Peter Theil and Robert Mercer, former co-CEO of the hedge fund company Renaissance Technologies. David McIntosh is president of Club for Growth.

Constitution Center

In 1988, President Ronald Reagan signed the Constitution Heritage Act, which established a private, nonpartisan, nonprofit organization called the National Constitutional Center in Philadelphia. Today it is the nation's leading platform for constitutional education and debate. The Center broke ground on its headquarters building in 2000 and opened its doors on

July 4, 2003. Since 2006, the Center has administered the Liberty Medal, awarded annually to men and women who strive to secure liberty to people around the world. Past recipients of the medal include President George W. and Laura Bush, for their support of veterans, Representative John Lewis, for his civil rights work, and activist Malala Yousafzai of Afghanistan, for her work on behalf of young women. In 2006, the Center launched its Constitution High School, a history- and civics-themed magnet school in Philadelphia. In 2008, the Center hosted a Democratic presidential primary debate between Hillary Clinton and then senator Barack Obama, as well as a town hall meeting with Republican senator John McCain. It also hosted a noteworthy speech on race by then senator Barack Obama. In 2010, the Center launched two online platforms: *Constitution Daily*, a blog, and Constitution Hall Pass, a free video lesson and live chat series exploring America's civic holidays and history that annually reaches millions of students. In 2011, the American Association of Museums accredited the Center. In 2013, the Center began displaying one of 12 surviving copies of the Bill of Rights, and its "We the People" institution began exhibiting the historic Constitution. Under a grant from the John Templeton Foundation, it began the "Interactive Constitution," a free, online tool exploring the meaning of each of the amendments to the Constitution. In 2016, it launched an "Interactive Constitution" mobile app. Today, the Center continues to gather scholars of government, public policy, and journalism from across the legal and political spectrum to explore and debate the role of the Constitution in American politics.

Democratic National Committee (DNC)

The DNC was founded in 1848 as the official national organization of the Democratic Party. It is headed by a chairperson elected at the national convention in presidential election years. The DNC supports and helps shape the policy agenda of the party, which is formally adopted at the national convention every four years and which tends to inform the presidential campaign for that election cycle. In 2016 and 2020, the Democratic platform was pro-choice, pro–gay marriage, pro–alternative energy, and for health-care reform, education reform, police and criminal justice reform, and comprehensive immigration reform. In 2020, it adopted planks to "Build Back Better," the economic recovery plan of President Biden, and support for H.R. 1, the "For the People Act," the most significant voting rights and democracy reform since the Voting Rights Acts of 1965 and 1968. It supports President Biden's COVID-19 vaccination plan and proposed global vaccination efforts. DNC is headquartered in Washington, DC, and chaired by Jaime Harrison. Mayor Keisha Lance Bottoms is its vice chair for civic engagement and voter protection, while Senate Majority Leader Chuck Schumer (D-NY) and Speaker of the House Nancy Pelosi (D-CA) are ex officio members.

Emily's List

Emily's List is a political action committee (PAC) to elect pro-choice and Democratic women to office at all levels—local, state, and national. Emily's List was founded in 1985 by Ellen Malcolm and is based in Washington, DC. Its president at this time of writing (late 2021) is Laphonza Butler, and Emily Cain serves as its executive director. It claims to be the nation's largest campaign-financing resource for women in politics, raising more than $700 million to elect Democratic women candidates since its founding and adding $50 million to that total annually. It also claims a grassroots community of five million members. Besides doing fundraising, Emily's List provides training for women candidates on how to successfully run for office. It also maintains a blog to engage new voters through its Creative Council and its Latina Advisory Council. It promotes progressive policy for education, health-care, voting rights, and economic reforms.

Federalist Society (FS)

The Federalist Society, also called the Federalist Society for Law and Public Policy Studies, began in 1982 as an organization of conservatives and libertarians to reform the judiciary. It was funded with a grant from the Institute for Educational Affairs and then by a grant of $5.5 million from the conservative Olin Foundation. Major financial supporters include the Robert Mellon Scaife Foundation, the Koch Family Foundation, Google, Chevron, and the Mercer Family Foundation. Headquartered in Washington, DC, its president is Eugene Meyer. The Society describes itself as an organization that advocates for a textualist and originalist interpretation of the U.S. Constitution and regards personal freedom and the separation of governmental powers as central values of the Constitution. It hosts forums for legal experts to interact with members of the legal profession, the judiciary, law students, academics, and public policymakers. During Republican administrations, and especially since the Trump administration, FS has played a substantial role in the nomination and confirmation of conservative judges to all levels of the federal bench.

FS has three divisions of members: Student, Lawyer, and Faculty. Its Student Division has more than 10,000 law students at approximately 200 ABA-accredited law schools, as well as 10 chapters at nonaccredited law schools. It supplies speakers and assists student chapters in organizing lectures, debates, and educational activities. Its Lawyers Division has more than 65,000 members and chapters in 90 cities. It hosts an annual National Lawyers Convention. Its speakers' bureau organizes lectures, debates, and 15 legal practice groups. Its Faculty Division, begun in 1999, fosters rigorous traditional legal scholarship. Five sitting Supreme Court justices are or were members: Brett Kavanaugh, Neil Gorsuch, Clarence Thomas, John Roberts, and Samuel Alito. President Trump appointed 54 judges to the U.S. appellate courts during his term in office from 2017 to 2021, the great majority of whom belonged to FS. It publishes the *Harvard Journal of Law and Public Policy*.

Federal Election Commission (FEC)

The FEC is an independent federal regulatory agency established in 1975 by an amendment to the Federal Elections Commission Act (FECA) of 1974. Congress established it to administer FECA, the law governing the financing of federal elections. The FEC discloses campaign financing of federal elections and enforces the provisions of FECA. It was supposed to oversee public funding of presidential elections. However, no presidential candidate of America's two major parties has ever opted to use federal funding. The commission has six members—three Democrats and three Republicans. Since 2016, FEC has been deadlocked on almost every issue brought before it, since by law four votes are required for any official FEC action. The chair rotates among the members each year, with no commission member serving more than once during the member's term. The hyperpartisan nature of current American electoral politics has resulted in the commission being quite toothless in enforcing FECA.

Green Party of the United States (GPUS)

GPUS describes itself as a federation of state parties (established in 30 states and DC). The state parties are each comprised of grassroots activists, environmentalists, social justice reform advocates, and ordinary citizens who oppose corporate-dominated politics. GPUS is a classic third-party that has occasionally played the role of "spoiler" in U.S. presidential elections by siphoning-off enough votes from the Democratic nominee to deliver victory to the Republican candidate (most pollsters and political scientists agree that most votes for Green Party candidates would otherwise go to Democrats, whose public policy positions are closer to the "Greens" than are the GOP's). As of late 2020, 117 officeholders in the United States were affiliated with GPUS, mostly in California and all at the local level.

The Green Party movement is worldwide and began in 1972. In the United States, GPUS was founded in 1984 in St. Paul, Minnesota. It has nominated a presidential candidate in every presidential race since 1996. It adopted GPUS as its name in 1999. Four "pillars" of the party are peace, ecology, social justice, and democracy. Its 2000 nominee, Ralph Nader, received about 3 percent of the popular vote but no Electoral College votes. Nader's performance was the party's best-ever showing in the presidential race. His Florida vote count exceeded the margin between Democratic candidate Al Gore and Republican candidate George W. Bush, and he arguably cost Al Gore the presidency. The party's nominee in 2012 and 2016 was Jill Stein. Many Democrats believe that her candidacy likely cost Democrat Hillary Clinton the election in 2016. In 2012, the party was on the ticket in 36 states and earned 469,628 votes (0.4 percent of the popular vote). In 2016, it won 1,457,222 votes (1.06 percent of the popular vote). In 2020, its nominee was Howie Hawkins, who garnered only 399,111 votes (0.3 percent of the popular vote). The party has never been on the presidential ballot in all 50 states and DC, which illustrates well the structural disadvantage of third (or minor) parties in U.S. elections.

League of Women Voters (LWV)

The LWV is a good example of a nonpartisan, voting-oriented activist organization that encourages informed and active public participation in government and the democratic process. The League was founded in 1920 by Carrie Chapman Catt, Susan B. Anthony, and Emma Smith DeVoe at the final meeting of the National American Women Suffrage Association. It is headquartered in Washington, DC, and is led by its president, Deborah Turner. A strictly nonpartisan political organization, it registers voters, educates and engages them, and seeks to reform campaign finance law (especially with respect to "dark money" in U.S. elections). The LWV was among the first organizations to receive official nongovernment organization (NGO) status from the United Nations. The League is organized into chapters at the local, state, and national levels, numbering more than 1,000 state and local chapters. It sponsors nonpartisan educational forums on ballot issues, publishes state- and local-specific voter guides, and has long supported and sponsored candidate- and issue-based forums. It sponsored presidential debates in 1976, 1980, and 1984. It regularly sponsors debate forums between candidates for state and local offices.

Although strictly nonpartisan, the League is firmly committed to promoting the values of diversity, equity, and inclusion. The LWV supported passage of the National Voter Registration Act in 1993 and the Bipartisan Campaign Reform Act in 2002. It vigorously opposed the Supreme Court's *Citizens United* (2010) decision. LWV supports a law to provide a path to citizenship for Dreamers. It supports progressive policy positions on issue areas such as universal health care, abortion rights, climate change, environmental regulation, and gun control. In 2012, LWV created National Voter Registration Day, and it hosts voter education through such programs as its Smart Voter and Voter's Edge. It also established www.VOTE411.org, an online resource that provides information, including stated positions on important public policy issues, for candidates for elected office at all levels of government, from presidential and U.S. Senate candidates to people running for seats in state legislatures across the country.

Lincoln Project

The Lincoln Project is a Republican, anti-Trump super political action committee (PAC) organization with the stated goal of protecting democracy by holding accountable those who violate their oaths to the Constitution. It was named after Republican president Abraham Lincoln, who had pledged to bind the wounds of the Civil War to move the nation forward together. It was formed in 2019 by a group of well-established Republicans who were part of the so-called Never Trumpers wing of the Republican Party. They wanted to defeat Trump's 2020 bid for reelection, and the group has described its anti-Trump stance as a battle to save the soul of the Republican Party. The organization's leadership has described Trumpism as a "clear and present danger" to the Constitution, democracy, and the Republic, and a promoter of authoritarianism rather than democracy.

Based in DC, the Project was founded by George Conway, Steve Schmidt, Rick Wilson, Jennifer Horn, Ron Steslow, Reed Galen, and Mike Madrid. Its executive director is Sarah Lenti.

In 2020, the Lincoln Project raised $90 million and spent more than $50 million on television ads, most of which attacked Trump for his handling of the pandemic, his alleged embrace of white nationalism, and his alleged role in the January 6, 2021, insurrection at the U.S. Capitol. Unlike most super PACs, according to OpenSecrets and to the Center for Responsive Politics, about 39 percent of the Lincoln Project's contributions came from small donors (contributing $200 or less).

Make America Great Again (MAGA) PAC/Save America PAC

The MAGA PAC was established in July 2015 to support the presidential bid of Donald Trump. Established by Leslie Caldwell, it raised more than $1 million to support his candidacy during the Republican primaries and raised more for the general election to fund anti–Hillary Clinton ads. It officially shut down in July 2016, however, when the FEC began investigating allegations that the super political action committee (PAC) was improperly coordinating with the Trump campaign.

In 2020, Trump established a successor PAC organization called the Save America PAC. It raised more than $200 million in contributions, although tens of millions had to be returned to donors because the PAC used an allegedly fraudulent "check the box" option that was prechecked to continue contributions in the same amount unless the contributor "unchecked" the box. In addition to its activities specifically in support of Trump's reelection, the Save America PAC was a financial supporter of WinRed, the conservative fundraising platform used by the Republic National Committee. Save America funds can be used for Mr. Trump's post–White House political operations, including keeping former campaign staff on the payroll, funding Mr. Trump's travel expenses when he is campaigning for other candidates, and helping finance rallies and events supporting other candidates or "issues" rather than Trump's 2024 events.

NAACP (National Association for the Advancement of Colored People)

The NAACP was founded in 1909. It is the oldest continuously active civil rights organization in the United States. The NAACP grew out of the Niagara Movement, a Black civil rights organization cofounded in 1905 by W. E. B. Du Bois, Mary White Ovington, Moorfield Storey, and Ida B. Wells. It began with a goal "to ensure political, educational, social, and economic equality of rights of all persons, and to eliminate racial hatred and discrimination." In the 1920s, NAACP worked against Jim Crow and disenfranchisement, and in the 1930s and 1940s, it became a prominent voice against racial segregation. In 1939, it established its Legal Defense Fund, which became an important force in the civil rights movement. Lawyers with the Legal Defense Fund were at the forefront of landmark civil rights victories in the courts, including such notable successes as *Brown v. Board of Education* (1954) and *NAACP v. Alabama* (1958). The organization's lead attorney, Thurgood Marshall, became the first Black justice on the U.S. Supreme Court, serving his country in that capacity from 1967 to 1991. In the 1960s, NAACP lobbied to help enact the Civil Rights Acts of 1964, 1965, and 1968, working closely with Martin Luther King Jr.'s Southern Christian Leadership

Conference (SCLC) and the Student Nonviolent Coordinating Committee (SNCC). In the 1990s, the NAACP established its National Voter Fund, pushed voter registration and Black voter turnout, and lobbied for LGBTQ rights. In recent years, NAACP has been at the forefront of legal challenges to Republican-led efforts to change election laws, decrying such efforts as racially targeted voter suppression. It also is deeply involved in such issues as police misconduct, workplace discrimination, and socioeconomic inequality. It was headquartered in Washington, DC but moved its national headquarters to Baltimore, Maryland, and to regional offices in New York, Michigan, Georgia, DC, and Texas. NAACP is governed by a 64-member board, and its president is Derrick Johnson. It operates with a budget of more than $24 million and has a membership of about 500,000.

National Conference of State Legislatures

The NCSL was established in 1975 to serve members and staff of state legislatures in the United States. It was the result of a merger of three separate organizations representing the organizational interests of state legislatures and their assorted staff. It was created to lobby as a means to support, defend, and strengthen state legislatures. It has helped to retain state legislatures' independence from Congress, and it claims to have saved state governments more than $1 billion by lobbying against unfunded legislative mandates proposed by the United States.

The NCSL monitors, tracks, and researches state and state-federal legislation that impacts state politics. It touts itself as a reliably nonpartisan source of information to the media on state government and recent state legislative efforts in nearly every state to enact legislation to reform or amend state law regarding elections, voter identification requirements, and the powers and duties of state election officials. The NCSL maintains offices in both Washington, DC, and Denver, Colorado. It provides staff support, manages a jobs clearinghouse, promotes legislative careers, compiles and publishes staff directories, provides a bill information service and links to legislative websites, runs a NCSL bookstore, and publishes *State Legislatures* magazine. NCSL also has established a nonprofit 501(c)(3) foundation.

National Democratic Redistricting Committee

Founded by former president Barack Obama and former U.S. attorney general Eric Holder, the National Democratic Redistricting Committee is a political action committee created to serve as a fundraising organization for executing a comprehensive redistricting strategy that shifts redistricting power to create fair districts that end gerrymandering and ensure that every person's vote counts. Its strategies include the use of litigation, the targeted mobilization of voters in key battleground states, electoral reform, and electoral politics. It is focused on such key battleground states as Pennsylvania, North Carolina, Ohio, Michigan, Virginia, Wisconsin, Nevada, and Florida. According to Ballotpedia, it raised $30 million in 2020.

National Rifle Association (NRA)

The NRA is a 501(c)(4) super political action committee (PAC) organization that was originally founded in 1871 by George Wood Wingate and William Conant Church. For its first century of existence, the NRA was a largely nonpartisan organization focused on gun safety training and rifle hunting for game. Since 1975, however, the NRA has become a fierce advocate for gun rights and has directly lobbied Congress and state legislatures for pro-gun laws. Since the 1990s the NRA has become a particularly powerful force in Republican politics, with virtual veto power over any gun control legislation. In recent years, however, the NRA's political clout has been diminished by internal power struggles and serious allegations of financial improprieties that have cast a shadow of uncertainty over the organization's leadership and future. The New

York State attorney general is even seeking dissolution of the organization for alleged fraud and financial misconduct by NRA leadership. In FY 2020, the NRA spent more than $72 million in legal fees. In 2019, the NRA reported revenues of $291 million and claimed more than five million members.

Pew Research Center

The Pew Research Center, founded in 2001, is a nonpartisan research organization that is a subsidiary of the Pew Charitable Trust. The Pew Research Center is a leading think tank and trusted source for nonpartisan research on public opinion on the issues, attitudes, and trends shaping the world, with an emphasis on U.S. politics in particular. For example, it regularly reports on factors influencing voting rates among ethnic and racial minorities. Pew's research is noted for timeliness, relevance, and scientific rigor, and it takes no advocacy positions for or against specific public policy proposals. It conducts public opinion polling, research on demographic trends, media content analysis, and related social science research. Pew Research Center is located in Washington, DC. Its research data are regularly reported on by the mass media, which thereby influence public opinion in such areas as electoral reform.

Priorities USA

Priorities USA is an independent expenditure-only 501(c)(4) political action committee (PAC), also known as a super PAC. It supports the election of Democratic candidates. It began in 2011, established by Bill Burton and Sean Sweeney, to reelect President Barack Obama. Since that time, it has become a permanent and important fixture in Democratic election efforts. It seeks to build a powerful progressive movement to inform, energize, mobilize, and empower average Americans to fight for their priorities and to build sustainable political power. It describes itself as an organization that strives to persuade and mobilize voters; conduct research for progressives and

Democrats; protect voting rights under attack in Republican-controlled states; and develop effective grassroots activism. It is headquartered in Washington, DC.

Republican National Committee (RNC)

The RNC was established in 1856 and is headquartered in Washington, DC. It provides official leadership for the Republican Party and, until the development of PACs and super PACs, was the main fundraiser for national elections to support Republican candidates for national offices (president and vice president, U.S. Senate, and U.S. House of Representatives). Like its Democratic National Committee (DNC) counterpart, the RNC is responsible for organizing its party's national convention, drafting the party platform, fundraising, and finalizing the election strategy for the forthcoming presidential campaign. After the 2016 convention, in 2017, the party selected Ronna McDaniel as its chairperson. Until the 2020 election cycle, RNC had a more aggressive and effective "get-out-the-vote" mail-in-vote and early vote effort than did the DNC. That changed in 2020 because of the election strategy of the Trump campaign, which promoted same-day voting and opposed the use of mail-in ballots, ballot drop boxes, and early voting despite the ongoing COVID-19 pandemic. At the 2020 national convention, the Republican Party elected cochairs to lead the RNC: Ronna McDaniel and Thomas Hicks Jr.

U.S. Department of Justice (DOJ)

The DOJ was established in 1870 by President Ulysses S. Grant. It is home to several divisions and bureaus that regularly involve the Justice Department in election-related matters. It established its Civil Rights Division in 1957, which on occasion led to conflict and First Amendment freedom cases—discrimination in voting rights in particular. In 1909, the DOJ established its Environment and Natural Resources Division, which has also been embroiled in First Amendment issues, for example, with Native American voting rights. The DOJ established a National Security Division in 2007. That division also tends to embroil the DOJ in controversies with minority religions, such as American Muslims.

The DOJ houses several law enforcement agencies: the U.S. Marshals Service and the Federal Bureau of Investigation (FBI, founded in 1908), the Federal Bureau of Prisons (FBP, 1930), the Bureau of Alcohol, Tobacco, Firearms and Explosives (ATF, 1972), the Drug Enforcement Agency (DEA, 1973), the Office of Inspector General (OIG, 1978), the Executive Office of Immigration Review (OIR, 1983), the Office of Immigration Litigation (OIL, 1983), and the Office of Tribal Justice (OTJ, 1995), all of which on occasion embroil the DOJ in federal judicial cases. In the past, the DOJ had "preclearance authority" to review proposed election-law changes in several southern states that had exhibited a history of racial discrimination in voting laws. For FY 2020, DOJ's budget for funding assistance for state, local, and tribal partners was $7 billion. The DOJ is led by the Attorney General of the United State (AG). During President Trump's term from January 2017 to January 2021, his two AGs, Jeff Sessions and William Bear, directed the DOJ in partisan political ways that were unprecedented. The current attorney general, Merrick Garland, appointed by President Joe Biden, has vowed to restore the department's tradition of strict political independence from the White House or other partisan political entities.

U.S. Elections Assistance Commission (EAC)

The EAC was established by a provision of the Help America Vote Act of 2002 (HAVA). HAVA mandated new mandatory minimum standards for states to follow in several important areas of election administration: provisional voting, voting information, updated and upgraded voting equipment, statewide voter registration databases, voter identification procedures, and election administration complaint procedures.

HAVA provides funding to help states meet the new standards, to replace noncompliant voting systems, and to improve election administration. HAVA established the EAC to assist states with HAVA compliance and to manage the distribution of HAVA funds to the states. The EAC is mandated to create voting-system guidelines and with operating the federal government's first voting-system certification program. It maintains the National Voter Registration system. It promotes shared best practices, distribution of information for voters, and other resources to improve elections.

Congress first created a National Clearinghouse for Information on Election Administration housed in the Government Accountability Office by the Federal Election Campaign Act of 1971. Congress established the Federal Elections Commission (FEC) in 1975. The clearinghouse assumed additional programs in 1980 and 1984. Enactment of the so-called Motor Voter Act in 1993 charged the clearinghouse with developing and maintaining a national mail voter registration form and with submitting a biannual survey to Congress on the impact of National Voter Registration Act and trends in voter registration. HAVA established the EAC to serve as the national clearinghouse in 2002. The EAC publishes reports on recertification of voting systems' hardware and software, information and training on the management of HAVA grants, and compilation of federal and state laws and procedures regarding election administration and voting.

WinRed

WinRed is an online platform that raises funds for Republican candidates. It was founded in 2019 by Gerrit Lansing as a direct response to the Democratic fundraising platform, ActBlue. It has since become the number one fundraising technology used by the Republican National Committee (RNC), the Republican Senate Legislative Conference, the National Republican Senate Campaign Committee, and the National Republican Congressional Campaign Committee. Donations to WinRed go directly to the candidate or organization that the voter specifies, using the latest digital fundraising technology. In July 2019, WinRed announced it would not offer financial or other support to any candidates who did not use WinRed. In 2020, WinRed was highly criticized for using an automatic check-off box device in its fundraising activities for the Trump reelection campaign. Specifically, WinRed charged regular monthly donations to one-shot contributors unless the contributor took the step of "unchecking" the box to stipulate that the donation was to happen only once. WinRed and the RNC were required to refund more than $10 million to political contributors who received the additional monthly charges. In 2020, it raised more than $2.24 billion for GOP campaigns and committees.

People

Becker, David (1968–)

David Becker is the founder and executive director of the Center for Election Innovation and Research (CEIR), a nonprofit think tank that works to improve election administration through research, data, and technology. Becker received his undergraduate and law degrees from the University of California–Berkeley. Prior to 2016, when he founded CEIR, Becker was director of the elections program at Pew Charitable Trusts (PEW), where he led PEW's election analysis and advocacy efforts and spearheaded the development of PEW's innovative Electronic Registration Information Center.

CEIR is a leader in election administration reform, using technology to help voters by providing information needed to cast their ballot, assessing election performance through better data, and upgrading voter registration systems. CEIR assisted a bipartisan group of about two dozen states to update and overhaul four million out-of-date voter records and to register almost a million new voters. Becker led campaigns in dozens of red, blue, and swing states

Prior to joining PEW, Becker served for seven years as a senior trial attorney in the Voting Section of the DOJ's Civil Rights Division. While at the DOJ, Becker worked in dozens of states, enforcing election laws and observing elections in thousands of precincts. He was lead trial counsel in many cases, including the landmark case of *Georgia v. Ashcroft* (2003). He has frequently appeared in print media outlets such as the *New York Times* and the *Washington Post.* Becker has also regularly appeared on broadcast media outlets such as MSNBC and NPR. He has authored articles in the *Stanford Social Innovation Review* and The Hill.

Bush, George W. (1946–)

George W. Bush served as the 43rd president of the United States, from 2001 to 2009. His election campaigns used social media outlets and innovated new fundraising approaches. George W. Bush was a litigant in the historic U.S. Supreme Court case of *Bush v. Gore* (2000) that settled the 2000 presidential election in his favor. George W. Bush is the son of President George H. W. Bush, the 41st president of the United States (POTUS; 1989–1993), and only the second son of a president to be himself elected president (the other being John Quincy Adams, who was America's sixth president; he was the son of the nation's second president, John Adams).

George W. Bush was born in New Haven, Connecticut. He graduated from Yale and earned a business degree from Harvard. His first foray in politics was an unsuccessful run for the U.S. House of Representatives, from Texas. He then co-owned the Texas Rangers baseball team. He ran for governor of Texas in 1994, and served as its 46th governor from 1995 to 2000. He was elected president in 2000 after a closely contested race against former vice president and senator Al Gore. Bush lost the popular vote to Gore but won the Electoral College vote (ECV) 271 to 266, when the Supreme Court, in a 5–4 decision along strictly partisan lines, awarded Bush the disputed ECVs of Florida.

Bush reorganized the U.S. intelligence services, passed major tax cuts, and engineered the passage of a major domestic education program—No Child Left Behind—that became the signature policy accomplishment of his first term and a key issue in promoting his 2004 reelection. In that election, Bush/Cheney won reelection over the Democratic ticket of Kerry/Edwards by 51 percent to 48 percent in the popular vote, and by 286 ECVs to 251 ECVs. Bush carried 31 states and received the most votes ever cast for a Republican nominee to that point in time.

Bush's popularity with the American public declined during his second term, as the military situations in both Iraq and Afghanistan became increasingly problematic and the wars increasingly unpopular. In 2008, the country fell into a deep economic recession after a collapse of the housing and financial markets. This dramatic economic downturn, which tanked Bush's approval ratings, helped Democratic candidate Barack Obama win the White House in 2008.

Clarke, Kristen (1975–)

Kristen Clarke served as president of the Lawyers' Committee for Civil Rights under Law from 2011 to June 2021, when she was appointed by President Joe Biden as the assistant attorney general for the DOJ's Civil Rights Division, the first Black woman to head the Division. Prior to her heading the Lawyers' Committee for Civil Rights under Law, Clarke managed the Civil Rights Bureau of New York State's Attorney General's Office.

Clarke is the daughter of Jamaican immigrants. She earned her BA from Harvard University, where she served as president of the Black Student Association. Clarke earned her JD from Columbia Law School in 2000. She began her legal career as a trial lawyer in the U.S. DOJ's Civil Rights Division, where she worked on voting rights and election-law reform. In 2011, she moved to the New York Attorney General's Office, where she carried out initiatives on criminal justice issues.

She was appointed president of the Lawyers' Committee for Civil Rights under Law in 2011, where she led its Election Protection program, a voter protection coalition. Clarke subsequently became one of the nation's leading lawyers and advocates for voting rights. In 2013, she handled the legal argument in federal district court for the landmark voting rights case, *Shelby County Alabama v. Holder*. In 2020, she successfully sued the U.S. Postal Service during the pandemic over USPS delays with delivery of ballots. She worked on disability rights under the Americans with Disabilities Act. Clarke supported the legal efforts of Cesar Vargas, who became the first undocumented person (a so-called Dreamer) to carry a law license in New York. Clarke is coauthor of two books: *Barack Obama and African American Empowerment* (2009) and *Seeking Higher Ground* (2008).

Elazar, Daniel (1934–1999)

Daniel Elazar was an eminent political scientist and scholar of American federalism. He is perhaps best known and most relevant here for his seminal studies of political culture in the United States. Elazar's research provided a theoretical foundation for understanding the diversity and determinants of political participation in American elections. Elazar was born in Minneapolis in 1934. He earned his MA and PhD from the University of Chicago. He was a professor at Bar-Ilan University in Israel and Temple University in Pennsylvania. At Temple, Elazar was founder and director of the Center for the Study of Federalism. Elazar was also the founder and president of the Jerusalem Center for Public Affairs, a major independent Jewish think tank concerned with analyzing and solving the problems facing Israel and world Jewry. In 1986, President Ronald Reagan appointed Elazar a citizen member of the U.S. Advisory Commission on Intergovernmental Relations, dealing with problems of federalism.

During his academic career, Elazar authored or edited more than 60 books and publications. He notably was the founding editor of *Publius: The Journal of Federalism*. Among his many books, his work on federalism includes: *The American Partnership* (1962); *American Federalism: A View from the States* (1972), widely viewed as the seminal work on political culture and American political behavior and voting; *Cities of the Prairie* (1984); *Exploring Federalism* (1987); and *The American Mosaic* (1994). Elazar was given numerous honorary degrees and awards for his distinguished scholarly contributions. He died in Jerusalem in 1999.

Feingold, Russ (1953–)

Russ Feingold is included here as the president of the American Constitution Society, an organization with the self-described mission of building a diverse legal community to advance and defend democracy, secure a government that serves the public interest, and guard against abuse of law and the concentration of power. Feingold is a former legislator, a diplomat, and a university professor. He was a Wisconsin state senator (1983–1993) and a U.S. senator (D-WI, 1993–2011) before serving as U.S. special envoy to the Great Lakes Region of Africa and the Democratic Republic of the Congo (2013–2015) in the Obama administration. During his 18 years in the U.S. Senate, Russ Feingold built a reputation as a principled and thoughtful lawmaker, and in 1999, he and fellow senator John McCain (R-Arizona) received the John F. Kennedy Profile in Courage Award for their legislative efforts to pass meaningful campaign finance reform legislation. He was the only senator who voted against passage of the USA Patriot Act, citing civil liberties concerns about the legislation. Feingold served on the following Senate Committees: Judiciary, Foreign Relations, Budget, and Intelligence; he was chairman or the ranking member of the Constitution Subcommittee. After being defeated in his reelection bid for his U.S. Senate seat in 2010, Feingold formed the Progressives United PAC.

Feingold earned a BA and MA from the University of Wisconsin–Madison, attended Magdalen College, Oxford, was a Rhodes Scholar, and took an MA from Oxford University. He earned his JD from Harvard University Law School. While in Congress or during his diplomatic service, he taught at various American law schools including Stanford Law, Yale Law, Marquette University Law, and Harvard Law. He also taught foreign policy to both graduates and undergraduates at Stanford, the University of Wisconsin, Yale, Lawrence University, and American University. Feingold is also the author of *While America Sleeps: A Wake-Up Call for the Post-9/11 Era* (2012).

Harrison, Jaime (1976–)

Jaime Harrison is a politician and current (2022) chair of the Democratic National Committee. He was nominated by President Joe Biden and elected by the Democratic National Convention. Prior to his DNC chairmanship, Harrison served as chair of the South Carolina Democratic Party (2013–2017), the first Black American to do so. In 2020, Harrison ran for the U.S. Senate from South Carolina against Senator Lindsey Graham (R-SC) but lost. Nonetheless, his strong showing in that race, and his notable fundraising prowess—Harrison raised a record-setting $109 million for his campaign, the most raised by any U.S. Senate candidate—contributed to his selection as chair of the DNC, an important fundraising arm of the Democratic Party.

Harrison attended Yale University on a scholarship, earning his BA in political science in 1998. He taught high school from 1998 to 1999 and served as the chief operating officer for College Summit, a nonprofit organization. Harrison earned his JD from Georgetown University Law Center in 2004. He has also worked as a lobbyist for the Podesta Group, United Way Worldwide, and the Association of Public and Land Grant Universities.

Hill, Erin

Erin Hill is the executive director of ActBlue, the Democratic Party's multibillion-dollar fundraising platform established in

2004. Erin also runs ActBlue Civics, its advocacy arm, and ActBlue Charities, its charitable arm. Since its creation in 2004 through the 2020 election, ActBlue has raised more than $3.5 billion. Prior to joining ActBlue, Hill worked in fundraising for the Democratic National Committee and as a fundraiser with the Kerry-Edwards ticket's campaign in 2004. Prior to her political fundraising work, Erin Hill was a Phi Beta Kappa graduate from Wellesley College, with a degree in English literature and a concentration in public policy studies. After graduation, she worked on legislative research for the Massachusetts State House and then on Capitol Hill for the Democratic National Committee.

Holder, Eric (1951–)

Eric Holder was the 82nd attorney general of the United States, serving from 2009 to 2015. Holder was the first Black attorney general in U.S. history. His impact on elections in America has been twofold: (1) as deputy attorney general and attorney general; (2) since leaving that office, in his capacity as cofounder and chairman of the National Democratic Redistricting Committee.

Eric Holder was born in New York City, the son of a father who was an immigrant to the United States from Barbados. He earned his BA degree in history from Columbia University in 1973 and a JD from Columbia Law School in 1976. He joined the Department of Justice in 1976 as a member of its Public Integrity Section. President Ronald Reagan appointed Holder a superior court judge in Washington, DC, in 1988. In 1993, President William Clinton appointed him U.S. attorney for the District of Columbia. In 1997, Holder became the deputy attorney general at DOJ, where he stressed citizen involvement in elections through the Lawyers for One America Project, which encouraged diversity in the legal profession. He left DOJ in 2001 to work for a DC law firm. In 2008, President Barack Obama nominated him to be attorney general in his incoming administration. Holder was confirmed by the Senate

75–21 in February 2009. He left the attorney general's office in April 2015 and was succeeded by Loretta Lynch. Holder returned to private practice in DC, where he notably worked in opposition to racial and political gerrymandering. In 2017, he cofounded, with former president Barack Obama, the National Democratic Redistricting Committee, with the purpose of transforming election maps in the United States and reducing the negative impacts of gerrymandering on American democracy. The Committee raised about $40 million in 2018 and worked in coalition with Forward America, which raised another $100 million, and with the Center for Popular Democracy Action, which raised $80 million. In 2018, the Committee targeted legislative and judicial election races in swing states such as Florida, Michigan, Ohio, Pennsylvania, North Carolina, Nevada, Virginia, and Wisconsin. It targeted 13 states in 2019–2020, working to change 13 gubernatorial offices and the party majority in 13 state legislatures. However, it suffered a net loss of one governorship, and the Republicans retained control of their state legislatures.

Koch, David (1940–2019)

David Koch was one of the single leading financial donors to Republican candidates and conservative political causes and organizations for much of his life. He was cofounder of a super PAC, Freedom Partners Action Fund, which became a major source of "dark money" in U.S. electoral politics after the U.S. Supreme Court ruled in *Citizens United v. FEC* (2010) that corporations and donors could spend unlimited amounts of money on elections on free speech grounds. Koch was born in Wichita, Kansas. He earned his BS degree from the Massachusetts Institute of Technology in 1970 and joined the family oil business. He and his older brother, Charles, built the company into Koch Industries, a diversified conglomerate corporation comprised of oil pipelines, oil refineries, building materials, paper towels, and Dixie Cups. Koch Industries had annual revenue of about $110 billion, and David Koch's personal worth at the time of his death in August 2019 was $42.4 billion.

In 1984, Koch cofounded two PACs: Americans for Prosperity, and Citizens for a Sound Economy. David Koch ran for vice president on the Libertarian ticket in 1980 (with Ed Clark for president), and like most third-party campaigns, the Clark-Koch ticket received less than 1 percent of the popular vote and no Electoral College votes.

In addition to his massive spending in American politics, Koch was a philanthropist who gave millions of dollars to the Johns Hopkins University School of Medicine for cancer research and to MIT's Institute for Integrative Cancer Research. He also gave more than $100 million over 10 years to renovate New York State Theater in the Lincoln Center for the Performing Arts and donated $10 million to renovate the fountain outside of the Metropolitan Museum of Art. He also donated millions to the Smithsonian Institution, funding its David Koch Dinosaur Wing at the Museum of Natural History.

David and Charles Koch ranked among the largest donors to the Republican Party for decades, and they built a massive network of donors to support libertarian economic policies. *Forbes* ranked Koch among the top 10 billionaires in the United States. Americans for Prosperity alone spent more than $1 billion over the past several election cycles in support of Republican candidates. David Koch did not back Donald Trump in 2016, however, concentrating instead on congressional races.

Limbaugh, Rush (1951–2021)

Rush Limbaugh was an entertainer, radio and television talk show host, writer, and arguably the nation's number one conservative political commentator, who had an enormous impact on Republican politics. Born in Cape Girardeau, Missouri, he attended but did not graduate from Southern Missouri State University. He worked for a number of years in radio as a disc jockey and sports news host until he began a politically conservative radio talk show in California in 1984. The show was such a hit that President Ronald Reagan called him the number one voice for conservatism in America. Limbaugh moved to New York City in 1988 to host his own show at WABC.

From 1992 to 1996, Limbaugh broadcast a half-hour syndicated television show produced by the late Roger Ailes, who later became the head of Fox News. His shows (both radio and television) were very successful, attracting a weekly cumulative audience of an estimated 13.25 million listeners, and at one time his talk show was the most listened-to show in America. His television show aired for three hours each weekday.

In 2008, he signed an eight-year contract to continue his syndicated radio program for $400 million. At the time of his death in February 2021, his estimated net worth was $600 million. *Forbes* ranked him as the 11th highest earning celebrity in the world. Limbaugh authored several books, including two best sellers: *The Way Things Ought to Be* (1993) and *I Told You So* (1993). Limbaugh received many awards, such as the Marconi Award for Syndicated Personality of the Year, in 1992, 1995, 2000, and 2004, and the William F. Buckley, Jr. Award for Media Excellence, in 2007. He received the Presidential Medal of Freedom, the nation's highest civilian award, in 2020 from President Trump.

McCain, John (1936–2018)

John McCain was a distinguished Republican U.S. senator from Arizona, serving from 1986 until his death in 2018. McCain was a political conservative but was noted for his willingness to work across the partisan divide. He was thus widely considered a maverick in the Senate, breaking with his fellow Republicans on policy positions related to health care, the tobacco industry, immigration reform, greenhouse gas emissions, reduction of pork-barrel spending, and regressive tax cuts. In 1989, he became embroiled in a savings-and-loan (S&L) industry fraud scandal in which he was accused of improperly intervening in an investigation of an S&L company that later collapsed spectacularly after engaging in widespread fraud. McCain survived the scandal, however, and became a champion of campaign finance reform. In that capacity, he coauthored the McCain-Feingold Bipartisan Campaign Reform Act of 2002.

McCain was the son and grandson of U.S. Navy four-star admirals. He graduated from the Naval Academy as a naval pilot and from the Naval War College. His plane was shot down in Vietnam in 1967 on his 23rd mission, and McCain was held as a prisoner of war in a North Vietnamese prison camp until 1973, during which time he was subjected to horrific torture. Upon his release and return to the United States, he was awarded the Silver Star and the Legion of Merit, the Bronze Star, a Purple Heart, a Distinguished Flying Cross, and a Naval Commendation Medal. He retired from the Navy as a captain in 1981 and moved to Arizona.

McCain was elected to the U.S. House of Representatives (R-AZ) in 1982 and served there until his election to the Senate in 1986. In the Senate, McCain served on the Armed Services Committee as both a ranking member and as chair, on the Committee on Homeland Security, and the Committee on Indian Affairs, important for electoral politics in Arizona. McCain was an ex officio member of the Committee on Intelligence, and he cochaired the Senate National Security Caucus. McCain lost his first bid for the Republican presidential nomination to George W. Bush in 2000. He supported the Iraq War and voted against repeal of the Bush tax cuts. McCain ran for the presidential nomination again in 2008, scoring a decisive win in the New Hampshire primary and taking a commanding lead in the primary races. After McCain won the nomination, he chose Alaska governor Sarah Palin as his running mate. The McCain/Palin ticket lost to the Obama/Biden ticket. He retained his Senate seat, and in 2013, McCain was one of the so-called Gang of Eight who negotiated a bipartisan immigration reform bill that, had it been enacted, would have provided a path to citizenship for undocumented immigrants. In the

2016 presidential race, he was highly critical of Donald Trump, and McCain crossed party lines to provide the critical vote to save the Affordable Care Act (a.k.a. Obamacare) in July 2017. He had to come back from brain tumor treatment to cast the determining and dramatic thumbs-down vote. He died from the brain tumor in August 2018. Over his lifetime, McCain authored seven books: *Faith of My Fathers* (1999), *Worth Fighting For: A Memoir* (2002), *Why Courage Matters* (2004), *Hard Call* (2007), *Thirteen Soldiers* (2014), and *The Restless Warrior* (2018).

McDaniel, Ronna (1973–)

Ronna Romney McDaniel was elected chairwoman of the Republican National Committee in 2017, only the second woman to ever hold that position. As RNC chair, McDaniel helped raise a record amount of funds and invested the most ever in its electoral ground game. She led the RNC in 2019 when it launched its fundraising internet platform, WinRed. As RNC chair, McDaniel approved several controversial decisions to spend large amounts of RNC campaign funds at Trump-owned properties and to use RNC funds to help pay legal fees for Trump and Trump family members, who were enmeshed in a wide range of lawsuits and criminal investigations throughout Trump's term in office She approved the WinRed controversial prechecked box system for automatic monthly campaign contributions, over which many donors sued the RNC for campaign finance fraud. After Trump's loss in 2020, McDaniel was elected cochair of the RNC, along with Thomas Hicks Jr.

Ronna Romney McDaniel was born in Austin, Texas, in 1973 and earned her BA from Brigham Young University. She is the granddaughter of former Republican governor of Michigan and U.S. presidential candidate George Romney, and the niece of Senator Mitt Romney, also a former GOP presidential nominee. McDaniel began her party activism at the grassroots level. She served as a precinct delegate, district committee executive member, state party committeewoman, an RNC committeewoman, and a delegate to the 2012 Republican National Convention. McDaniel served on a land-planning and public-safety commission and was active with her local Parent-Teacher Association. She serves on the executive board of the Romney Institute of Public Policy in the Marriott School of Business at Brigham Young University.

Nader, Ralph (1934–)

Ralph Nader exemplifies the attorney/activist turned electoral politician. Nader famously sparked reform movements for auto safety, consumer advocacy, and environmentalism from the 1960s through the 1980s, during which time he founded or cofounded several consumer protection and good government organizations, including the Public Interest Research Group (more commonly and derisively called "Nader's Raiders") and the Center for Study of Responsive Law. Nader also ran for U.S. president as an independent or on the Green Party ticket in every election from 1992 to 2008. In the 2000 election, many critics claim his Green Party candidacy cost Democratic nominee Al Gore the presidency, which went to Republican George W. Bush in a closely contested and controversial election that actually saw Gore win the popular vote.

Nader was born in 1934 in Connecticut into a family that instilled in him a strong sense of social justice. He graduated from Princeton University and Harvard Law School, where Nader edited the *Harvard Law Record*. He served in the U.S. Army and began to practice law in Hartford while teaching history and government at the University of Hartford. In 1965, he worked part-time for the Department of Labor, conducting research that led him to write his breakout book, *Unsafe at Any Speed* (1965). The publication of the book, which offered a withering assessment of the American auto industry's indifference to driver safety, led to significant reforms within the automobile industry. It also increased public support for government regulation of industry. In 1968, Congress passed and President Lyndon Johnson signed into law the National Traffic and Motor Vehicle Safety Act that established the National Highway Traffic Safety Administration. In 1970, Nader sued General Motors for harassment and intimidation after the company tried to prevent him from releasing his book, *Unsafe at Any Speed.* Claiming invasion of privacy and intentional infliction of emotional distress, Nader won a judgment of $425,000 from General Motors. He used this money to found the Center for Auto Safety and several other public interest groups. Nader also led a campaign on food safety that led to passage of the Wholesome Meat Act (1967). Nader has written dozens of books besides *Unsafe at Any Speed*, including *The Menace of Atomic Energy* (1977), *Who's Poisoning America* (1981), *Good Works* (1981), and *No Contest* (1996).

Obama, Barack (1961–)

Barack H. Obama served as the 44th president of the United States (POTUS). He is an example of a community activist turned professional politician who uses electoral politics to pave the way to minority inclusion. Barack Obama was born in Hawaii in 1961. He is the first African American to serve as U.S. president. He was educated at Occidental College, Columbia University (BA), and at Harvard Law School (JD), at which he was the first African American editor of the prestigious *Harvard Law Review.* After graduation from Columbia University, he moved to Chicago, where he worked as a community activist with a group of churches to help rebuild communities devastated by the closure of local steel plants. He attended Harvard Law and after graduation, instead of joining some lucrative Wall Street law firm, Obama returned to Chicago to lead a voter registration drive and teach constitutional law at the University of Chicago, and he remained active as a community organizer and activist in Illinois electoral politics. He served in the Illinois State Senate (2005–2008), where he sponsored a bill that was the first major ethics reform law in 25 years.

He authored several best-selling books, notably *Dreams from My Father* (1995), *The Audacity of Hope* (2008), *Change We Can Believe In* (2008), and *Of Thee I Sing* (2010). His quotes and other comments are the focus of a book published in 2008 by Lisa Rogak, titled *Barack Obama in His Own Words*. He released *A Promised Land* in 2020, a NYT Bestseller.

President Obama appointed two associate justices of the Supreme Court: Sonia Sotomayor, in 2009, and Elena Kagan, in 2010. He appointed more minority judges to the federal bench than did any other U.S. president. He was awarded the Profile in Courage Award in 2017. He continues to affect electoral politics in America through his cofounding and work on, with Eric Holder, the National Democratic Redistricting Committee.

Reagan, Ronald (1911–2004)

Ronald Reagan was the 40th president of the United States. Elected in November 1980, he served in the White House from 1981 to 1989. Reagan was the highly influential voice of modern conservatism, and his presidency is considered to have been a transformative one. His impact on conservatism and the Republican Party's policy priorities was immense, and he was a prodigious fundraiser for his party as well. Reagan built a new coalition of voters that included all the traditional Republican constituencies as well as a significant number of blue-collar, working-class Democrats, dubbed "Reagan Democrats" by political journalists. Reagan was the first Republican president since Dwight Eisenhower to win and serve two terms. In the 1980 election, Reagan defeated incumbent president Jimmy Carter, carrying 44 states and winning 489 ECVs. He survived an assassination attempt in 1981 and went on to win reelection in 1984 over former vice president Walter Mondale. Reagan won 49 states and 525 ECVs, the most ever by any president in U.S. presidential election history.

Reagan was born in Illinois. In 1932, he graduated with a BA degree from Eureka College. He twice served as president of the Screen Actors Guild (1947–1952 and 1959–1960). It was during his stint as guild president that he led the effort to drive communists and communist sympathizers out of the film industry, and as a result of that campaign, Reagan changed his political orientation from a liberal supporter of FDR (prior to 1962) to a conservative Republican (1962 to 2004). In 1964, he gave a speech, "A Time for Choosing," that made him a national conservative spokesman and became the core of his 1980 presidential election "stump speech." In 1966, Reagan was elected California's 33rd governor, serving from 1967 to 1975. In 1976, he ran, unsuccessfully, for the Republican nomination for president. He won the office in 1980. In his postpresidency, Reagan was busy initially as a much sought-after public speaker and in work on his presidential library. He was awarded the Presidential Medal of Freedom in 1993 and the Congressional Gold Medal in 2000. He authored five books: *A Time for Choosing* (1983), *Abortion and the American Conscience* (1984), *An American Life* (1990), *Reagan* (2003), and posthumously, *The Reagan Diaries* (2007). He succumbed to Alzheimer's disease and died in Los Angeles in 2004.

Rehnquist, William (1924–2005)

William Rehnquist was born in Milwaukee, Wisconsin, in 1924. He married Natalie Cornell in 1953. Rehnquist graduated from Harvard University (with a BA and an MA in political science) and earned his JD from Stanford Law School, graduating in the same law class as Sandra Day O'Connor. Rehnquist also served in the U.S. Army Air Force during World War II.

With a total of 33 years on the Supreme Court bench, William Rehnquist was one of the longest-serving U.S. Supreme Court justices. He was an associate justice from 1972 to 1986 and was chief justice from 1986 to 2005. While serving as associate justice, William Rehnquist often wrote dissenting opinions, sometimes even notable solo dissents (Tushnet 2008; Vile

2014). As chief justice, Rehnquist wrote several notable majority opinions. His record on civil rights and liberties cases can be described as consistently conservative rather than expansive of such rights.

Chief Justice Rehnquist led the Court toward what has been described as ""judicial activism of the Right," tilting the Court increasingly toward conservative rulings (Schwartz 2003). During Rehnquist's years as chief justice, the Supreme Court trended toward more split-decision rulings (i.e., more 5–4 or 6–3 decisions, as opposed to the 7–2, 8–1, or even unanimous rulings more common during the Warren Court). Justice Rehnquist presided over the U.S. Senate impeachment trial of President William Jefferson Clinton as well as the Supreme Court's highly controversial 5–4 decision in *Bush v. Gore* (2000). The *Bush v. Gore* ruling has been criticized by Democrats and many legal experts as blatantly partisan, and the decision injected the Court into electoral politics in a way that historically has been more often eschewed by the Court. Rehnquist was still serving as chief justice of the Court when he died of thyroid cancer in September 2005.

Richards, Cecile (1957–)

Cecile Richards was president of the Planned Parenthood Federation of America and the Planned Parenthood Action Fund from 2006 to 2018. She exemplifies the activist approach to electoral politics. Planned Parenthood is the grassroots and national movement that for nearly a century has worked to build a national network of 700 clinics, centers, and women's health-care providers who serve nearly three million patients annually. Planned Parenthood also provides sex education to more than one million persons. Before joining Planned Parenthood, Cecile Richards was the deputy chief of staff to Speaker of the House Nancy Pelosi. In 2004, Richards founded and served as president of America Votes, a coalition of 42 national grassroots organizations working to maximize registration, voter education, and voter participation. In

2011, Richards led a national campaign to preserve Planned Parenthood services through federal programs. She led a campaign to expand advocacy for health-care coverage and services under the Affordable Care Act. She oversaw the doubling of Planned Parenthood's supporters, reaching seven million persons. She began her career organizing low-wage workers in the hotel, health-care, and janitorial services industries in California, Louisiana, and Texas. She is a frequent speaker and commentator on women's rights, reproduction rights, voting rights, and sex education and a regular contributor to HuffPost. Richards serves on the board of directors of the Ford Foundation. After leaving Planned Parenthood, Cecil Richards cofounded (with Alicia Garza and Ai-jen Poo) Supermajority, a women's political action group. Supermajority is a membership-based political action committee (PAC) that is a one-stop shop for advocacy, community building, and electoral participation in an intergenerational, multiracial movement advocating for women's equity. In the 2019–2020 election cycle, Supermajority raised more than $3.5 million, spent more than $3 million, and launched its Majority Leaders program. Cecile Richards is the daughter of former Texas Democratic governor Ann Richards. She is a graduate of Brown University. She lives with her husband, Kirk Adams, and three children in New York City.

Roberts, John (1959–)

In 2005, President George W. Bush nominated judge John Roberts to serve as chief justice of the U.S. Supreme Court, taking the seat vacated with the death of William Rehnquist. The Roberts nomination was approved by the U.S. Senate on a 78–22 vote on September 29, 2005. Justice Roberts was born in Buffalo, New York, in 1959. He attended Harvard College (BA, 1976) and Harvard Law (JD, 1979). He served as law clerk for Associate Justice William Rehnquist in 1980. He was special assistant to the attorney general, Department of Justice (DOJ), from 1981 to 1982, and then served as associate counsel to President Ronald Reagan, in the White House Counsel's Office, from 1982 to 1986. He was principal deputy solicitor general, DOJ, from 1989 to 1993. Roberts was appointed to the U.S. Court of Appeals in 2003 by President George W. Bush.

With regard to election law, Justice Roberts has been critically involved in three important Supreme Court cases, all decided by a 5–4 vote. Chief Justice Roberts wrote the majority opinion in *FEC v. Wisconsin Right to Life, Inc.* (2007) that ruled against the Federal Election Commission and held that issue ads may not be banned from the months preceding a primary or general election. In perhaps the Court's most consequential campaign finance reform decision, *Citizens United v. FEC* (2010), Justice Roberts voted with the majority in essentially gutting the Bipartisan Campaign Reform Act. The Citizens United decision held that the First Amendment's right to free speech prohibited the FEC from limiting contributions from "independent expenditure" organizations, such as corporations and unions. The ruling spurred the use of super PACs and dark money in U.S. elections, as it freed corporations and individual donors to spend unlimited amounts of money on political campaigns. Justice Roberts also joined the majority in *McCutcheon v. the FEC* (2014), which banned the limits that the FEC had placed on individual campaign contributions.

Roberts has already had a long tenure on the Court, and he will unquestionably influence future election-law jurisprudence, both through his majority opinions and by his management of the opinions in decisions in which he votes in the minority. With the Court's docket including legal challenges to several state election reform laws (or voter suppression laws from the perspective of progressives), Chief Justice Roberts will continue to impact electoral politics in the United States. Indeed, the Supreme Court upheld partisan gerrymandering as constitutional in *Rucho v. Common Cause* (2019) and upheld (6–3) two Arizona voter suppression laws on July 1, 2021, in *Brnovich v. DNC.*

Roosevelt, Franklin D. (1882–1945)

Franklin Delano Roosevelt was the 33rd president of the United States, serving from 1932 until his death in 1945. He was the only president in U.S. history to be elected four times. The Roosevelt era marked a fundamental shift in the American electorate that reshaped American life and politics. FDR is one of a handful of presidents whose tenure in the White House is regarded by historians as transformative.

Roosevelt was born in Hyde Park, New York, in 1882. In 1900, he entered Harvard University. In 1905, he married Eleanor Roosevelt, a distant cousin who was also the niece of former president Theodore Roosevelt. Franklin attended Columbia Law School and passed the bar in 1909. In 1910, he was elected to the New York State Senate at age 29. In the Woodrow Wilson administration, Roosevelt served as assistant secretary of the navy. In 1921, Roosevelt contracted poliomyelitis, better known as polio. Although crippled by the disease, he continued his political career, and in 1928 he was elected governor of New York, where he earned a reputation in the early years of the Great Depression as a "reform governor," although he was able to work well with New York's urban machine politicians.

In 1932, Roosevelt was elected president, and his 1932 and 1936 elections are considered to be realigning elections. He crafted a new coalition of voting blocs that gave the Democratic Party unprecedented dominance. In his 1932 victory, Roosevelt won 57.4 percent of the popular vote to 39.6 percent for Republican Herbert Hoover. He carried 44 of the then 48 states and won the Electoral College vote by 472 to 59. He campaigned on a platform of "Relief, Recovery, and Reform." In his first term, he innovated the bully pulpit of the presidency with radio talks, called "fireside chats," that enabled him to directly mold public opinion in support of his ambitious "New Deal" programs.

He set a new precedent of successful enactment of legislation in his first 100 days that has been the challenge for every president since. Historians mark two "New Deal" periods: 1932 to 1935 and 1936 to 1938, in which he launched 14 major programs, perhaps most notably Social Security in 1935. For Roosevelt, one electoral challenge with respect to immigrant voters and their children was reforming the urban machines. Roosevelt understood the need to build a nation-state with welfare programs of the national government replacing the welfare work previously done by those machines. Roosevelt worked with Democratic urban politicians, making them partners in the New Deal and crafting a national welfare system. From 1932 to 1940, he used his campaign manager, Jim Farley, as first postmaster general, and the DNC chair as his chief dispenser of the New Deal patronage system. Roosevelt acted as something akin to a "national boss" of the Democratic Party. Roosevelt won an unprecedented third term in 1940 and a fourth term in 1944. He successfully led the nation through two national crises: the Great Depression and World War II. Roosevelt died in office at his retreat at Warm Springs. Georgia, just months after his fourth inauguration.

Sanders, Bernie (1941–)

Bernie Sanders is a third-term U.S. senator (I-VT) who was a major contender for the Democratic presidential nomination in 2016 (losing to New York senator Hillary Clinton, but winning 45 percent of the primary vote) and in 2020 (losing to former vice president Joe Biden). Sanders was born in Brooklyn, New York, the son of Jewish immigrants from Poland. He attended Brooklyn College and graduated from the University of Chicago in 1964. It was in Chicago that Sanders began his anti-war and pro–civil rights political activism, joining the Young People's Socialist League, the Congress on Racial Equality, and the Student Nonviolent Coordinating Committee. At that point in his political career, he was a political protest activist.

Sanders was a member of the Liberty Union Party, from 1970 to 1977, and the anti-war People's Party. Sanders moved to Vermont and became a Head Start teacher. In 1981, he turned to standard electoral politics to pursue his reformist policy agenda. Sanders was elected mayor of Burlington, Vermont, where he served for four terms (1981–1989). Sanders lectured at the John F. Kennedy School of Government at Harvard University, and at Hamilton College in upstate New York. In 1991, Sanders won a seat in the U.S. House of Representatives despite running as an Independent rather than a Democrat or Republican. He served in that seat for the next 16 years, winning election a total of eight times. His membership in the House from 1991 to 2007 made him the longest-serving Independent member of Congress in U.S. history.

Although Sanders spent much of his career as an Independent, he regularly caucused with the Democrats, whom he saw as more interested in helping poor and working-class Americans than the Republicans were. In paperwork filed with the Democratic National Committee (DNC) for the 2020 presidential campaign, Sanders affirmed that he considered himself a Democrat and would serve in the White House as a Democrat if elected. Sanders has been a member of the Congressional Progressive Caucus, the Democratic Caucus, and the Senate AfterSchool Caucus. From 1996 to 2021, Sanders received a 100 percent rating for his Senate voting record by the NAACP in nine different years.

In his 2016 and 2020 bids for the Democratic presidential nomination, Sanders pioneered the "small donor" strategy, eschewing super political action committee (PAC) donations and raising $73 million from 2.5 million donations and an average contribution of $27.16. His campaign worked closely with ActBlue and helped it rise to its current prominence. He also pioneered the use of social media in his campaigns, and in his 2016 presidential bid, he drew huge crowds to his campaign rallies.

Sanders is the author or coauthor of five books: *Outsider in the White House* (1999); *The Speech* (on the filibuster, 2011, 2015); *Our Revolution* (2016); *Bernie Sanders Guide to Political Revolution* (2017); and *Where We Go from Here* (2018).

Schumer, Charles (1950–)

Charles "Chuck" Schumer is the senior U.S. senator from New York and, since 2021, the Senate majority leader. He was born in Brooklyn, where he resides with his wife. They have two daughters. In 1980, Schumer joined the U.S. Congress when he won the seat of New York's Ninth Congressional District. He served in the House for eight years before winning election to the U.S. Senate in 1988. Schumer became the senior U.S. senator from New York when the late Daniel Patrick Moynihan retired in 2000. Schumer was reelected in 2004 and served on the Senate Finance Committee.

Important for electoral politics, Schumer was chair of the Democratic Senate Campaign Committee for two election cycles: 2004 and 2008. In 2006, he was selected as vice chair of the Democratic Conference and, in 2010, as chair of the Democratic Policy and Communications Center. Schumer led the effort to mount a "50-states" strategy, competing vigorously in many states and districts in which the party had previously been largely noncompetitive. Prior to becoming majority leader, Schumer was the ranking member of the powerful Senate Rules Committee, which oversees federal elections, voting rights, campaign finance, and the operations of the Senate complex

As Senate majority leader, Schumer has been a vocal advocate for Senate Bill 1, the "For the People Act," with its myriad provisions to shore up voting rights and protect American democracy and elections. He also is a supporter of the John Lewis Voting Rights Act, which if enacted, would restore and strengthen parts of the Voting Rights Act of 1965 that were struck down in the U.S. Supreme Court case of *Shelby County v. Holder* (2013) and further weakened by *Brnovich v. DNC* (2021). However, neither bill has, nor is expected to pass in the Senate because two Senate Democrats (Joe Manchin of West Virginia and Kyrsten Sinema of Arizona) don't agree on a strategy to circumvent Republican filibusters of both these bills, preventing them for coming up for a vote in 2021 and 2022.

Stein, Jill (1950–)

Dr. Jill Stein was the Green Party presidential candidate in 2012 and 2016. Stein was born in Chicago and graduated with her BA from Harvard in 1973 and from Harvard Medical School in 1979. She is a physician, political party organizer, and pioneering environmental-health advocate. Jill Stein was the principal organizer for the Global Climate Convergence for People, Planet, and Peace-Over-Profit, a direct-action and education campaign to provide coordinated action on global climate change across national borders. Stein began her political activism as a physician in the 1990s, exposing the link between exposures to toxic chemicals and illness. She worked as a grassroots activist to pass an election reform law by voter referendum in Massachusetts, only to see it later overturned in the state legislature. In 2002, Jill Stein was recruited by the Green-Rainbow Party to run for Massachusetts governor against Mitt Romney, which was her first foray into electoral politics as a candidate for office. She was twice elected to town government in Lexington, Massachusetts. In 2003, Stein cofounded the Coalition for Healthy Communities, a nonprofit organization. She was the Green-Rainbow Party candidate in two additional elections: for state representative in 2004 and for secretary of state in 2006. Stein has received numerous awards for her efforts and activism regarding public health and environmental protection. She has coauthored two reports: *In Harm's Way: Toxic Threats to Child Development* (2002), and *Environmental Threats to Healthy Aging* (2009). After the 2016 election, some critics maintained that her third-party run was partially the reason Hillary Clinton lost the Electoral College vote in several states, giving the election to Trump. They contend that for most voters who pulled the lever for Stein, Clinton would have been their second choice. Like Ralph Nader, Jill Stein illustrates the "spoiler role" that third-party candidates can sometimes play in closely contested elections.

Trump, Donald (1946–)

Donald J. Trump was elected the 45th president in 2016 and sworn into office in January 2017. He lost the popular vote to Democratic nominee Hillary Clinton but won the Electoral College vote (ECV) 306–232. Even as a former one-term president and the only president to have been twice impeached, he continues to totally dominate Republican Party electoral politics.

Trump was born in New York City in 1946, the son of a multimillionaire real estate tycoon. He attended Fordham University and then the Wharton School of the University of Pennsylvania. He built on the family real estate empire and also became a television celebrity as the host for the first 14 seasons of a reality TV program called *The Apprentice* (2004–2015).

In the 2020 election, the Trump-Pence ticket lost to the Biden-Harris ticket by seven million votes in the popular vote (49.96 percent to 51.37 percent), and by 306 to 232 ECV. President Trump was twice impeached by the U.S. House of Representatives but was acquitted both times in the U.S. Senate. In both cases, a majority of senators voted to impeach him but the tally didn't reach the necessary two-thirds supermajority for conviction. The first impeachment charged him with, among other things, abuse of power of his office by soliciting foreign interference in the 2016 election. The second impeachment charged him with inciting the insurrection to overturn the 2020 election by interfering with Congress's certification of the ECV results. Since losing the 2020 presidential election, Trump continues to allege, without any proof and having lost 59 court challenges and numerous recounts in the swing states he lost (Arizona, Georgia, Michigan, Pennsylvania, and

Wisconsin), that he only lost due to widespread voter fraud. Throughout 2021, he pushed for partisan "audits" of election results in those swing states and attacked both Democratic and Republican state and local election officials, who refused to overturn the election results in the 2020 presidential race. Trump's falsehoods about the accuracy of the elections in both 2016 and 2020 have been widely cited as the single greatest driver of public doubts about the integrity of American elections. In 2021, he was banned from using the major social media platforms (Facebook and Twitter) for having used them to spread disinformation and falsehoods about the 2020 election results and his role in the January 6, 2021, riot at the Capitol.

Turner, Deborah Ann (1970–)

Deborah Turner is the 20th president of the League of Women Voters (LWVUS). She was elected at the National Convention of the LWVUS in June 2020 and will serve until June 2022. She joined the Des Moines Metropolitan League in 2012, where she served until 2015 and helped to revitalize its membership. Turner served on the LWV Iowa board and as the Iowa state vice president and became copresident of the state league in 2015. While on the Iowa board, she strengthened the relationship between local leagues and the state board. She was elected to the LWVUS national board of directors in 2016.

At the national board level, Turner focused on organizational cultural change by emphasizing racial equality, international dynamics, socioeconomic differences, gender identity, and interpersonal engagement. Turner received her BS from Iowa State University and her MD from the University of Iowa. She practiced gynecological oncology for 35 years. She also received her JD from Drake University in 2007. Since 2016, she has served as associate medical director of Planned Parenthood of the North Central States, a position that involved her in Planned Parenthood's electoral advocacy work and the fight against the GOP-led campaign to defund Planned Parenthood and to overturn *Roe v. Wade*. As chair of the LWVUS Voter Education Fund, she leads its efforts to promote nonpartisan electoral reforms in campaign finance reform, against racial- and minority-oriented gerrymandering, and against voter suppression laws.

Van Buren, Martin (1782–1862)

Martin Van Buren was the eighth president of the United States, serving from 1837 to 1841, and played a central role in establishing the two-party system that prevails in the United States today. Just five feet tall, he was known as the "little magician" to his friends and as the "sly fox" to his political opponents (in recognition of his electoral political cunning.)

Van Buren was born in New York, the son of Dutch immigrants, and spoke Dutch and English. Van Buren was the first U.S. president born a citizen of the United States and not a British subject. He was educated in the law as a legal apprentice, as was the prevailing practice, and was elected as the ninth governor of New York. Van Buren established the Albany Regency, a prototype political party that served as the model for the Democratic Party, also known as the Jacksonian Democratic Party, a coalition of Jeffersonian Republicans and supporters of Andrew Jackson. The New York Albany Regency was a disciplined organization that doled out financial and political benefits in exchange for party loyalty, a state of affairs that came to be known as "the spoils system." Van Buren essentially managed the Jackson campaign to secure the presidential nomination by caucus in 1828. This was before any party had held a national nominating convention (the Whigs were the first to do so in 1831). In 1827–1828, Van Buren was de facto chair of the Jeffersonian Republican Party.

Van Buren helped create the Jacksonian Democratic Party as the nation's first true mass political party. The mass party organization approach was successful. It increased voter turnout from 26.5 percent in 1824 to 56.3 percent in 1828. After the 1828 election, in which the Jacksonian Democrats beat the Whigs (at the time the second major party) and the Anti-Masonic Party, which was the first U.S. third party, President Andrew Jackson made Van Buren his secretary of state and, in 1831, minister (ambassador, in today's terminology) to Great Britain. In 1832, after the Democrats held their first national nominating convention, Van Buren was the Democrat's first vice presidential nominee. In the 1832 election, the Jackson-Van Buren ticket easily won against the Whig Party ticket. Between 1832 and 1836, the mass party system, with its spoils system, matured, resulting in even greater democratization of the U.S. electorate. Voting restrictions based on property-ownership requirements fell left and right, extending the franchise to non-property-owning white males, and Democrats encouraged the party's rank-and-file supporters to participate in electoral politics. In 1836, with the support of President Jackson, Van Buren easily won the Democratic Party nomination for president and went on to defeat the Whig Party nominee, William Henry Harrison.

Van Buren's administration was plagued by the economic Panic of 1837 (what would be called a depression today), and Van Buren lost his reelection in 1840 to Harrison, who died after serving only 31 days in office, the shortest-ever presidency in American history. Van Buren tried to win the White House again in 1844 but lost the party nomination to James Polk. In 1848, Van Buren made his last attempt to return to the White House when he ran as a member of the antislavery Free Soil Party. He lost again, but his contribution of establishing the two-party and mass party system was secure.

Warren, Earl (1891–1974)

As was noted above, Chief Justice William Rehnquist is often characterized as a "judicial activist of the Right." Chief Justice Earl Warren, by contrast, is widely viewed as the Supreme Court's primary judicial activist of the Left (Belknap 2005; Newton 2006; Tushnet 1996). Warren was chief justice of the

U.S. Supreme Court from 1953 to 1969. He led the Court during its most activist period regarding civil rights and civil liberties. Warren guided the Court when it developed and most often used the judicial doctrine of incorporation to extend the protections of the Bill of Rights to state and local governments (Powe 2000; Urofsky 2001).

Warren was born in Los Angeles in 1891. He attended the University of California–Berkeley, earning his BA in political science in 1913 and his LLB in 1914. During World War I, Warren served in the U.S. Army as a first lieutenant (1917–1918). He was chair of the Republican Party of California from 1932 to 1939 and was district attorney of Alameda County from 1925 to 1939. Earl Warren was elected attorney general of California in 1938, and while Attorney General Warren supported the Japanese relocation and internment programs in 1942. It was a decision he came to regret by 1944. In his memoirs, Warren wrote, "Whenever I thought of the innocent little children who were torn from home, school, friends, and congenial surroundings, I was conscience stricken. . . . It was wrong to react so impulsively, without positive evidence of disloyalty" (Warren 1977). At the time, however, it was a popular decision that helped him win the race for governor of California in 1942. Warren served as governor of California from 1943 to 1953. He was appointed as chief justice of the Supreme Court in 1953 by President Dwight Eisenhower, who thought that Warren would be a reliably conservative vote on the Court. Eisenhower was mistaken, and he later indicated that he regarded his appointment of Warren as one of his biggest mistakes as president (Hitchcock 2018).

As chief justice, Warren wrote the majority opinion in a number of landmark civil rights–relevant cases: *Brown v. Board of Education* (1954, a unanimous ruling), *Klopfer v. North Carolina* (1967, a unanimous Sixth Amendment ruling), *Reynolds v. Sims* (1964, an 8–1 ruling), *Miranda v. Arizona* (1966, a 6–3 decision), and *Loving v. Virginia* (1967, a unanimous ruling). In managing the Court, Warren worked hard to hand down decisions that reflected unanimity or a high level of consensus among the nine justices.

Under Warren, the Court also issued "incorporation" rulings in several landmark cases, two of which directly concerned voting and elections: *Reynolds v. Sims* (1964), and *Wesberry v. Sanders* (1964). The Court also upheld the constitutionality of the 1964 Civil Rights Act in *Heart of Atlanta Motel, Inc. v. United States* (1964).

After President John F. Kennedy's assassination in 1963, Warren led the government's investigation into the murder. The findings of the so-called Warren Commission, which attributed the assassination to a lone gunman, have been challenged by various conspiracy theories in the decades since Kennedy's death. Earl Warren retired from the Court in 1969. He timed his retirement to enable President Lyndon B. Johnson, a Democrat, to replace him on the Court. Warren died in California in 1974.

Bibliography

Anderson, Carol. 2019. *One Person, No Vote: How Voter Suppression Is Destroying Our Democracy*. New York: Bloomsbury.

Anton, Michael. 2019. *After the Flight 93 Election: The Vote That Saved America and What We Still Have to Lose*. New York: Encounter Books.

Bear, Kenneth. 2000. *Reinventing Democrats*. Lawrence: University Press of Kansas.

Belknap, Michael. 2005. *The Supreme Court under Earl Warren, 1953–1969*. Columbia: University of South Carolina Press.

Biden, Joe. 2017. *Promise Me Dad*. New York: Flatiron Books.

Booker, Cory. 2016. *United*. New York: Random House.

Brewer, Mark, and Jeffrey Stonecash. 2015. *Polarization and the Politics of Personal Responsibility*. Oxford: Oxford University Press.

Brookhiser, Richard. 2018. *John Marshall: The Man Who Made the Supreme Court*. New York: Basic Books.

Castro, Julian. 2018. *An Unlikely Journey*. Boston: Little, Brown.

Ceasar, James W., and Andrew Busch. 2001. *The Perfect Tie: The True Story of the 2000 Presidential Election*. Lanham, MD: Rowman and Littlefield.

Cole, David. 2016. *Engines of Liberty: The Power of Citizen Activists to Make Constitutional Law*. New York: Basic Books.

Dinken, Robert J. 1987. *Campaigning in America: A History of Election Practices*. Westport, CT: Greenwood Press.

Fiorina, Morris, Samuel Abrams, and Jeremy Pope. 2017. *Culture War? The Myth of the Polarization of America*. 3rd ed. New York: Longman.

Garrow, David. 2017. *Rising Star: The Making of Barack Obama*. New York: William Morrow/Harper Collins.

Hanson, Victor. 2019. *The Case for Trump*. New York: Basic Books.

Harris, Kamala. 2019. *The Truths We Hold: An American Journey*. New York: Penguin Press.

Hitchcock, William. 2018. *The Age of Eisenhower: America and the World in the 1950s*. New York: Simon & Schuster.

Hudson, David. 2006. *The Rehnquist Court: Understanding Its Impact and Legacy*. New York: Praeger Press.

Irving, Curtis L., and Joshua Bassett, eds. 2011. *America's Urban Crisis and the Advent of Color Blind Politics*. Lanham, MD: Rowman and Littlefield.

Johnstone, David Cay. 2016. *The Making of Donald Trump*. New York: Melville House.

Kaufman, Eric. 2018. *White Shift: Populism, Immigration, and the Future of White Majorities*. New York: Abrams Press.

King, Desmond S., and Roger Smith. 2011. *Still a House Divided: Race and Politics in Obama's America*. Princeton, NJ: Princeton University Press.

Klobuchar, Amy. 2015. *The Senator Next Door*. New York: Henry Holt.

Lee, Percy, Louise Young, and Ralph Young. 1989. *In the Public Interest: The League of Women Voters, 1920–1970*. Westport, CT: Greenwood Press.

LeMay, Michael C. 2009. *The Perennial Struggle: Race, Ethnicity, and Minority Group Relations in the United States*. 3rd ed. Upper Saddle River, NJ: Prentice-Hall.

LeMay, Michael C. 2017. *The American Political Party System: A Reference Handbook*. Santa Barbara, CA: ABC-CLIO.

LeMay, Michael C. 2018. *U.S. Immigration Policy, Ethnicity, and Religion in American History*. Santa Barbara, CA: ABC-CLIO.

LeMay, Michael C. 2020. *First Amendment Freedoms: A Reference Handbook*. Santa Barbara, CA: ABC-CLIO.

Mayor, Jane. 2016. *Dark Money: The Hidden History of the Billionaires behind the Rise of the Radical Right*. New York: Anchor Books.

Murray, Charles. 2012. *Coming Apart: The State of White America, 1960–2010*. New York: Crown Forum.

Newton, Jim. 2006. *Justice for All: Earl Warren and the Nation He Led*. New York: Riverhead Books.

Norris, Pippa, and Ronald Inglehart. 2019. *Cultural Backlash: Trump, Brexit, and Authoritarian Populism*. Cambridge: Cambridge University Press.

Obermayer, Herman. 2009. *Rehnquist: A Personal Portrait of the Distinguished Chief Justice of the United States*. New York: Oxford University Press.

Olsen, Henry. 2017. *The Working Class Republicans: Ronald Reagan and the Return of Blue-Collar Conservatism*. New York: Broadside Books.

Powe, Lucas. 2000. *The Warren Court and American Politics*. Cambridge, MA: Belknap Press/Harvard University Press.

Sanders, Bernie. 2016. *Our Revolution: A Future to Believe In.* New York: Thomas Dunne Books.

Schwartz, Herman, ed. 2003. *The Rehnquist Court: Judicial Activism of the Right.* New York: Hill and Wang.

Shafer, Byron E., and Richard Spady. 2014. *The American Political Landscape.* Cambridge, MA: Harvard University Press.

Sides, John, Michael Tesler, and Lynn Vavrek. 2018. *Identity Crisis: The 2016 Presidential Campaign and the Battle for the Meaning of America.* Princeton, NJ: Princeton University Press.

Simon, James. 2003. *What Kind of Nation: Thomas Jefferson, John Marshall, and the Epic Struggle to Create a United States.* New York: Simon & Schuster.

Sloan, John. 2008. *FDR and Reagan: Transformative Presidents with Clashing Visions.* Lawrence: University Press of Kansas.

Strang, Stephen E. 2020. *God, Trump, and the 2020 Election.* New York: Frontline.

Thomas, G. Scott. 2019. *Presidential Election Record Book.* New York: Niawanda Books.

Tushnet, Mark. 1996. *The Warren Court in Historical and Political Perspective.* Charlottesville: University of Virginia Press.

Tushnet, Mark. 2005. *A Court Divided: the Rehnquist Court and the Future of Constitutional Law.* New York: W. W. Norton.

Tushnet, Mark. 2008. *Dissent: Great Opposing Opinions in Landmark Supreme Court Cases.* Boston: Beacon Press.

Urofsky, Melvin. 2001. *The Warren Court: Justices, Rulings, and Legacy.* Santa Barbara, CA: ABC-CLIO.

Vile, John R. 2014. *Essential Supreme Court Decisions: Summaries of Leading Cases in U.S. Constitutional Law.* 16th ed. Lanham, MD: Rowman and Littlefield.

Warren, Earl. 1977. *The Memoirs of Earl Warren*. Garden City, NY: Doubleday.

Wilentz, Sean. 2016. *The Politicians and the Egalitarians*. New York: W. W. Norton.

Witcover, Jules. 2003. *Party of the People*. New York: Random House.

Zentner, Scot, and Michael LeMay. 2020. *Party and Nation: Immigration and Regime Politics in American History*. Lanham, MD: Lexington Books.

5 Data and Documents

Introduction

Since the country's inception, elections in America have been shaped by guidance contained in the Constitution, laws enacted by the U.S. Congress and various state legislatures, and U.S. Supreme Court decisions concerning the franchise. This chapter presents a synopsis of critical actions, both legislative and judicial, that have impacted U.S. elections over time. In the first section of the chapter, data on various aspects of American elections and political trends are presented in 16 tables. These are followed by a primary documents section that presents excerpts from some key federal legislative actions on elections and voting, as well as excerpts from a dozen landmark U.S. Court decisions that have shaped the way elections and election campaigns are conducted today. The documents are presented in chronological order.

Supporters of President Donald Trump demonstrate at the U.S. Capitol following a "Stop the Steal" rally protesting the ratification of President-elect Joe Biden's Electoral College victory over President Trump in the 2020 election, January 6, 2021, in Washington, DC. Hundreds breached the Capitol building, as lawmakers were set to sign off on President-elect Joe Biden's electoral win in what was supposed to be a routine process headed to Inauguration Day. For the first time in U.S. history, the outgoing president refused to peacefully transfer the government. (Alex Gakos/Shutterstock)

Data

The original 13 states ran their elections in the manner they did as colonies. Those states that joined after 1800, however, set their laws governing campaigns and elections at the same time that political parties were gaining prominence. Those states that joined after 1830 reflected the expansion of the franchise, while those that joined after the Civil War reflected the impact of the Civil War Amendments. States that joined the Union after 1920 were impacted by the 19th, 23rd, 24th, and 26th Amendments. Table 5.1 provides a rundown of all 50 states by the order in which they officially achieved statehood.

Table 5.1 States Ranked by Date of Entrance to the Union

Rank	State	Date of Entrance to the Union
1	Delaware	December 7, 1787
2	Pennsylvania	December 12, 1787
3	New Jersey	December 18, 1787
4	Georgia	January 2, 1788
5	Connecticut	January 9, 1788
6	Massachusetts	February 6, 1788
7	Maryland	April 28, 1788
8	South Carolina	May 23, 1788
9	New Hampshire	June 21, 1788
10	Virginia	June 25, 1788
11	New York	July 26, 1788
12	North Carolina	November 21, 1789
13	Rhode Island	May 29, 1790
14	Vermont	March 4, 1791
15	Kentucky	June 1, 1792
16	Tennessee	June 1, 1796
17	Ohio	March 1, 1803
18	Louisiana	April 30, 1812
19	Indiana	December 11, 1816
20	Mississippi	December 10, 1817
21	Illinois	December 3, 1818

(*continued*)

Table 5.1 *(continued)*

Rank	State	Date of Entrance to the Union
22	Alabama	December 14, 1819
23	Maine	March 15, 1820
24	Missouri	August 10, 1821
25	Arkansas	June 15, 1836
26	Michigan	January 26, 1837
27	Florida	March 3, 1845
28	Texas	December 29, 1845
29	Iowa	December 28, 1846
30	Wisconsin	May 29, 1848
31	California	September 9, 1850
32	Minnesota	May 11, 1858
33	Oregon	February 14, 1859
34	Kansas	January 29, 1861
35	West Virginia	June 20, 1863
36	Nevada	October 31, 1864
37	Nebraska	March 1, 1867
38	Colorado	August 1, 1876
39	North Dakota	November 2, 1889
40	South Dakota	November, 2, 1889
41	Montana	November 8, 1889
42	Washington	November 11, 1890
43	Idaho	July 3, 1850
44	Wyoming	July 10, 1850
45	Utah	January 4, 1896
46	Oklahoma	November 16, 1907
47	New Mexico	January 6, 1912
48	Arizona	February 14, 1912
49	Alaska	January 3, 1959
50	Hawaii	August 21, 1959

Table 5.2 provides an alphabetical list of the 50 states and the chief election official within each state.

Table 5.2 State Election Officials by State

State	Title of Chief Election Official	Selection	Appointing Authority
Alabama	Secretary of State	Elected	
Alaska	Lieutenant Governor	Elected	
Arizona	Secretary of State	Elected	
Arkansas	Secretary of State	Elected/Board	
California	Secretary of State	Elected	
Colorado	Secretary of State	Elected	
Connecticut	Secretary of State	Elected	
Delaware	Commissioner of Elections	Appointed	Governor
Florida	Secretary of State	Appointed	Governor
Georgia	Secretary of State	Elected/Board	
Hawaii	Chief Election Officer	Board	State Elections Commission
Idaho	Secretary of State	Elected	
Illinois	Executive Director	Board	State Board of Elections
Indiana	Secretary of State	Elected/Board	
Iowa	Secretary of State	Elected	
Kansas	Secretary of State	Elected	
Kentucky	Secretary of State	Elected/Board	
Louisiana	Secretary of State	Elected	
Maine	Secretary of State	Appointed	State Legislature
Maryland	Administrator of Elections	Board	State Board of Elections
Massachusetts	Secretary of State	Elected	
Michigan	Secretary of State	Elected	
Minnesota	Secretary of State	Elected	
Mississippi	Secretary of State	Elected	
Missouri	Secretary of State	Elected	
Montana	Secretary of State	Elected	
Nebraska	Secretary of State	Elected	
Nevada	Secretary of State	Elected	
New Hampshire	Secretary of State	Appointed	State Legislature
New Jersey	Secretary of State	Appointed	Governor
New Mexico	Secretary of State	Elected	
New York	Co-Directors	Board	State Board of Elections
North Carolina	Director	Board	State Board of Elections
North Dakota	Secretary of State	Elected	

(*continued*)

Table 5.2 (*continued*)

State	Title of Chief Election Official	Selection	Appointing Authority
Ohio	Secretary of State	Elected	
Oklahoma	Secretary/Board of Elections	Appointed	State Senate
Oregon	Secretary of State	Elected	
Pennsylvania	Secretary of Commonwealth	Appointed	Governor
Rhode Island	Secretary of State	Elected/Board	
South Carolina	Executive Director	Board	State Election Commission
South Dakota	Secretary of State	Elected	
Tennessee	Secretary of State	Appointed/ Board	State Legislature
Texas	Secretary of State	Appointed	Governor
Utah	Lieutenant Governor	Elected	
Vermont	Secretary of State	Elected	
Virginia	Commissioner	Appointed	Governor
Washington	Secretary of State	Elected	
West Virginia	Secretary of State	Elected/Board	
Wisconsin	Administrator	Board	State Elections Commission
Wyoming	Secretary of State	Elected	

Source: NCSL 2021; Hale, Montjoy, and Brown 2015

Table 5.3 lists those states that split the responsibility for managing elections among multiple election officials.

Table 5.3 States with Multiple Election Officials

State	Names of Election Offices
Alabama	Probate Judge; Clerk of Circuit Court; Sheriff; Board of Registrars
Arizona	Director or Administrator
Arkansas	County Board of Election Commissioners; County Clerk
Connecticut	Registrars of Voters; Town Clerk
Georgia	Judge of Probate; County Board of Registrars
Indiana	County Election Board; Clerk of Circuit Court; Board of Registration
Louisiana	Clerk of District Court; Registrar of Voters
Maine	Town/City Clerk; Registrar of Voters
Massachusetts	City/Town Clerk; Board of Registrars of Voters; County Clerk

(*continued*)

Table 5.3 (*continued*)

State	Names of Election Offices
Michigan	County Election Commission; City/Township Clerk; City/Township Election Commission
Mississippi	County Board of Election Commissioners; County Registrar; Clerk of Circuit Court
Nevada	County Clerk; Registrar of Voters in Clark and Washoe Counties; Moderator
New Hampshire	Town/City Clerk; Superintendent of Checklist (towns); Board of Registrars (cities)
New Jersey	County Clerk; County Board of Elections
New Mexico	County Board of Registration; County Clerk
South Carolina	County Board of Registration; Commissioners of Elections; County Clerk
Texas	County Clerk; County Tax Assessor/Collector
Virginia	County/City Electoral Boards; County/City Registrars

Source: Hale, Montjoy, and Brown 2015; NCSL 2021

Table 5.4 presents a rundown of the various types of primary elections found across the United States, as well as the specific states that employ each type.

Table 5.4 Types of Primary Elections Used in the American States

Election Type Used	States Using Type
Closed Primaries	Delaware, Florida, Kentucky, Maryland, Nevada, New Mexico, New York, Oregon, Pennsylvania
Partially Closed Primaries	Alaska, Connecticut, Idaho, North Carolina, Oklahoma, South Dakota, Utah
Partially Open Primaries	Illinois, Indiana, Iowa, Ohio, Tennessee, Wyoming
Open to Unaffiliated Voters	Arizona, Colorado, Kansas, Maine, Massachusetts, New Hampshire, New Jersey, Rhode Island, West Virginia
Open Primaries	Alabama, Arkansas, Georgia, Hawaii, Michigan, Minnesota, Mississippi, Missouri, Montana, North Dakota, South Carolina, Texas, Vermont, Virginia, Wisconsin
Top-Two Primaries	California, Washington
Caucus States/Territories	Iowa, Nevada, North Dakota, Wyoming, Kentucky (Republican Party only), Territories: American Samoa, U.S. Virgin Islands, Guam

Source: Table by author; data from National Conference of State Legislatures. Accessed September 30, 2020. https://www.ncsl.org/research/elections-and-campaign/primary-type.

Table 5.5 presents data from an ABC News exit poll after the 2020 election showing the percentage of respondents who identified themselves as either Democrat or Republican by various characteristics of the voters as to gender, race or ethnicity, age, and level of formal education. As political scientists and campaign officials alike well know, these demographic factors have a statistically significant impact on voting behavior.

Table 5.5 Political Party Percentage from 2020 Exit Polls (ABC News)

Characteristic	Percent Democrat	Percent Republican
Gender		
Male	45	53
Female	57	42
Race		
White	41	58
Black	87	12
Hispanic	65	32
Asian	61	34
Other	55	41
Nonwhite	71	21
White Men	38	61
White Women	44	35
Black Men	79	19
Black Women	90	9
Latino Men	59	36
Latino Women	69	30
All Other Races	58	38
Age		
18–29	60	36
30–44	52	46
45–64	49	50
65+	47	52
Education		
College	55	43
No College	48	50
New Voters	64	32

Source: Table by author; data from ABC News. Accessed January 12, 2022. https://abcnews.go.com/Elections/exit-polls-2020-us-election.

Table 5.6 lists six major U.S. Supreme Court decisions regarding the 10th and 14th Amendments.

The 10th Amendment specified that powers not specifically granted to the national government, such as the conduct of elections, were reserved to the states. The 14th Amendment stipulated that states may not make or enforce any law that abridged the rights and privileges or immunities of citizenship to any citizens, born or naturalized, in the jurisdiction of the state—nor deny them the equal protection of the laws, including laws regarding the right to vote.

Table 5.6 Six U.S. Supreme Court Cases Involving the 10th and 14th Amendments

Name of Case	Citation	Vote	Ruling
The Slaughter House Cases	83 U.S. 361873	5–4	Citizens "privileges and immunities" versus a Louisiana law (state citizenship)
Plessy v. Ferguson	163 U.S. 5371896	7–1	Louisiana "Separate Cars Act" upheld, doctrine of "separate but equal" legalizes segregation
Brown v. Board of Education, Topeka	347 U.S. 4831954	9–0	Segregation laws inherently unequal and therefore unconstitutional
Citizens United vs. FEC	558 U.S. 3102010	5–4	Upheld that corporations and other outside groups can spend unlimited money on elections
Bond v. United States	564 U.S. 2112011	9–0	Individuals have standing to raise 10th Amendment challenges to federal laws
Shelby County v. Holder	570 U.S. 5292013	5–4	Voting Rights Act procedures re: preclearance held unconstitutional

Source: Table by author.

Since the U.S. Civil War, Congress has enacted several laws that have had an important although sometimes rather temporary impact on elections in the United States. These laws are listed in Table 5.7 by their formal title and date of enactment and by the more common name by which they are known.

Table 5.7 Major Civil Rights Acts Passed by the U.S. Congress, 1866–1993

Title and Year	Citation	A.K.A.
Civil Rights Act of April 6, 1866	14 Stat. 27-60	Overrode Veto by Pres. Andrew Johnson
Civil Rights Act of March 3, 1875	18 Stat. 335	The Enforcement Act
Civil Rights Act of August 9, 1957	71 Stat. 634	Eisenhower Civil Rights Act
Civil Rights Act of May 6, 1960	74 Stat. 89	Voter Registration/Poll Tax
Civil Rights Act of July 2, 1964	78 Stat. 241	Equal Employment Opportunity Act
Civil Rights Act of August 6, 1965	79 Stat. 437	Voting Rights Act
Civil Rights Act of April 11, 1968	82 Stat. 73	The Fair Housing Act/ Indian Civil Rights Act
Civil Rights Act of November 21, 1991	105 Stat. 1071	Equal Opportunity Act
Civil Rights Act of May 20, 1993	107 Stat. 77	National Voter Registration Act

Source: Table by author.

Since the 1940s, and particularly since the Citizens United *decision in 2010, political action committees and especially so-called super PACs have had an increasingly consequential impact on U.S. elections. Table 5.8 lists 20 of the most powerful super PACs.*

Table 5.8 Exemplary Powerful Super PACs

Number	Name of Super PAC/Interest Group
1	National Association of Realtors
2	National Beer Wholesalers Association
3	Honeywell International PAC
4	National Auto Dealers Association
5	Lockheed Martin
6	American Bankers Association
7	AT&T
8	Credit Union National Association
9	International Union of Operating Engineers
10	International Brotherhood of Electrical Workers
11	National Rifle Association
12	U.S. Chamber of Commerce

(*continued*)

Table 5.8 *(continued)*

Number	Name of Super PAC/Interest Group
13	American Medical Association
14	AARP
15	Americans for Prosperity
16	MoveOn.org
17	America Israel PAC
18	AFL-CIO
19	NARAL Pro-Choice America
20	NAACP

Source: Table by author; data from OpenSecrets, list of the most powerful super PACs as of 2020. Accessed January 12, 2022. https://www.opensecrets.org/political-action-committees-pacs/super-pacs/2020.

The cost of running a campaign for an elective office has skyrocketed over the last several decades, largely due to the spiraling cost of buying advertising on various media. Table 5.9 compares the total cost of U.S. elections in billions of dollars by year between 1998 and 2020. The data reflect the difference in total costs in midterm election cycles versus presidential-year cycles.

Table 5.9 The Cost of U.S. Elections, 1998–2020

Year	Total Cost ($)	Congressional Races ($)	Presidential Race ($)
1998	1,618,936,265	1,618,936,265	NA
2000	3,082,340,937	1,669,244,553	1,413,116,289
2002	2,181,682,066	2,181,682,066	NA
2004	4,147,304,003	2,237,073,141	1,910,230,862
2006	2,852,658,140	2,852,658,140	NA
2008	5,285,680,863	2,485,952,737	2,799,728,146
2010	3,631,712,836	3,631,712,836	NA
2012	6,285,557,223	3,664,141,430	2,621,415,712
2014	3,845,393,700	3,845,393,700	NA
2016	6,511,181,587	4,124,304,874	2,386,876,712
2018	5,725,183,133	5,725,183,133	NA
2020	14,403,966,687	8,703,050,547	5,700,916,140

Source: Table by author; data from OpenSecrets.org 2021. Accessed May 27, 2021. https://www.opensecrets.orgt/elections-overview/cost-of-elections?cycle.

The use of ethnic, racial, and partisan gerrymandering has been a perennial problem in U.S. elections due to the mandatory redistricting of electoral boundaries after each decennial census. Table 5.10 lists landmark Supreme Court decisions on gerrymandering since 1960 and specifies the vote of the Court in each decision. The table also breaks the cases down by various aspects of gerrymandering (redistricting, redistricting commissions, partisanship, and race). Note that the rulings have become more often close (5–4 rulings) as the partisan split and the liberal versus conservative ideological divide among the justices on the Supreme Court became more evident since 1960.

Table 5.10 Supreme Court Cases Impacting Gerrymandering

Re: Redistricting	Citation	Year	Vote
Gomillion v. Lightfoot	364 U.S. 81	1960	9–0
Baker v. Carr	369 U.S. 186	1962	6–2
Wesberry v. Sanders	376 U.S. 1	1964	6–3
Reynolds v. Sims	377 U.S. 533	1964	8–1
Gaffney v. Cummings	412 U.S. 735	1973	6–3
Karcher v. Daggett	462 U.S. 725	1983	5–4
Shaw v. Reno	509 U.S. 630	1993	5–4
Miller v. Johnson	515 U.S. 900	1995	5–4
Hubt v. Cromartie	526 U.S. 541	1999	9–0
Re: Redistricting Commission			
Arizona State Legislature v. Arizona Independent Redistricting Commission	576 U.S. 135	2015	5–4
Re: Partisanship			
Gaffney v. Cummings	412 U.S. 735	1975	6–3
Davis v. Bandemer	478 U.S. 109	1986	7–2
Vieth v. Jubelirer	541 U.S. 267	2004	6–3
Rucho v. Common Cause	588 U.S. ___	2019	5–4
Re: Race			
Thornburg v. Gingles	478 U.S. 30	1986	6–3
Shaw v. Reno	509 U.S. 630	1993	5–4
Miller v. Johnson	515 U.S. 900	1995	5–4
Bush v. Vera	517 U.S. 952	1996	5–4
Bartlett v. Strickland	556 U.S. 1	2009	5–4
Shelby County v. Holder	570 U.S. 529	2013	5–4

(*continued*)

Table 5.10 *(continued)*

Re: Redistricting	Citation	Year	Vote
Alabama Legislative Black Caucus, et al. v. Alabama, et al.	575 U.S. 135	2015	5–4
Cooper v. Harris	581 U.S. 137	2017	5–3

Source: Table by author; data from NCSL, April 25, 2019. https://www.ncsl.org/research/redistricting/redistricting -and-the-supreme-court-the-most-significant-cases.

Congress and the Supreme Court have had different approaches to the issue of campaign finance reform laws ever since the U.S. Civil War. Congress has enacted laws to regulate the financing of elections, often imposing restrictions, such as limitations on contributions, or imposing the mandatory reporting of campaign contribution sources on the states or on candidates, organizations, or political parties, to regulate the impact of money on elections or to better address the potential corrupting effects of unlimited secret contributions. The Supreme Court has tended to see the issue as one of free speech rather than one of undue corruption or has viewed the problem as an issue to be resolved in the political arena of elections rather than through the court system. Table 5.11 presents a timeline of campaign finance reform laws passed by the Congress and significant Supreme Court rulings.

Table 5.11 Campaign Finance Laws and Supreme Court Decisions Timeline

Year	Description of Action
1867	Congress passes first law for campaign regulation.
1890	Naval appropriations bill bans seeking campaign donations from dockyard workers—law also known as the Battleship Act of 1890.
1907	Tillman Act prohibits banks and corporations from directly contributing money to campaigns.
1910	Federal Corrupt Practices Act (FCPA) requires candidates for U.S. House of Representatives to disclose campaign spending and source of contributions.
1911	Congress amends FCPA of 1910, adding U.S. Senate candidates to required campaign funding and spending reports.
1921	The Supreme Court rules in *Newberry v. U.S.* the FCPA unconstitutional regarding spending limits.

(continued)

Table 5.11 *(continued)*

Year	Description of Action
1925	Congress amends FCPA to set rules regarding sources of contributions above certain amounts to conform to *Newberry* decision.
1935	Public Utilities Act, a.k.a. the Wheeler-Rayburn Act, bans campaign contributions from public utilities.
1939	Hatch Act bars most federal employees from contributing to political campaigns and participating in most campaign activities.
1943	Smith-Connelly Act bans labor union contributions. In response, the CIO creates the first political action committee (PAC) in 1944.
1947	The Taft-Hartley Act also bans union banks and corporations from making contributions to candidates for federal office.
1971	Revenue Act establishes a federal fund for presidential candidates, and Congress passes Federal Elections Campaign Act (FECA).
1974	Congress amends FECA after Watergate scandal, setting new spending and contribution caps.
1976	Supreme Court decision in *Buckley v. Valeo* overturns many provisions of FECA, and Congress amends FECA as per the *Buckley* ruling.
1979	Congress further amends FECA.
2002	Bipartisan Campaign Reform Act (BCRA), a.k.a. McCain-Feingold Act, bans "soft money" and further defines "issue ads."
2003	Supreme Court decision in *McConnell v. FEC* (540 U.S. 93, 12/10/2003) upholds the major provisions of BCRA by a 5–4 vote.
2007	In *FEC v. Wisconsin Right to Life*, Supreme Court rules 5–4 that laws that ban ads by corporations and unions in weeks leading up to an election are unconstitutional infringement of free speech.
2010	In *Citizens United v. FEC,* in 5–4 decision along partisan lines, Supreme Court dismantles the McCain-Feingold Act
2014	In *McCutcheon v. FEC* ruling, the Supreme Court strikes down caps on total spending by individuals to federal campaigns and to political parties.
2015	In *Alabama Legislative Black Caucus, et al. v. Alabama, et al.* Court rules 5–4 that claims of racial gerrymandering have to be examined on a district-by-district basis rather than by statewide effects; in *Arizona State Legislature v. Arizona Independent Redistricting Commission, et al.* the Court in a 6–3 decision upholds constitutionality of the Independent Redistricting Commission.
2016	In *Harris et al. v. Arizona Independent Redistricting Commission, et al.* the Court unanimously upholds the Arizona redistricting plan.
2017	In *North Carolina, et al. v. North Carolina State Conference of the NAACP, et al.,* the Supreme Court denies a writ of certiorari regarding a challenge to North Carolina's voting law requiring voter photo ID, reducing early voting period, and eliminating same-day registration.

(continued)

Table 5.11 (continued)

Year	Description of Action
2018	In *Abbott, Governor of Texas, et al. v. Perez, et al.* by a 5–4 vote, the Court upholds controversial Texas congressional redistricting plan.
2020	In *Democratic National Committee, et al. v. Wisconsin State Legislature, et al.* the Supreme Court declines to reinstate special absentee ballot accommodations made by the state in response to COVID-19 public health concerns after an appeals court stopped the accommodations from being implemented.

Source: Table by author; data accessed May 27, 2021, from https://www.ncsl.org/research/elections-and-campaigns/campaignfinance-and-the-Supreme-Court/ and https://www.infoplease.com/history/us/campaign-finance-reform-history-and-timeline.

Table 5.12 presents the states ranked by the percent of voters eligible to participate (VEP) in elections by their turnout rate for the 2020 election.

Table 5.12 States Ranked by Percent VEP Turnout Rate, 2020 U.S. Election

Rank	State	VEP Turnout (%)	Rank	State	VEP Turnout (%)
1	Minnesota	79.96	26	Idaho	67.69
2	Colorado	76.41	27	Ohio	67.43
3	Maine	76.32	28	Illinois	67.02
4	Wisconsin	75.77	29	Missouri	66.26
5	Washington	75.71	30	South Dakota	65.97
6	Oregon	75.52	31	Arizona	65.92
7	New Hampshire	75.46	32	Kansas	65.86
8	New Jersey	74.28	33	Rhode Island	65.65
9	Vermont	74.21	34	Nebraska	65.36
10	Michigan	73.90	35	Kentucky	64.94
11	Iowa	73.25	36	Louisiana	64.61
12	Montana	73.10	37	Wyoming	64.56
13	Virginia	73.00	38	South Carolina	64.51
14	Massachusetts	72.11	39	North Dakota	64.45
15	Florida	71.66	40	New York	63.36
16	Connecticut	71.49	41	Alabama	63.13
17	North Carolina	71.48	42	Indiana	61.37
18	Maryland	70.71	43	New Mexico	61.25

(*continued*)

Table 5.12 (*continued*)

Rank	State	VEP Turnout (%)	Rank	State	VEP Turnout (%)
19	Pennsylvania	71.05	44	Texas	60.42
20	Delaware	70.68	45	Mississippi	60.17
21	Nebraska	69.89	46	Tennessee	59.81
22	Utah	69.17	47	West Virginia	57.58
23	Alaska	68.76	48	Hawaii	57.52
24	California	68.50	49	Arkansas	56.07
25	Georgia	67.72	50	Oklahoma	54.99

Source: Table by author; data from WorldPopulationReview.com, 2021.

Table 5.13 presents the ranking of states by their partisan voting using the Cook Partisan Voting Index (CPVI), which is calculated by the average Democratic or Republican share of the vote for the last two presidential elections compared to the national average. These data are presented by the 23 Republican-leaning states, then the 7 battleground (or swing) states, and then by the 20 Democratic-leaning states.

Table 5.13 States Ranked by the Cook Partisan Voting Index (CPVI), 2020

Name of State	CPVI Score
Republican-Leaning States:	
Wyoming	R+26
West Virginia	R+23
Oklahoma	R+20
North Dakota	R+20
Idaho	R+19
South Dakota	R+16
Kentucky	R+16
Arkansas	R+16
Texas	R+15
Alabama	R+15
Tennessee	R+14
Utah	R+13
Nebraska	R+13

(*continued*)

Table 5.13 (*continued*)

Name of State	CPVI Score
Louisiana	R+12
Montana	R+11
Kansas	R+11
Indiana	R+11
Missouri	R+10
Mississippi	R+9
Alaska	R+9
South Carolina	R+8
Ohio	R+6
Iowa	R+6
Battleground States:	
North Carolina	R+3
Georgia	R+3
Florida	R+3
Arizona	R+3
Wisconsin	R+2
Pennsylvania	R+2
Michigan	R+1
Democratic-Leaning States:	
New Hampshire	D+0
Nevada	D+0
Minnesota	D+1
Maine	D+1
Virginia	D+2
New Mexico	D+3
Colorado	D+3
Oregon	D+6
New Jersey	D+6
Illinois	D+7
Connecticut	D+7
Washington	D+8
Rhode Island	D+8
New York	D+10
Massachusetts	D+14
Maryland	D+14
California	D+14
Vermont	D+15
Hawaii	D+15

Source: Table by author; data accessed January 12, 2022, from https://www.cookpolitical.com/analysis/national/pvi/introducing-2021-cook-political-report-partisan-voter-index. First introduced in 1997.

Table 5.14 presents the Electoral College votes (ECVs) awarded to each state as of the 2020 presidential election.

Table 5.14 Electoral College Vote (ECV) by State, 2020

Name of State	ECV	Name of State	ECV	Name of State	ECV
Alabama	9	Kentucky	8	North Dakota	3
Alaska	3	Louisiana	8	Ohio	18
Arizona	11	Maine	4	Oklahoma	7
Arkansas	6	Maryland	10	Oregon	7
California	55	Massachusetts	11	Pennsylvania	20
Colorado	9	Michigan	16	Rhode Island	4
Connecticut	7	Minnesota	10	South Carolina	9
Delaware	3	Mississippi	6	South Dakota	3
District of Columbia	3	Missouri	10	Tennessee	11
Florida	29	Montana	3	Texas	38
Georgia	16	Nebraska	5	Utah	6
Hawaii	4	Nevada	6	Vermont	3
Idaho	4	New Hampshire	4	Virginia	13
Illinois	20	New Jersey	14	Washington	12
Indiana	11	New Mexico	5	West Virginia	5
Iowa	6	New York	29	Wisconsin	10
Kansas	6	North Carolina	15	Wyoming	3

Source: Table by author; data accessed January 12, 2022, from https://www.archives.gov/electoral-college/2020.

Table 5.15 lists the percent of voters claiming a party identification by annual averages, years 2010–2020.

Table 5.15 Party Identification, Annual Averages, 2010–2020

Year	Percent Democrat	Percent Independent	Percent Republican
2010	31	38	29
2012	31	40	28
2014	30	43	26
2016	30	39	28
2018	30	42	28
2020	30	39	29

Source: Table by author; data accessed January 12, 2022, from https://www.statista.com/statistics/1078383/political-party-identification-in-the-us.

Table 5.16 lists the most popular source platforms for news about government and political as of November 2020.

Table 5.16 Most Popular News Platforms for Government and Politics, November 2020

News websites = 25 percent
Social media sites = 18 percent
Local TV = 16 percent
Cable TV = 16 percent
National TV Networks = 13 percent
Radio = 8 percent
Print Newspapers and Magazines = 3 percent
No Answer = 1 percent

Source: Table by author; data accessed January 12, 2022, from https://www.pewresearch.org/fact-tank/2020/04/01/americans-main-sources-for-political-news-vary-by-party-and-age.

Documents

Acts of Congress

The Constitution empowers Congress to carry out a census of the population every 10 years. The Constitution gives Congress the power to determine how the census is undertaken. At various times, the Supreme Court and federal district courts have weighed in on the issue of the census, for example, holding that the Constitution requires the counting of all persons, not just citizens, and that the census may collect such additional information as Congress deems to be "necessary and proper." Important for the number of Electoral College votes each state is entitled to, Congress by the Act of June 18, 1929, fixed permanently the number of seats in the U.S. House of Representatives at 435, necessitating redistricting after every decennial census. Doc. 5.1 cites the census clause in the Constitution.

Doc. 5.1: Census Clause of the U.S. Constitution, Article I, Section 2, Clause 3

Representatives and direct Taxes shall be apportioned among the several States which may be included within this Union, according to their respective Numbers, which shall be determined by adding to the whole Number of free persons, including those bound to service for a Term of Years, and excluding Indians not taxed, three fifths of all other Persons. The actual Enumeration shall be made within three Years after the first Meeting of the Congress of the United States, and within every subsequent Term of ten Years, in such Manner as they shall by Law direct. The Number of Representatives shall not exceed one for every thirty Thousand, but each State shall have at least one Representative, and until such enumeration shall be made, the State of New Hampshire shall be entitled to chuse three, Massachusetts eight, Rhode Island and Providence Plantation one, Connecticut five, New York six, New Jersey four, Pennsylvania eight, Delaware one, Maryland six, Virginia ten, North Carolina five, and Georgia three.

Source: American Civil Liberties Union. *The Constitution of the United States of America, Article I, Section 2, Clause 3.*

Doc. 5.2: The Hatch Act

In 1939, the Congress passed the Act of August 2 (53 Stat. 1147), known as the Hatch Act after its author, Senator Carl Hatch (D-NM). The Hatch Act was passed to curb the growing power of the Works Progress Administration (WPA) and its chief administrator, Harry Hopkins. President Franklin D. Roosevelt opposed the Hatch Act as an anti–New Deal bill, but it passed despite his opposition. At the time, Roosevelt was struggling to purge the Democratic Party of its more conservative and anti–New Deal members, most of whom represented southern states. Doc. 5.2 excerpts 9 of its 11 provisions.

Be it enacted by the Senate and House of Representatives in Congress assembled, That it shall be unlawful for any person to intimidate, threaten, or coerce, or to attempt to intimidate, threaten, or coerce any person to vote for any candidate or for the purpose of interfering with the right of such person to vote or to vote as he may choose, or of causing such person to vote for, or not to vote for, any candidate for the office of a President, Vice President, Presidential elector, Member of the Senate, or Member of the House of Representatives at any election held solely or in part for the purpose of selecting a President, Vice President, or any Member of the Senate or any Member of the House of Representatives, Delegate, or Commissioner from the Territories or insular possessions.

Sec. 2. It shall be unlawful for any person employed in any administrative position by the United States, or by any department, independent agency, or other agency of the United States (including any corporation controlled by the United States or any agency thereof, and any corporation all of the capital stock of which is owned by the United States or any agency thereof), to use his official authority for the purpose of interfering with, or affecting the election or the nomination of any candidate for the Office of President, Vice President, Presidential elector, Member of the Senate, or Member of the House of Representatives, Delegates, or Commissioners from the Territories or insular possessions.

Sec. 3. It shall be unlawful for any person, directly or indirectly, to promise any employment, position, work, compensation, or other benefit, provided for or made possible in whole or in part by any Act of Congress, to any person as consideration, favor, or reward for any political activity or for the support of or opposition to any candidate or any political party in any election.

Sec. 4. Except as may be required by the provisions of any subsection (b), section 9 of this Act, it shall be unlawful for any person to deprive, attempt to deprive, or threaten to deprive, by any means, any person of any employment, position, work, compensation, or benefit provided for or made possible by any Act of Congress, appropriating funds for work relief or relief purposes, on account of race, creed, color, or any political activity of, or opposition to any candidate or any political party in any election.

Sec. 5. It shall be unlawful for any person to solicit or receive or be in any manner concerned in soliciting or receiving any assessment, subscription, or contribution for any political purpose whatever from any person known by him to be entitled to or receiving compensation, any list or names of persons receiving compensation, employment, or other benefit provided for or made possible by any Act of Congress appropriating funds for work relief or relief purposes.

Sec. 6. It shall be unlawful for any person for political purposes to furnish or to disclose, or to aid in furnishing or disclosing, any list of names of persons receiving compensation, employment, or benefits provided for by any Act of Congress appropriating, or authorizing the appropriation of funds for any work relief or relief purposes, to a political candidate, committee, campaign manager, or to any person for delivery to a political candidate, committee, or campaign manager, and it shall be unlawful for any person to receive any such list or names for political purposes.

Sec. 7. No part of any appropriation made by any Act heretofore or hereafter enacted, making appropriations for work relief, relief, or otherwise to increase employment by providing loans or grants for public-works projects, shall be used for the purpose of, and no authority conferred by any such Act upon any person shall be exercised for or administered for the purpose of interfering with, restraining, or coercing any individual in the exercise of his right to vote in any election.

Sec. 8. Any person who violates any of the foregoing provisions of this Act upon conviction thereof shall be fined not more than $1,000 or imprisoned for not more than one year, or both.

Sec. 9 (a). It shall be unlawful for any person employed in the executive branch of the Federal Government, or any agency or department thereof, to use his official authority or influence for the purpose of interfering with an election or affecting the results thereof. No officer or employee in the executive branch of the Federal Government, or any agency or department thereof, shall take an active part in political management or in political campaigns. All such persons shall retain the right to vote as they may choose or to express their opinions on all political subjects. . . .

Sec. 9 A. It shall be unlawful for any person employed in any capacity by any agency of the Federal Government, whose compensation, or any part thereof, is paid for by funds authorized or appropriated by any Act of Congress, to have membership in any political party or organization which advocates the overthrow of our constitutional form of government in the United States.

Source: Act of August 2, 1939, 53 Stat. 1147.

Doc. 5.3: The McCarran-Walter Act

Congress passed the Immigration and Naturalization Act of June 27, 1952 (66 Stat. 163), also known as the McCarran-Walter Act. It was an omnibus law of more than 200 pages in the Code of Statutes. Although it mostly reenacted the various quota laws and in particular *the 1917 Immigration act's provisions, better known as the Barred-Zone Act (39 Stat. 8741), in its naturalization section it did provide for the naturalization (and thereby voting rights) of racial groups (the Japanese and Koreans) previously excluded from becoming citizens based on their race. That provision alone was critically important for the Japanese American Citizens League to vigorously lobby for its enactment. Doc. 5.3 presents an excerpt, Sec. 311, of chapter 2 of the Act, on Naturalization.*

Chapter 2: Nationality and Naturalization

Sec. 311. The right of a person to become a naturalized citizen of the United States shall not be denied or abridged because of race or sex or because such a person is married. Notwithstanding section 405(b), this section shall apply to any person whose petition for naturalization shall hereafter be filed or shall have been pending on the effective date of this Act.

Source: Act of June 27, 1952, 66 Stat. 163.

Doc. 5.4: The Voting Rights Act of 1965

The Voting Rights Act of August 6, 1965 (79 Stat. 437, Public Law 89-110), is arguably the most significant and effective federal civil rights law ever enacted and one of the farthest-reaching civil rights laws in U.S. history. The impact of this law and its five subsequent amendments can hardly be exaggerated. It was designed to secure the right to vote for all racial minorities. Signed into law by President Lyndon Johnson during the height of the civil rights movement, the legislation was crafted to overcome legal barriers at the state and local levels that prevented Black Americans from exercising their right to vote under the 15th Amendment to the U.S. Constitution. It was challenged and upheld in two decisions of the Supreme Court, South Carolina v. Katzenbach, *393 U.S. 301, 1968 and* Allen v. State Board of Elections, *393 U.S. 544, 1969. Section 5 of the law was eviscerated, however, in the 2013 decision of the Supreme Court in* Shelby v. Holder (570 U.S. 529) *The Voting Rights Act of 1965 is excerpted in Doc. 5.4.*

An Act to enforce the fifteenth amendment to the Constitution of the United States and for other purposes.

Be it enacted by the Senate and the House of Representatives of the United States in Congress assembled, That this Act shall be known as the "Voting Rights Act of 1965."

Sec. 2. No voting qualifications or prerequisite to vote, or standard or procedure shall be imposed or applied by any State or political subdivision thereof to deny or abridge the right to vote of any citizen of the United States to vote on account of race or color.

Sec.3 (a). Whenever the Attorney General institutes a proceeding under any statute to enforce the guarantees of the fifteenth amendment by any State or political subdivision the court shall authorize the appointment of Federal examiners by the United States Civil Service Committee, in accordance with section 6, to serve for such period of time and for such political subdivisions as the court shall determine is appropriate to enforce the guarantees of the fifteenth amendment (1) as part of any interlocutory order if the court determines that the appointment of such examiners is necessary to enforce such guarantees or (2) as part of any final judgment if the court finds that violations of the fifteenth amendment justifying equitable relief have occurred in such State or subdivision: Provided, That the court need not authorize the appointment of examiners if any incident of denial or abridgment of the right to vote on account of race or color (1) have been few in number and have been promptly and effectively corrected by State or local action, (2) the continuing effect of such incidents have been eliminated, and (3) there is no reasonable probability of their re-occurrence in the future. (b) If in a proceeding instituted by the Attorney General under any statute to enforce the guarantees of the fifteenth amendment in any State or political subdivision the court finds that a test or device has been used for the purpose or with the effect of denying or abridging the right of any citizen of the United States to vote on account of race or color, it shall suspend the use of such tests and devices in such State or subdivisions as the court shall determine is appropriate and for such period as it deems necessary. . . .

Sec. 4 (a) To assure that the right of citizens of the United States to vote is not denied or abridged on account of race or color, no citizen shall be denied the right to vote in any Federal, State, or local election because of failure to comply with any test or device in any state with respect to which determinations have been made under subsection (b).

Source: The Voting Rights Act of August 6, 1965, 79 Stat. 437, P.L. 89-110.

Doc. 5.5: The Federal Election Campaign Act of 1971

The Federal Election Campaign Act (FECA) of 1971 was signed into law by President Richard Nixon on February 7, 1972 (86 Stat. 3, enacted February 7, 1972, as Public Law 92-225). It regulated the financing of federal election campaigns, including money raised and spent by both candidates and the political parties to which they belonged. The bill to enact FECA was extensively amended after the Watergate scandal that led to Nixon's resignation in disgrace. It was amended in 1974 as to the limits an individual could contribute to any federal campaign or to a political party or the amount any committee could contribute to a candidate per election. The law, often simply referred to as the Campaign Finance Act, runs for more than 130 pages in the code of statutes. The following excerpts from FECA show how complex the wording of any legislation aimed at regulating campaign finance must by necessity be.

An Act to promote fair practices in the conduct of election campaigns for Federal offices and for other purposes.

Be it enacted by the Senate and House of Representatives of the United States of America in Congress assembled, That this Act may be cited as the "Federal Election Campaign Act of 1971."

Sec. 101. This title may be cited as the "Campaign Communications Reform Act."

Sec. 104 (a)(1). Subject to paragraph (4) no legally qualified candidate in an election (other than a primary or primary runoff election) for a Federal elective office may—

(A) Spend for the use of communication media on behalf of his candidacy in such election a total amount in excess of the greater part of

(i) 10 cents multiplied by the voting age population . . . of the geographic area in which then election for such office is held, or

(ii) $50,000, or

(B) Spend for the use of broadcast stations on behalf of his candidacy in such election in total amount in excess of 60 percent of the amount under paragraph (A) with respect to such election.

(2) No legally qualified candidate in a primary election for nomination to a Federal office, other than President, may spend—

(A) for the use of communications media, or

(B) for the use of broadcast stations on behalf of his candidacy in such elections in excess of the amounts determined under paragraph (1)(A) or (B), respectively, with respect to the general election for such office. For purposes of this subsection a primary runoff election shall be treated as a separate primary election. . . .

(3)(A) No person who is a candidate for presidential nomination may spend—

(i) for the use in a State of communications media, or

(ii) for the use in a State of broadcast stations, on behalf of his candidacy for presidential nomination a total amount in excess of the amount which would have been determined under paragraph (1)(A) or (B) respectively, had he been a candidate for election for the Senate from such State. . . .

(C) The Comptroller General shall prescribe regulations under which any expenditure by a candidate in presidential nomination for the use in two or more states of a communication medium shall be attributed to such candidate's expenditure limitation in each such State, based on the number of persons in such State who can reasonably be expected to be reached by such communication medium.

Source: Act of February 7, 1972 (FECA), 86 Stat. 3, P.L. 92-225.

Doc. 5.6: The Bipartisan Campaign Reform Act of 2002

The Bipartisan Campaign Reform Act of 2002 (BCRA, 116 Stat. 81, PL 107-155) is a federal law amending the FECA of 1971. Its chief sponsors were Russ Feingold (D-WI) and John McCain (R-AZ). It was the first major amendment to the 1971 law after the Watergate scandal of 1974. The primary purpose of the BCRA was to eliminate the increased use of so-called soft money in American politics. It was signed into law by President George W. Bush on March 27, 2002 and became effective on November 6, 2002. It was the most serious bipartisan attempt to reform campaign finance law but was effectively gutted by subsequent Supreme Court decisions, most notably Citizens United v. FEC *(2010).*

An Act to amend the Federal Election Campaign Act of 1971 to provide bipartisan campaign reform. Be it enacted by the Senate and House of Representatives of the United States in Congress assembled,

Sec. 1 (a) Short Title—This Act may be cited as the "Bipartisan Campaign Reform Act of 2002."

Sec. 101. Soft Money of Political Parties.

(a) National Committees—

(1) IN GENERAL. A National Committee of a political party (including a national congressional campaign committee of a political party) may not solicit, receive, or direct to another person a contribution, donation, or transfer of funds or any other thing of value, or spend any such funds, that are not subject to the limitations, prohibitions, and reporting requirements of this Act.

(2) APPLICABILITY—The prohibition established by paragraph (1) applies to any such national committee acting on behalf of such committee or entity), or by an association or similar group of candidates for

State or local office or of individuals and officer or agent, any officer or agent acting on behalf of such a national committee, and any entity that is directly or indirectly established, financed, maintained, or controlled by such a national committee.

(b) STATE, DISTRICT, AND LOCAL COMMITTEES.

(1) IN GENERAL—Except as provided in paragraph (2), an amount that is expended or distributed for Federal election activity by a State, district, or local committee of a political party (including an entity that is directly or indirectly established, financed, maintained, or controlled by a State, district, or local committee of a political party or an officer or agent acting on behalf of such committee or entity), or by an association or similar group of candidates for State or local office or of individuals holding State or local office, shall be subject to the limitations, prohibitions, and reporting requirements of this Act.

(2) APPLICABILITY

(A) IN GENERAL—Notwithstanding clause (i) or (ii) of section 301 (20)(A), and subject to paragraph (B) paragraph (1) shall not apply to any amount expended or distributed by a State, district, or local committee of a political party for any activity described in either such clause to the extent the amounts expended or disbursed for such activity are allocated (under regulations described by the Commission) among amounts (i) which consist solely of contributions subject to the limitations, prohibitions, and reporting requirements described in subparagraph (B)(iii), and (ii) other amounts which are not subject to the limitations, prohibitions, or reporting requirements of this subsection.

Source: Bipartisan Campaign Reform Act of 2002 (116 Stat. 81, PL. 107-155).

Supreme Court Decisions

Doc. 5.7: Reynolds v. Sims, *377 U.S. 533, 1964*

In the 1960s, the U.S. Supreme Court under Chief Justice Earl Warren issued a series of decisions that impacted reapportionment in the states and subsequent federal, state, and local elections. In Baker v. Carr, *decided on March 26, 1962, the Court held that federal courts could "enter the political thicket" and hear cases regarding reapportionment by the states. In* Wesberry v. Sanders (February 17, 1964, 376 U.S. 1), *the Court ruled 6–3 that all federal congressional districts within each state had to be made up of a roughly equal number of voters. And in* Reynolds v. Sims, *handed down on June 15, 1964, in an 8–1 decision, the Court applied the principle of "one man, one vote" to U.S. legislative bodies. These decisions had a major impact on the state of Alabama and on state legislatures in many states that had to change their system of representation per the decision. Doc. 5.7 presents excerpts from the majority opinion of Chief Justice Earl Warren in* Reynolds v. Sims.

Involved in these cases are an appeal and two cross-appeals from a decision of the Federal District Court for the Middle District of Alabama holding invalid, under the Equal Protection Clause of the Federal Constitution, the existing and two proposed plans for the apportionment of seats in the two houses of the Alabama legislature and ordering into effect a temporary apportionment plan comprised of parts of the proposed but judicially disapproved measures.

On August 21, 1961, the original plaintiffs . . . residents, taxpayers, and voters of Jefferson County, Alabama, filed a complaint in the United States District Court for the Middle District of Alabama, in their own behalf and on behalf of all similarly situated Alabama voters, challenging the apportionment of the Alabama Legislature. Defendants below . . . sued in their representative capacities, were various state and political party officials charged with the performance of certain duties in connection with state elections. The complaint alleged a deprivation of rights under the Alabama Constitution and under the Equal Protections Clause of the Fourteenth Amendment, and asserted that the District Court had jurisdiction under provisions of the Civil Rights Act. . . .

The complaint stated that the Alabama Legislature was composed of a Senate of 35 members and a House of Representatives of 106 members. It set out relevant portions of the 1901 Alabama Constitution, which prescribe the numbers of the two bodies of the State Legislature and the method of apportioning seats among the State's 67 counties, [including] Art. XVIII, Section 284, "Representation in the legislature shall be based on population, and such basis of representation shall not be changed by constitutional amendments. . . .

35. We indicated in *Baker*, however, that the Equal Protection Clause, provides discoverable and manageable standards to use by lower courts in determining the constitutionality of a state apportionment scheme. . . .

51. Legislators represent people, not trees or acres. Legislators are elected by voters, not farms or cities or economic interests. As long as ours is a representative form of government, and our legislatures are those instruments of government elected by and directly representative of the people, the right to elect legislators in a free and unimpaired fashion is a bedrock of our political system. . . . And if a state should provide that the votes of citizens in one part of the state should be given two times, or five times, or 10 times the weight of votes of citizens in another part of the state, it could hardly be contended that the right to vote of those residing in the disfavored areas have not been effectively diluted. . . .

68. In *Wesberry v. Sanders,* supra, the Court stated that congressional representation must be based on equal population as nearly as practicable. . . ."

80. The Court goes much beyond the necessities of this case in laying down a new "equal population" principle for state legislative apportionment. This principle seems to be an offshoot of *Gray v. Sanders,* 372 U.S. 168 (1963), i.e., 'one person, one vote' modified by the 'nearly as is practicable' admonition of *Wesberry v. Sanders,* 376 U.S. 1 (1964).

Source: *Reynolds v. Sims,* June 15, 1964, 377 U.S. 533.

Doc. 5.8: Excerpts of the Case Summary in Bush v. Gore, *2000*

In December 2000, the U.S. Supreme Court handed down a momentous decision that settled a recount dispute concerning Florida's presidential election results. The dispute was a high-stakes one, because Florida's Electoral College votes (ECVs) would determine whether Democratic nominee Al Gore or Republican nominee George W. Bush became the 43rd president of the United States. The Court's 5–4 decision broke down along party lines, with the five conservative justices carrying the day. Their decision effectively decided the presidential election in favor of Bush, even though Gore won the popular vote. Chief Justice William Rehnquist was joined by four associate justices, Sandra Day O'Connor, Antonin Scalia, Anthony Kennedy, and Clarence Thomas, in siding with Bush. Four justices joined in dissent: John Paul Stevens, Ruth Bader Ginsburg, David Souter, and Stephen Breyer. Doc. 5.8 excerpts the summary of the case.

On December 8, 2000, the Florida Supreme Court ordered, inter alia, the manual recount of ballots for the recent Presidential election were required in all Florida counties where so-called "undercounts" had not been subject to manual tabulation, and that manual recounts should begin at once. Noting the closeness of the election, the court explained that, on the record before it, there could be no question that there were uncounted "legal" votes, i.e., those in which there was a clear indication of the voter's intention in sufficient numbers to place the results of the election in doubt. Petitioners, the Republican candidates for President and Vice President who have been certified as the winners in Florida, filed an emergency application for a stay of this mandate on December 9. This Court granted the stay application, treated it as a petition for a writ of certiorari, and granted certiorari. . . .

Held: Because it is evident that any recount seeking to meet 3 U.S. C. 5's December 12 "safe harbor" date would be unconstitutional under the Equal Protection Clause, the Florida Supreme Court's judgment ordering manual recounts is reversed.

Source: *Bush v. Gore,* December 12, 2000, 534 U.S. 98.

Doc. 5.9: FEC v. Wisconsin Right to Life, Inc., *2007*

Another 5–4 decision of the Supreme Court was in the landmark case of FEC v. Wisconsin Right to Life, Inc. *(551 U.S. 449, 2007). The Court held that so-called issue advocacy ads may not be banned in the months preceding a primary or general election. Decided on June 25, 2007, this decision upheld a district court ruling that the electioneering communications financing restrictions of the BCRA were an infringement on the constitutional free speech rights of Wisconsin Right to Life, Inc., a 501(c)(4) nonprofit corporation.*

Section 203 of the Bipartisan Campaign Reform Act (BCRA) makes it a crime for a corporation to use its general treasury funds to pay for any "electioneering communication," (2 U.S.C. 41 (b) (2)), which BCRA defines as any broadcast that refers to a candidate for federal office aired within 30 days of a primary election or 60 days of a general election in the jurisdiction where the candidate is running. . . . On July 26, 2004, appellee Wisconsin Right to Life, Inc. (WRTL), began running advertisements declaring that a group of Senators was filibustering to delay and block federal judicial nominees and telling voters to contact Wisconsin Senators Feingold and Kohl to urge them to oppose the filibuster. WRTL planned to run the ads throughout August 2004 and financed the ads with its general treasury funds. Recognizing that

As of August 15, 30 days before the Wisconsin primary, the ads would be illegal "electioneering communications" under BCRA section 203 . . . but believing that it nonetheless had a First Amendment right to broadcast them, WRTL filed suit against the FEC, seeking declaratory and injunctive relief and alleging that section 203's prohibition was unconstitutional as applied to the three ads in question. . . . This Court vacated that judgment [*McConnell*'s reasoning that section 203 was not facially overbroad], holding that *McConnell* did not purport to resolve future as applied challenges to section 203 . . . on remand, the District Court granted WRTL summary judgment, holding section 203 unconstitutional as applied to the three ads. The court first found that the adjudication was not barred by mootness because the controversy was capable of repetition yet evading review. On the merits, it concluded the ads were genuine issue ads, not expressly advocacy or its "functional equivalent" under *McConnell* and held that no compelling interest justified BCRA regulation of such ads.

The judgment is affirmed.

Source: *FEC v. Wisconsin Right to Life, Inc.*, June 25, 2007, 551 U.S. 449.

Doc. 5.10: Citizens United v. FEC, *2010*

The Supreme Court, in yet another 5–4 decision reflecting the Court's partisan divide, issued a landmark decision concerning section 203 of the Bipartisan Campaign Reform Act in a case that revolved around the relationship between campaign finance and free speech. In Citizens United v. FEC *(558 U.S. 310, 2010), which was decided on January 21, 2010, the Court held that the free speech clause of the First Amendment prohibited the government from restricting independent expenditures for political campaigns by corporations, wealthy billionaires, and super political action committees (PACs) established for the purpose of fundraising. The majority opinion by Justice Anthony Kennedy, which essentially ruled that money was speech, was joined in by Chief Justice Roberts, and Justices Antonin Scalia, Samuel Alito, and Clarence Thomas. The dissenting opinion by Justice Stevens was joined by Justices Ruth Bader Ginsburg, Stephen Breyer, and Sonia Sotomayor.*

The Citizens United *decision called into question laws in 24 states (including Connecticut, where the case originated), that prohibited corporations from making independent political expenditures from their general treasury. The* Citizens United *decision spurred an explosion in political campaign spending by major corporations, industries, and wealthy donors. Doc. 5.10 excerpts the majority opinion in the case.*

As amended by section 203 of the Bipartisan Campaign Reform Act (BCRA), federal law prohibits corporations and unions from using their general treasury funds to make independent expenditures, for speech that expressly advocates the election or defeat of a candidate. . . . An election communication is "any broadcast, cable, or satellite communication" that "refers to a clearly identified candidate for Federal office" and is made within 30 days of a primary election . . . and that is "publicly distributed" . . . which means that the communication [c]an be received by 50,000 or more persons in a State where a primary election is being held within 30 days. Corporations and unions may establish a political action committee (PAC) for express advocacy or electioneering purposes. . . . This Court upheld limits on electioneering communication in a facial challenge, relying on the holding in *Austin v. Michigan Chamber of Commerce*, 494 U.S. 652, that political speech may be banned based on the speaker's corporate identity. . . .

Because the question of whether section 441b applies to *Hillary* cannot be resolved on other, narrower grounds without chilling political speech, this Court must consider the continuing effect of the speech suppression upheld in *Austin* . . . (c) This Court is confronted with conflicting lines of precedent: a pre-*Austin* line forbidding speech restrictions based on the speaker's corporate identity, and a post-*Austin* line permitting them. Neither *Austin's* anti-distortion rationale nor the Government's other justifications support section 441 b/s restrictions. . . .

For these same reasons, this Court affirms the application of the sections 201 and 311 disclaimers and disclosure requirements to *Hillary*. Reversed in part, affirmed in part, and remanded.

Source: *Citizens United v. FEC*, June 21, 2010, 558 U.S. 310.

Doc. 5.11: McCutcheon v. FEC, *2014*

In the case of McCutcheon v. FEC *(572 U.S. 185), decided April 2,2014, the Supreme Court held that Section 441 of the Federal Elections Campaign Act, which imposed a limit on contributions an individual can make over a two-year period to national party and candidate committees, was unconstitutional. In a 5–4 decision that broke down along partisan lines, Chief Justice John Roberts wrote the majority opinion, joined by Justices Antonin Scalia, Anthony Kennedy, Samuel Alito, and Clarence Thomas. The dissenting opinion by Justice Stephen Breyer was joined by Justices Ruth Bader Ginsburg, Sonia Sotomayor, and Elena Kagan. The Court held that the limits are unconstitutional under the First Amendment. Doc. 5.11 excerpts the majority opinion in the case.*

The right to participate in democracy through political contributions is protected by the First Amendment, but that right is not absolute. Congress may regulate campaign contributions to protect against corruption or the appearance of corruption (See e.g., *Buckley v. Valeo*, 424 U.S. 1, 26-27). It may not, however, regulate contributions simply to reduce the amount of money in politics, or to restrict the political participation of some in order to enhance the relative influence of others. . . . Federal Elections Campaign Act of 1971 (FECA), as amended by the Bipartisan Campaign Reform Act of 2002 (BCRA), imposes two types of limits on campaign contributions. Base limits restrict how much money a donor may contribute to a particular campaign committee, while aggregate limits restrict how much money a donor may contribute in total to all candidates or committees (2 U.S.C. section 441 a).

In the 2011–2012 election cycle, Appellant McCutcheon contributed to 16 different candidates, complying with the base limits applicable to each. He alleges that the aggregate limits prevented him from contributing to 12 additional candidates and to a number of noncandidate political committees.

He also alleges that he wishes to make similar contributions in the future, all within the base limits. McCutcheon and appellant Republican National Committee filed a complaint before a three-judge District Court, asserting that the aggregate limits were unconstitutional under the First Amendment. The District Court denied their motion for a preliminary injunction and granted the Government's motion to dismiss, assessing that the base limits appropriately served the Government's anti-corruption interests, the District Court concluded that the aggregate limits survived First Amendment scrutiny because they prevented evasion of the base limits.

Held: The judgment is reversed, and the case is remanded.

Source: *McCutcheon v. FEC*, April 2, 2014, 572 U.S. 185.

Doc. 5.12: Rucho v. Common Cause, *2019, Justice Kagan's Dissenting Opinion*

In another 5–4 ruling in a landmark case concerning partisan gerrymandering, Rucho v. Common Cause, *decided June 27, 2019, the Court ruled that while partisan gerrymandering may be incompatible with democratic principles, the federal courts cannot review such allegations as they present nonjusticiable political questions outside the review jurisdiction of federal district courts. The majority opinion was by Chief Justice John Roberts, joined by Justices Clarence Thomas, Samuel Alito, Neil Gorsuch, and Brett Kavanaugh. There was ample precedent, however, for the Court to review gerrymandering cases. In* Baker v. Carr, *decided March 26, 1962 (369 U.S. 186), the Court ruled 6–2 that redistricting did qualify as a justiciable question under the 14th Amendment. The dissenting opinion of Justice Elena Kagan was joined by Justices Ruth Bader Ginsburg, Stephen Breyer, and Sonia Sotomayor. In effect, the Roberts majority decided to stay out of the "political thicket," refusing to provide any legal remedies for partisan gerrymandering. Justice Kagan's blistering dissenting opinion expressed disbelief at the majority's stance. Doc. 5.12 presents excerpts of Justice Kagan's dissenting opinion in the Rucho decision.*

For the first time ever this court refuses to remedy a constitutional violation because it thinks the task beyond judicial capabilities. And not just any constitutional violation, the partisan gerrymander in those cases deprived citizens of the most fundamental of their constitutional rights. The rights to participate equally in the political process, to join with others to advance political beliefs and to choose their political representatives. In doing so, these gerrymandered districts dishonored our democracy, turning upside down the core American idea that all government power derives from the people. These gerrymandered districts enabled politicians to entrench themselves in office against voters' preferences. They promoted partisanship above respect for the popular will. They encouraged a politics of polarization and dysfunction left unchecked. As the court does today, gerrymanders like these may irreparably damage our system of government. Consider what happened in these cases. What politicians in North Carolina and Maryland did to entrench themselves in political office regardless of what voters wanted. And as I relate some of these facts, which the chief justice has also related, ask yourselves one simple question: Is this how democracy is supposed to work? In North Carolina, Republican legislators voted to create a district plan that would ensure that Republicans captured 10 of the 13 seats in the state's congressional delegation. The mapmaker did everything he could to carry out those instructions, pretty much guaranteeing that Republicans would get 10 seats no matter what the statewide vote. . . . The committee chair explained, as the chief justice told you, that this was the way the map was drawn, because, well, it's just not possible to draw a map with eleven Republicans. He also announced, I think electing Republicans is better than electing Democrats, so I drew this map to help foster what I think is better for the country. Now, usually we think that choice is better left to the American people. But so far, the map has worked just as the Republican legislators and the mapmakers planned. Even though Democrats have won up to 50 percent of the state's statewide vote. In Maryland, much the same thing happened. But here it was Democrats creating the voter proof map. For years Maryland had six reliably Democratic districts and two reliably Republican districts, reflecting the two areas of the state in which Republicans form a natural majority. But the Democrats who control the state House and legislature decided to press their advantage. . . . A party in office at the right time can keep itself there for a decade or more. No matter what the voters would prefer. The core principle of republican government is that the voters should choose their representatives, not the other way around. Partisan gerrymandering turns it the other way around. By that mechanism, politicians can cherry pick voters to ensure their re-election, and then the power becomes not the people over the government. . . . Partisan gerrymandering of the kind here violates individual's constitutional rights as well. Once again, this court has long recognized the fact that gerrymandering like these violates the 14th Amendment by making the votes of some people count less than those of others. And these gerrymandered districts violate the First Amendment too, because they effectively penalize people for their political views and associations. Nearly every justice who has served on this court during the last several decades has agreed with everything I've just said, and notably today's majority doesn't contest it. The majority just says it can't do anything about the problem. In the face of grievous harm to democratic governance and flagrant infringements on constitutional rights, in the face of escalating partisan manipulation whose compatibility with this nation's values and laws no one defends. The majority declares that it can't provide a remedy because it can't find a manageable legal standard to apply. The majority, as you have just heard, gives two reasons for thinking so. First, it says there is no neutral baseline from which to measure injury. Partisan gerrymandering claims, the majority contends, will inevitably require courts to decide for themselves what electoral outcomes are fair, so that they can measure the results of gerrymandering against that ideal. And second, the majority argues that after doing so the court will have no way to answer the question, how much is too much? How far from the ideal a gerrymander must go to prompt a constitutional remedy. . . . But the state's own district and criteria whatever that might be, all the courts did was to determine how far the state had gone off that state-determined track because of its politicians' efforts to maintain their hold on political power and deciding whether the state went too far off that track is not so hard. Think about these two cases. North Carolina went too far off that track. Maryland went too far off that track. . . .

The question here whether vote dilution is substantial is no less a subset susceptible of judicial resolution, and the standard the district court used to set the bar high, that standard enabled courts to intervene only in the most extreme partisan gerrymander. It made sure that courts would not meddle in state electoral politics. But still that they would act to protect democracy and restore voting rights when most needed. In all these respects the district court's decision . . . are worth a read. They are detailed and thorough and painstaking. They evaluated with immense care the legal arguments and factual evidence that the parties presented. They used neutral and manageable and strict legal standards. They had not a shred of politics about them on every page. They refute the majority's idea that the law provides insufficient tools to remedy the blatant constitutional injuries. These cases present the courts below did what anyone would want a decision maker to do when so much hangs in the balance. They looked hard at the facts and the law, and they went where the facts and law led them. One of the oldest tenants of our legal system . . . is that it is emphatically the province and duty of the judicial department to say what the law is. And of all times to abandon the court's duty to declare the law, this was not the one. The practices challenged in these cases imperil our system of government. Part of the court's role in that system is to defend its foundations. None is more important than free and fair elections. With respect and deep sadness, Justices Ginsburg, Breyer, Sotomayor, and I dissent.

Source: *Rucho v. Common Cause*, June 27, 2019, 588 U.S.___.

Electoral
College
MY PUSSY

6 Resources

Introduction

This chapter briefly annotates major sources of information that the reader is encouraged to consult for further research and study on elections and campaign politics in the United States. It begins with print resources, discussing both scholarly books and major scholarly journals that regularly publish on election and voting issues. The chapter closes with a list of useful websites and documentary films to consult, for further nonprint sources of information on elections in America.

Books

Ackerman, Bruce, ed. 2002. *Bush v. Gore: The Question of Legitimacy.* New Haven, CT: Yale University Press.

Ackerman's book brings together a collection of prominent legal scholars to examine the larger questions raised by *Bush v. Gore* and the Court's actions in that case. It asks if the Court violated the rule of law and whether the decision inaugurated an era of hyper-politicized jurisprudence. The book exemplifies the pitfalls for the Court, and for the nation's democracy, when it enters the political arena in an obviously partisan manner.

Having lost the popular vote by an estimated three million votes, President Trump was among the least popular presidents ever at the time of his inauguration. Women, in particular, protested his election, as depicted here during the women's march in Los Angeles on January 21, 2017, with approximately 750,000 activists joining in. (Joe Sohm/Dreamstime.com)

Ackerman, Bruce, and Ian Ayres. 2004. *Voting with Dollars: A New Paradigm for Campaign Finance*. New Haven, CT: Yale University Press.

Two leading law professors challenge the conventional wisdom about the agenda for campaign finance reform. They propose a provocative system of "secret donation booths" for campaign contributions. Their proposal would have the U.S. government issue a special credit card account containing 50 "patriot dollars" to be used for presidential elections to eligible voters, who could send their patriot dollars anonymously to their favorite candidates or political organizations. The book details the problems of money—and secret money in particular—in the electoral process, as well as the difficulties in crafting campaign finance reforms.

Acosta, Jim. 2020. *The Enemy of the People: A Dangerous Time to Tell the Truth in America*. New York: HarperCollins.

In this *New York Times* best seller, CNN's Chief White House correspondent Jim Acosta presents a firsthand account of the dangers he faced reporting on the Trump White House and confronting the falsehoods spread by President Trump, his administration, and his allies. This book discusses Trump's practice of attacking any critical news coverage as "fake news" and the efforts of the administration and its allies to paint Acosta and fellow journalists as the "enemy of the people." Acosta's book offers up a damning portrait of the bureaucratic dysfunction, daily deceptions, and hostility to democratic institutions and norms that he believes characterized the Trump White House. Costa also details the frequent threats on his life with words as well as physical violence. And the book covers some of the other key personalities of the Trump administration, including Sarah Huckabee Sanders, Stephen Miller, Steve Bannon, Sean Spencer, Hope Hicks, and Jared Kushner.

Aldrich, John. 2012. *Why Parties? A Second Look.* Chicago: University of Chicago Press.

Aldrich goes beyond arguments about whether American political parties are in resurgence or decline and reexamines the foundations of the American party system and its role in citizens seeking office, mobilizing voters, and achieving majorities to accomplish policy goals. The book offers a full consideration of the party system, especially the two-party system. He explains why he believes the party system is necessary for effective democracy.

Amar, Akhil Reed. 1998. *The Bill of Rights: Creation and Reconstruction.* New Haven, CT: Yale University Press.

This award-winning history by Amar, a Yale Law School scholar and a leading constitutional law authority, provides insight into the impact, flexibility, and timeliness of the Bill of Rights, which guarantees personal rights, including the right to vote and to petition government for redress through political action and campaigns. He shows how the Bill of Rights shields society against authoritarianism. Amar emphasizes the counter-majoritarianism aspects of the Bill of Rights and its impact over time, especially on state and local governments, as the courts have incorporated the Bill of Rights by the 14th Amendment.

Anderson, Carol. 2019. *One Person, No Vote: How Voter Suppression Is Destroying Our Democracy.* New York: Bloomsbury/Macmillan.

In this stinging polemic, Anderson presents a condensed history of voting rights and disenfranchisement. She challenges the reader to think about who counts the vote and whose votes count. She illustrates specific historical injustices that she assesses as putting American democracy in crisis. Anderson's tone is urgent and indignant, and the book exemplifies investigative journalism as well as popular history. It traces the ugly history of disenfranchisement, gerrymandering, and voter suppression efforts aimed at disabling democracy, and Anderson deftly ties the GOP's current voter suppression efforts to the legacy of Jim Crow's racial apartheid system. She contends that racial discrimination underlies many state government–sanctioned laws and practices, such as photo ID requirements and political gerrymandering, by demonstrating how these suppression efforts disproportionately target ethnic and racial minorities.

Anton, Michael. 2019. *After the Flight 93 Election: The Vote That Saved America and What We Still Have to Lose.* New York: Encounter Books.

Anton's book is a thoughtful, insightful, and succinct summation of the factions of the political Right. It explores trends in conservative thought regarding political strategies, voting rights, and America's democratic institutions.

Appiah, Kwame. 2014. *Lines of Dissent: W. E. B. Du Bois and the Empire of Identity.* Cambridge, MA: Harvard University Press.

Appiah traces the twin lineages of Du Bois's American experience and his German apprenticeship in Berlin. He shows how those two shaped Du Bois's ideas of race and social identity. He argues that Du Bois's challenge was to take the best of German intellectual life without its parochialism. His book illustrates the impact Du Bois had on American politics and on the participation of Blacks in the electoral process, as well as his work to establish and strengthen Black social identity in America.

Araiza, Lauren. 2014. *To March for Others: The Black Freedom Struggle and the United Farm Workers.* Philadelphia: University of Pennsylvania Press.

Araiza's book adds to the body of scholarship on African American and Latinx organizational relationships within the context of American politics. She explores how the United Farm Workers (UFW) created alliances of varying length and strength with five leading Black civil rights organizations. In doing so, the author illuminates the role of activism by Black and Hispanic groups to open up American electoral politics to minority groups.

Baker, Jean. 2004. *Women and the United States Constitution, 1776–1920.* Washington, DC: American Historical Association.

Women played a peripheral role in America's constitutional history until 1920. Baker looks at their role as it developed throughout the 19th century, culminating with the passage of the 19th Amendment in 1920, which granted women's suffrage. She describes the epic struggle of suffrage advocates to secure the franchise for women, as well as the subsequent political impact of women voters.

Banks, Dennis, and Richard Erdoes. 2005. *Ojibwa Warrior: Dennis Banks and the Rise of the American Indian Movement.* Norman: University of Oklahoma Press.

Dennis Banks tells his own story to writer and photographer Richard Erdoes. He details the founding of the American Indian Movement (AIM) and traces its rise. The book offers an insider's understanding of AIM and its many political protest events and drive to secure Native American political rights, including voting rights, and the political impact of "off-reservation" Native Americans. Banks contends that the political and social activism of AIM was essential in expanding Native American political participation in electoral politics.

Barnes, Kenneth. 2016. *Anti-Catholicism in Arkansas: How Politicians, the Press, the Klan, and Religious Leaders Imagined an Enemy.* Fayetteville: University of Arkansas Press.

Barnes's book illustrates how the dominant Protestant majority portrayed Catholics as a feared and disliked "other," a phenomenon that was particularly strong in Arkansas starting in the 1880s. His book examines in detail the period of 1910–1960 and shows how anti-Catholic forces in much of the South, such as the Klan and fundamentalist Protestant groups used violence and other means to suppress the Catholic vote in Arkansas.

Barry, Jeffrey, and Clyde Wilcox. 2018. *The Interest Group Society*. 6th ed. New York: Routledge.

This book is a classic on interest-group politics that analyzes interest groups within the framework of democratic theory. It guides readers to a better understanding of interest groups, their variety of types, and their workings within the context of the nation's political system. It is comprehensive in its coverage, covering labor unions, farm organizations, trade associations, citizen groups, public interest organizations, corporations, and public interest firms. This sixth edition updates the role of money in interest-group political activity following the *Citizens United* Supreme Court decision. Barry and Wilcox cover newer interest groups and movements such as the Tea Party and Occupy Wall Street. The volume examines new developments in interest-group activity in health-care and environmental policy and discusses the role social media increasingly play in interest-group politics, both electoral and lobbying.

Barzilas, Gad. 2002. *Communities and Law: Politics and Culture of Legal Identities*. Ann Arbor: University of Michigan Press.

Barzilas tackles such important questions as how minorities use or avoid state laws, legal ideology, and communal laws to pursue their political aims, and the relations between violent and nonviolent means, litigation, and legal mobilization. The book probes the relations between individuals, communities, and the state and why democracies should encourage the collective rights of nonruling communities (his category for minority groups).

He examines six dimensions of community: nationality, social stratification, gender, religion, ethnicity, and legal consciousness. The book effectively narrates debates about the embedded self; about communitarianism as a theoretical approach to study state–society relations; about communal legal cultures; about the intersection between nonruling communities, state ideology, and legal ideology; and about the comprehension of nonruling communities through their own voices and texts.

Bass, Harold, Jr. 2000. *Historical Dictionary of United States Political Parties*. New York: Scarecrow Press.

Bass's book provides concise entries on U.S. parties both past and present, providing coverage of both major and minor political parties and the role they have played in the nation's political history. It also includes brief biographical sketches of major party leadership figures, all presidents and vice presidents, and any minor party candidates who won Electoral College votes. The book also includes coverage of congressional party leadership and national party chairs. It includes a bibliography covering the political party system, the parties, and their leadership.

Bay, Mia. 2004. *To Tell the Truth Freely: The Life of Ida B. Wells*. New York: Hill & Wang.

Mia Bay presents a detailed profile of the civil rights pioneer from her early life in Mississippi and Tennessee to her famous campaign for justice, and her fight, as a journalist, against lynching and racial injustice. Wells's life exemplifies the role of pioneering civil rights activists whose efforts culminated in greater political participation for historically disenfranchised groups, but only after decades of concerted and focused political protest action.

Bedell, Kenneth B. 2017. *Realizing the Civil Rights Dream: Diagnosing and Treating American Racism*. Santa Barbara, CA: ABC-CLIO.

Bedell proposes a civil rights dream that grows out of American history yet speaks to 21st-century reality. He makes the case that by adopting a larger perspective about the role of racism in preserving social, cultural, economic, and political institutions and practices, Americans can better understand why it has been so difficult to fulfill the promises of the 1960s civil rights movement. He uses sociological theories to explain why racism is still so prevalent in the United States. He concludes with identifying steps necessary to overcome racism in American society.

Belknap, Michael. 2005. *The Supreme Court under Earl Warren, 1954–1969.* Columbia: University of South Carolina Press.
Belknap recounts the eventful history of the Warren Court and its controversial judicial decisions, many of which are still hotly debated. He draws on internal memoranda as well as published opinions of the justices to reveal the philosophical debates and the personality conflicts behind the Court's major decisions during Warren's years as chief justice. He also places them in their political and social context, detailing how some Supreme Court decisions in the 1960s opened the pathway to greater political participation by Blacks and other ethnic and racial minorities.

Berman, Art. 2015. *Give Us the Ballot: The Modern Struggle for Voting Rights in America.* New York: Farrar, Straus and Giroux.
Berman's book is compelling history but also a cry for help in the recurring struggle to protect what is supposed to be an inalienable right. Berman is a political correspondent for *Nation* and a fellow at the Nation Institute. His book, which reflects the journalist's liberal political orientation, is an excellent examination of the ongoing struggle for voting rights and how continuous and necessary that struggle remains.

Berson, Robin K. 2004. *Jane Addams: A Biography.* Westport, CT: Greenwood Press.

Berson chronicles Jane Addam's privileged childhood, her thirst for education, and her search for purpose and self-fulfillment. The book describes her help in cofounding the NAACP (National Association for the Advancement of Colored People) and her championing of women's suffrage. Berson's biography highlights the greatness of this lesser-known civil rights leader to a new generation and emphasizes how essential voting rights are to achieving and protecting other civil rights.

Bos, Angela L., and Monica Schneider, eds. 2017. *The Political Psychology of Women in U.S. Politics*. New York: Routledge.
The editors provide a comprehensive resource for students and political practitioners interested in women and politics. The book draws on the best available research in psychology and political science. It summarizes interdisciplinary research on how and why women and men differ as citizens, as voters, as political candidates, and as officeholders. It documents the growing power and influence of women in American electoral politics.

Bowen, Michael. 2011. *The Roots of Modern Conservatism*. Chapel Hill: University of North Carolina Press.
Bowen traces the power struggle emerging between 1944 and 1953 between Thomas Dewey and Robert Taft and how their struggle led to a divide of ideology that determined the Republican Party's political identity and what "true" Republicanism came to mean. It provides a foundational understanding of the impact of conservative ideology on power struggles over political participation.

Brinkley, Douglas. 2005. *Rosa Parks: A Life*. New York: Penguin.
Historian Brinkley brings to life midcentury America in this compelling examination of the life of an iconic heroine of the civil rights movement. It shows how her quiet dignity, hope, courage, and humor made her a living legend. His biography documents Parks' critically important

role in securing political power for Black Americans and illustrates the increasing clout that women of color have in American electoral politics.

Broadwater, Jeff. 2006. *George Mason: Forgotten Founder*. Chapel Hill: University of North Carolina Press.

Broadwater provides a comprehensive account of the birth of the governments of Virginia and the United States and the contributions made to both by George Mason. It shows his impact on the founding period of American history. His in-depth portrait of Mason and his times is a rich resource for the period and helps readers understand how expansion of voting rights was built into the foundational documents of both the United States and of individual states such as Virginia.

Brown, Donathan L., and Michael L. Clemons. 2015. *Voting Rights under Fire: The Continuing Struggle for People of Color*. Santa Barbara, CA: Praeger.

Brown and Clemons show how the struggle for voting rights continues to this day for people of color. This interdisciplinary book connects past and present issues in the political debates, historical development, and court decisions on race and voting rights in America. It documents and illuminates how and why that struggle is ever necessary and why voting rights are foundational to all other civil rights.

Brown, Mitchell, Kathleen Hale, and Bridget King, eds. 2019. *The Future of Election Administration: Cases and Conversations*. London and New York: Palgrave Macmillan.

This edited volume covers American election administration and how its landscape is changing as a result of major court cases, national and state election laws, changes in professionalism, and the evolution of voting equipment and security measures. The book presents a series of case studies that collectively highlight practical responses to changes in election administration on national, state, and local levels. It focuses on voting technology and presents the experiences of practitioners in key areas of election administration, with an emphasis on the practical aspects of electoral administration.

Brown, Nadia, and Sarah Gershon, eds. 2016. *Distinct Identities: Minority Women in U.S. Politics*. New York: Routledge.

The authors present studies of minority women that highlight both their similarities and differences to other groups of women or minorities. It presents current demographic and political trends that are in the forefront of shaping U.S. politics, and studies the growing importance of identity politics. The book provides a particularly detailed look at how minority women utilize their sheer numbers, their collective voting behavior (bloc voting), their policy preferences, and their roles as elected officials to impact American electoral politics. The book challenges readers to think more holistically about identity politics.

Brown, Nikki L. M., and Barry M. Stentiford, eds. 2014. *Jim Crow: A Historical Encyclopedia of the American Mosaic*. Santa Barbara, CA: Greenwood Press.

This reference encyclopedia examines a broad range of topics related to the establishment, maintenance, and eventual dismantling of the discriminatory system known as Jim Crow, which trapped generations of African Americans in deep political, economic, and social inequality across the South. The book documents the methods used to create the system and how courts and laws and the civil rights movement finally dismantled it. The book is a volume within the American Mosaic series and follows the format of the series.

Bruns, Roger. 2018. *Documents of the Chicano Movement*. Santa Barbara, CA: ABC-CLIO.

This book provides original source documents regarding the Chicano movement from the 1960s through the 1970s. It covers key events, individuals, and political developments of *La Causa* and how Chicanos united to free themselves from exploitation. It documents their struggle to gain access to political participation and to make themselves an effective voting bloc. It illustrates an early example of how and why identity politics became increasingly impactful in American electoral politics.

Bullock, Charles, Ronald Gaddle, and Justin Wert, eds. 2016. *The Rise and Fall of the Voting Rights Act.* Norman: University of Oklahoma Press.

The authors trace the development of the Voting Rights Act of 1965 from its inception by exploring the political and legal aspects of the Jim Crow electoral regime. They detail the subsequent struggle to enact laws to end Jim Crow systems across the South, as well as the impact of legal challenges to the Act. The authors contend that decisions by the Supreme Court's conservative majority have gutted the Voting Rights Act by overturning key provisions of the law.

Bullough, Vern L., ed. 2002. *Before Stonewall: Activists for Gay and Lesbian Rights in Historical Context*. New York: Harrington Park Press.

This book illuminates the lives of 50 individuals involved in the early struggles for gay and lesbian rights. It explores the early history of the movement through concise biographies of the pre-1969 barrier breakers. It illustrates how social movements are often necessary precursors to subsequent political power movements, and how such movements pave the way for gains in electoral politics by minority groups.

Burden, Barry, and David Kimball. 2004. *Why Americans Split Their Tickets: Campaigns, Competition, and Divided Government*. Ann Arbor: University of Michigan Press.

This book addresses the fundamental puzzles of American politics by explaining the causes of the increasingly evident divided government. The authors debunk the myth that voters prefer division of power over one-party control. The book describes the decline in ticket splitting, evident in recent election cycles, and shows how ticket splitting shapes policy differences between the two major parties. The authors detail why the ideological positions of candidates for elective office still matter in American elections. They provide careful, deftly used, and thorough statistical analysis of the split-ticket voting that drives the outcomes of many electoral contests at various levels of government.

Caro, Robert. 2012. *The Years of Lyndon Johnson: The Passage of Power*. New York: Knopf.

This book is the fourth in the award-winning series on the life of Lyndon Johnson. It is a definitive history of his presidency. It details his impact on American society and particularly on civil rights policy and law during the tumultuous years of the 1960s. It also documents his important role in securing the Civil Rights Acts of 1964, 1965, and 1968, each of which had important and long-lasting impacts on American elections and voting patterns.

Carroll, Susan, and Richard Fox, eds. 2018. *Gender and Elections: Shaping the Future of American Politics*. 4th ed. New York: Cambridge University Press.

This fourth edition of the book offers a systematic, lively, and multifaceted examination of the role of gender in the electoral process, covering elections through the 2016 election cycle. This book is a timely yet enduring volume, balancing its coverage of the most important developments for women as both voters and candidates in the 2016 elections with in-depth analysis of the myriad ways in which gender has shaped the contours and the outcomes of U.S. electoral politics over the decades.

Individual chapters cover the importance of gender to the understanding and interpretation of such topics as presidential elections, presidential and vice presidential candidates, voter participation and turnout, voting choices, congressional elections, political involvement of Latinas, the participation of African American women, the support of political parties and women's organizations, candidate communication with voters, and state elections. It is a comprehensive, reliable, and trustworthy resource on the role of gender in electoral politics.

Ceasar, James W., and Andrew Busch. 2001. *The Perfect Tie: The True Story of the 2000 Presidential Election*. Lanham, MD: Rowman and Littlefield.

The authors continue their study of national elections and the broader implications of presidential elections on American politics and society. It is an extensively researched study of electoral politics and a penetrating discussion of divided government, independent candidates, party platforms, realignment theory, campaign strategies, and the effects of the Electoral College.

Chemerinsky, Erwin. 2014. *The Case against the Supreme Court*. New York: Penguin.

An eminent constitutional scholar presents a hard-hitting analysis of the Supreme Court over its more than 200-year history. He argues that the Supreme Court has often failed at its most important tasks at its most important moments—such as in rulings handed down over the last several years that, according to the author, have wreaked enormous damage on American voting rights.

Chemerinsky, Erwin. 2017. *Constitutional Law: Principles and Policies*. 6th ed. New York: Wolters Kluwer.

A treatise on constitutional law, the book identifies how the Constitution impacts policy issues and political considerations in such areas as congressional power, presidential power, abortion, voting rights, and freedom of speech and religion.

Congressional Quarterly Press. 2005. *Presidential Elections, 1789–2008*. Washington, DC: Congressional Quarterly Press.

This classic provides a comprehensive resource that explains in detail and with clarity the evolution of presidential elections, from 1789, when the first such election was held, through Barack Obama's victory in 2008. In addition to providing full coverage of the McCain/Obama contest, the book explains the complexities of the Electoral College system and the party primary and caucus systems. It provides summary data on the popular vote and the Electoral College vote for all presidents from 1789 to 2008, as well as a biographical directory of all U.S. presidential and vice presidential candidates.

Congressional Quarterly Press. 2009. *National Party Conventions, 1831–2008*. Washington, DC: Congressional Quarterly Press.

The book provides focused, detailed, and wide-ranging information on national party conventions and their key role in U.S. electoral processes and politics since the early 19th century. It provides a comprehensive history of the evolving structure of the convention that helps the reader to better understand how presidential leaders are chosen in the United States. For each convention, it provides excerpts of the party platforms, key ballots in the nominating process, and significant votes on rules and delegation disputes. Its broad scope provides a reliable resource for experienced scholars and election professionals alike.

Cook, Franklin Rhodes. 2003. *Presidential Nominating Process: A Place for Us?* Washington, DC: Congressional Quarterly Press.

Cook explains the sprawling presidential-nominating process used every four years in the election of the president. The book explains how the field of contenders is narrowed from a plethora of aspirants to the two finalists who carry the banner of the two major parties. It emphasizes that whereas more than 100 million Americans regularly participate in the general election for presidents, only a small percentage of voters have a meaningful voice in the nominating process. The book discusses how we got to this point and how the current system works, and it compares the U.S. system to that used in other countries. It discusses how the process might be changed in ways to give a more meaningful voice to a much larger number of voters.

Crotty, William, ed. 2014. *Polarization Politics: The Impact of Divisiveness in the U.S. Political System.* Boulder, CO: Lynne Rienner Publishing.

Crotty's book provides an excellent collection of cutting-edge research on the nature and causes of political division within American government and American politics. It is a comprehensive examination of polarization and resulting political dysfunction. The book emphasizes the relationship between polarization and U.S. income inequality. It analyzes racial, ethnic, religious, age, and ideological divisions. The book systematically considers the way that various constitutional provisions contribute to polarization. Crotty details how special-interest influence created primary and campaign finance systems that have been captured by intensely partisan political groups using their immense wealth resources, and how political parties have evolved from umbrella organizations to more nationalized, ideological parties. The book shows how the ties between major religious groups and political parties have changed over time and explains how African American and Latinx groups became core constituencies of the Democratic Party.

Cushman, Clare. 2001. *Supreme Court Decisions and Women's Rights*. Washington, DC: Congressional Quarterly Press.

Cushman's book examines a range of hot-button women's issues before the Supreme Court, from the 19th century to *Roe v. Wade*. Featuring more than 100 cases, it provides a complete study of all the important issues and movements involving the Supreme Court—and the role the Court plays in shaping women's rights—through the close of the 20th century.

Dailey, Jane, Glenda Gilmore, and Bryant Simon, eds. 2000. *Jumpin' Jim Crow: Southern Politics from the Civil War to Civil Rights*. Princeton, NJ: Princeton University Press.

This book presents a clear picture of the white supremacist roots of Jim Crow laws across the American South and how the civil rights movement was able to dismantle those laws over the course of the 1950s and 1960s.

Davis, Hugh. 2011. *We Will Be Satisfied with Nothing Less: The African American Struggle for Equal Rights in the North During Reconstruction*. Ithaca, NY: Cornell University Press.

Historian Hugh Davis examines two issues that African Americans in the North considered the most essential: Black male suffrage, and equal access to public schools. His book focuses on specific campaigns in cities such as Cincinnati, Detroit, and San Francisco and details the valuable work of such organizations as the National Equal Rights League and the National Executive Committee of Colored Persons.

Dershowitz, Alan. 2020. *Cancel Culture: The Latest Attack on Free Speech and Due Process*. Pittsburgh, PA: Hot Books.

Dershowitz, a prominent and controversial legal scholar, contends in this book that so-called cancel culture poses a dire threat to American guarantees of free speech and due process. Dershowitz argues that greater restraint and care need to be present in decisions about whom and what is to be cancelled, boycotted, denied a social media platform, or otherwise barred from public life. He offers recommendations as to for whom, why, and to what degree those steps may be appropriate. He acknowledges that the "cancel culture" movement does seek to use it to create meaningful, positive change in American society, but he also describes it as the greatest challenge and threat to free speech and due process since McCarthyism.

Dierenfield, Bruce J. 2008. *The Civil Rights Movement*. Oxfordshire, UK: Routledge/Taylor Francis.

Dierenfield recounts the extraordinary and all-too-often bloody story of how thousands of ordinary African Americans overcame long odds to end segregation, exercise the right to vote, and improve their economic standing. He shows how their struggle required great personal courage, as many activists sacrificed their homes, jobs, and even their lives for the cause of equal rights.

Dorrien, Gary. 2015. *The New Abolition: W. E. B. Du Bois and the Black Social Gospel*. New Haven, CT: Yale University Press.

Dorrien describes the early history of the Black social gospel from its 19th-century roots to its close association in the 20th century with civil rights icon W. E. B. Du Bois. His book offers a new perspective on modern Christianity and the civil rights era. It delineates the traditions of social justice theology and activism that thrived during this era—and explores how they laid the groundwork for the mid-20th-century civil rights movement and passage of the Civil Rights Acts of 1964, 1965, and 1968. It illustrates how the Black church has for more than a century led the way for Black activism and Black voting and cultivated a tradition of "souls to the polls."

Dray, Philip. 2008. *Capitol Men: The Epic Story of Reconstruction through the Lives of the First Black Congressmen*. New York: Houghton Mifflin.

In his deep look at the first African American congressmen during the Reconstruction era, Dray offers a look at the different issues in post–Civil War America. He shows how the congressmen attempted to fulfill the notion of post–Civil War democracy and equality, and how they came to be denied representation for nearly a century thereafter due to the rise and spread of Jim Crow laws.

Epps, Garrett. 2006. *Democracy Reborn: The Fourteenth Amendment and the Fight for Civil Rights in Post–Civil War America.* New York: Holt.

This narrative of the adoption of the 14th Amendment shows how it revolutionized the Constitution and shaped the United States as it emerged from the ashes of the Civil War. Over time, Epps argues, it provided African Americans with full citizenship by prohibiting the states from denying any citizen due process and equal protection under the law. The book recounts the struggle from the halls of Congress to the bloody streets of Memphis and New Orleans. It shows how the 14th Amendment was foundational for Black voting rights.

Epstein, David. 2012. *Left, Right, Out: A History of Third Parties in America.* London: Arts and Imperium Press.

Epstein explores the lesser-told story of the ways in which so-called third parties in U.S. politics influenced American history from the country's founding to the present. By examining the nation and its politics through the lens of third-party politics, whether short-lived or long-lasting, the book provides an interesting vantage point from which to study the great social, economic, and political forces that informed the evolution of the nation.

Farrelly, Maura Jane. 2017. *Anti-Catholicism in America: 1620–1860.* Cambridge, UK: Cambridge University Press.

Farrelly's book reveals the ironic role anti-Catholicism played during the 18th and 19th centuries in defining and sustaining some of the core elements of American identity. Those values, she shows, animate our religious and political discussions today. Her book provides a framework for understanding what is at stake in the debate over the place of Muslims and other non-Christian groups in American politics and society.

Feldman, Paul, ed. 2013. *Routledge Revivals: Encyclopedia of American Civil Liberties*. Oxfordshire, UK: Routledge Press.

This comprehensive, three-volume set covers a broad range of topics on civil liberties in America. In includes such topics as free speech, press, religion, assembly and petition, the Bill of Rights, slavery, censorship, crime, and war. It takes a multidisciplinary approach and provides extensive coverage of civil liberties issues related to voting, elections, and political campaigns.

Finley, Keith. 2008. *Delaying the Dream: Southern Senators and the Fight against Civil Rights, 1936–1965*. Baton Rouge: Louisiana State University Press.

Finley explores the gradation in opposition to equal rights by examining how senators addressed the civil rights question and developed a concerted plan to thwart legislation by using a strategy of delay. His book goes beyond traditional images of the quest for racial equality. It adds a fresh perspective to the canon of the civil rights era in modern American history.

Fireside, Harvey. 2003. *Separate and Unequal: Homer Plessy and the Supreme Court Decision that Legalized Racism*. Gretna, LA: Pelican Press.

Fireside presents a powerful account of the *Plessy v. Ferguson* decision. His book combines judicial records with historical photographs to provide a richly evocative portrait of Jim Crow–era Louisiana. His book presents a history less well known but every bit as explosively influential as that of Rosa Parks.

Flores, Lori. 2016. *A Grounds for Dreaming: Mexican Americans, Mexican Immigrants, and the California Farm Workers Union*. New Haven, CT: Yale University Press.

Flores's book provides a sweeping and critical history of how Mexican Americans organized for their rights in the decades leading up to the political activism of Cesar Chavez and the United Farm Workers in the 1960s and 1970s. It looks at the U.S.-born, the Bracero workers, and undocumented workers and how they confronted and interacted with one another. It is an incisive study of labor, migration, gender, citizenship, and class.

Gans, Marshall. 2009. *Why David Sometimes Wins: Leadership, Organization, and Strategy in California's Farmworkers Movement*. New York: Oxford University Press.

This book tells the story of Cesar Chavez and the UFW and how and why they succeeded. It offers insights from a longtime movement organizer and scholar about turning short-term advantage into long-term gain. It is an authoritative and important contribution to learning about the movement's struggles and successes.

Gierzynski, Anthony. 2011. *Saving American Elections: A Diagnosis and Prescription for a Healthier Democracy*. Amherst, NY: Cambria Press.

The author employs a medical metaphor of diagnosis to present a big-picture understanding of what ails American elections and what may be done to save them and why. Gierzynski covers such critical issues as redistricting, campaign finance, political parties, election administration, the impact of the media, the electoral structure, and the role of the public and public opinion in electoral problems. The book is a balanced yet provocative look at every flaw that people complain about regarding American government and the American electoral system.

Ginsburg, Ruth Bader. 2018. *My Own Words*. New York: Simon & Schuster.

This is a witty, engaging, serious, and playful collection of Ginsburg's writings and speeches covering a wide range of topics. She demonstrates the value of looking beyond U.S. shores when interpreting the Constitution. It is a fascinating glimpse into the life of one of America's most influential women, including her steadfast support for women's rights.

Goff, Michael. 2005. *The Money Primary: The New Politics of the Early Presidential Nomination Process*. Lanham, MD: Rowman and Littlefield.

Goff's book makes an important historical contribution to our understanding of the evolving role of money in presidential-nominating politics. He labels the race for financial support among candidates that takes place before the primaries as the money primary, and he details how various factors in addition to money must be acquired early on in any campaign for the presidential nomination. Goff stresses the importance of securing what he terms "candidate viability"—including media coverage and endorsements garnered during this early phase—and how candidate performance in these areas is increasingly seen as the first decisive test of a candidate's presidential strength. The book was especially timely for the 2008 race. He notes how the "early money primary" is effectively expanding the race for the presidential nomination to three years before the actual Election Day. Goff demonstrates how the ability to raise campaign funds has direct bearing on the ability to get elected. He focuses on the early campaigns in 1988 through the 2000 presidential races.

Gould, Lewis. 2003. *Grand Old Party: A History of the Republicans*. New York: Random House.

In this comprehensive, if dated, history of the Republican Party, Gould traces the evolution of the GOP from its emergence as an antislavery coalition in the 1850s to its priorities in the early years of George W. Bush's presidency. It concludes with an assessment of the party's historical legacy.

Gould, Lewis. 2010. *1968: The Election That Changed America.* Chicago: Ivan R. Dee.

Gould's book is a detailed narrative of the 1968 election and how Republican nominee Richard M. Nixon came to win the presidency over Democratic nominee Hubert H. Humphrey. It explores how events and issues at the forefront of that election shaped national affairs during the two decades that followed.

Grinspan, Jon. 2021. *The Age of Acrimony: How Americans Fought to Fix Their Democracy, 1865–1915.* New York: Bloomsbury Publishing.

Grinspan charts the rise and fall of 19th-century America's unruly politics viewed through the prism of the lives of a remarkable father-daughter dynasty: radical congressman William "Pig Iron" Kelly and his fiery Progressive daughter, Florence Kelly. The book details how their friendships, feuds, campaigns, and crusades provide a narrative of U.S. democracy in crisis. The book reveals how America's divisive political system endures by reinventing itself.

Grofman, Bernard, Andre Blais, and Shaun Bowler, eds. 2009. *Duverger's Law of Plurality Voting.* New York: Springer Verlag.

The editors of this insightful volume examine four major examples of plurality voting—in Canada, India, the United Kingdom, and the United States—using French political scientist Maurice Duverger's seminal argument on the topic. It discusses such issues as the favorable impact of plurality voting for two-party systems as well as the ways that proportional representation favors a multiparty system. They present national-level data about Duverger's hypothesis in the four longest-lived and most successful democracies. Other chapters examine the mechanical and psychological effects predicted by "Duverger's law." The editors collect incisive analyses of electoral and political party dynamics.

Gutzman, Kevin. 2007. *The Politically Incorrect Guide to the Constitution*. Washington, DC: Regnery Publishing.

Gutzman's book argues that there is little relationship between the constitution as ratified by the original states and the constitutional law imposed by judges since then. He argues that the Supreme Court interpreted the 14th Amendment to twist the use of the Bill of Rights.

Hacker, Andrew. 2003. *Two Nations: Black and White, Separate, Hostile, Unequal*. New York: Scribner.

Hacker's book explains the origins and meaning of racism and clarifies conflicting theories of equality and inferiority. His book paints a stark picture of racial inequality in America and explores controversial policies that cause the gap between the races. He illuminates why Blacks have to continuously struggle to achieve political equality.

Hagedorn, Sara L., and Michael C. LeMay. 2019. *The American Congress: A Reference Handbook*. Santa Barbara, CA: ABC-CLIO.

The book thoroughly examines the operations and politics of the U.S. Congress. It guides readers to their own assessment of congressional politics and presents the major functions of Congress and how they evolved. It provides readers with the bases for future reading and study of the subject. It illustrates the role of Congress in achieving and securing basic civil rights, including voting rights.

Hale, Kathleen, and Mitchell Brown. 2020. *How We Vote: Innovation in American Elections*. Washington, DC: Georgetown University Press.

Hale and Brown examine the complexity of voter administration from the perspective of the values of access and integrity of the electoral system. They demonstrate how elections are run, how administration determines how ballots are cast and counted, and how various jurisdictions have tried to innovate the process while still protecting the security of the voting process. They show how election officials work in a difficult intergovernmental environment with ongoing change and intense partisanship. They examine variations in voting practices and the funding of elections from state to state. They show how multiple government agencies, judiciaries at both the state and national levels, voting equipment vendors, nonprofit groups, and citizen activists all influence the voting process. The authors use original data from state and local election officials across the United States. The book analyzes innovations in such areas as registration, voting options, voter convenience, support for voting in languages other than English, the integrity of the voting process, and voting-system technology.

Hale, Kathleen, Robert Montjoy, and Mitchell Brown. 2015. *Administering Elections: How American Elections Work*. London and New York: Palgrave Macmillan.

This book examines contemporary American electoral administration by employing a systems perspective. It provides insight into the interconnectedness of all elements of election administration. The authors shed light on the potential consequences of reforms that fail to recognize and incorporate that interconnectedness. The authors are three widely recognized experts of election administration and election strategies, program evaluation, intergovernmental relations, and the role of professional associations.

Handley, Lisa, and Bernard Grofman, eds. 2008. *Redistricting in Comparative Perspective*. New York: Oxford University Press.

Handley and Grofman collect and present basic data on redistricting practices in democracies around the world. The book also provides a series of case studies that detail particular countries with regard to the institutions and practices that have evolved in recent years as well as the political debates that have been spurred by that evolution. The contributing authors examine in comparative perspective the consequences of alternative redistricting mechanisms, showing the trade-offs among competing redistricting criteria. The book compiles contributions from leading specialists on redistricting in their respective countries, and the chapters reflect a mix of country-specific data with more broadly comparative perspectives that are more methodological in nature.

Harris, Kamala. 2019. *The Truths We Hold: An American Journey*. New York: Penguin.

This book is a memoir by the vice president, written when she was the junior U.S. senator from California. It discusses the core truths that, she argues, unites us as Americans and the long struggle to discern them and how best to act upon them.

Hartman, Thom. 2004. *Unequal Protection: The Rise of Corporate Dominance and the Theft of Human Rights*. Emmaus, PA: Rodale Books.

Hartman tells a startling story, uncovering original eyewitness accounts of the Boston Tea Party and showing that it was provoked by specific actions of the East India Tea Company and the commercial interests of the British elite. He then describes the history of the 14th Amendment and shows how corporate lawyers used it to extend business rights far more than those of the freed slaves. He proposes specific legal remedies to the excessive power of corporate America.

Head, Tom. 2009. *Civil Liberties: A Beginner's Guide.* London: Oneworld Publications.

This thought-provoking guide to civil liberties weaves history, philosophy, and practical advice for activists. It demonstrates the important roles activists play in the struggle to secure and protect civil liberties.

Holzer, Harold, and Sara Vaughn Gabbard, eds. 2007. *Lincoln and Freedmen: Slavery, Emancipation, and the Thirteenth Amendment.* Carbondale: Southern Illinois University Press.

This comprehensive book presents Lincoln's responses to slavery as a politician, president, writer, orator, and commander-in-chief. A collection of essays, the book explores slavery as a constitutional issue, from the Founders' original intent to Lincoln's decision to issue the Emancipation Proclamation.

Issacharoff, Samuel, Pamela Karlan, Richard Pides, and Nathaniel Persily. 2016. *The Law of Democracy: Legal Structures of the Political Process.* 5th ed. New York: Foundation Press.

This book offers a systematic account of the legal construction of American democracy. It covers the Voting Rights Act, campaign finance, and political corruption issues. It examines the struggle over gerrymandering, the relationship of the states to political parties, and the tensions between majority rule and minority rights.

Ivery, Curtis L., and Joshua Bassett, eds. 2011. *America's Urban Crisis and the Advent of Color-Blind Politics.* Lanham, MD: Rowman and Littlefield.

Two experts in the field of civil rights and urban studies present a book that provides an overview of the scholarship on the urban underclass. The book looks at modern racial politics in America's cities and encourages the readers to be aware of inequities and to engage in efforts to change them.

Johnson, Troy. 2007. *Red Power: The Native American Civil Rights Movement*. New York: Chelsea House.

This book is one in a series covering landmark events in Native American history. It examines the Red Power movement within the broader context of the Native American struggle for civil rights and political power.

Johnston, David Cay. 2016. *The Making of Donald Trump*. New York: Melville House.

The Pulitzer Prize–winning investigative journalist has followed the career of Donald Trump for 30 years. The book takes readers on a journey from the origins of the family fortune to Trump's tumultuous gambling and real estate dealings in New York and Atlantic City, offering a searing indictment of Trump's business practices along the way.

Keck, Thomas M. 2004. *The Most Activist Supreme Court in History: The Road to Modern Judicial Conservatism*. Chicago: University of Chicago Press.

Keck astutely analyzes the Rehnquist Court and how its decisions related to broader tendencies in political and social change. It delves into the relationship between constitutional decision-making and the political and social forces that influence the process. It shows how the conservative-activist Court impacts basic civil rights and has paved the way for today's even more consequential conservative judicial activism in such areas as campaign finance, voter access, voter suppression, and political gerrymandering.

Kerstein, Andrew. 2006. *A. Philip Randolph: A Life in the Vanguard*. Lanham: Rowman and Littlefield.

Kerstein's book explores the significance and accomplishments of Randolph as a labor and a civil rights leader from the 1920s, when he founded the country's first major Black labor union (the Brotherhood of Sleeping Car Porters), through the 1960s, when he helped organize the historic 1963 March on Washington. He shows how Randolph's political philosophy and his involvement in the labor and the civil rights movements shaped his quest to improve the lives of American workers and African American families.

Keyssar, Alexander. 2009. *The Right to Vote: The Contested History of Democracy in the United States*. 2nd ed. New York: Basic Books.

Keyssar's book was a widely acclaimed account of the evolution of suffrage from the American Revolution through the close of the 20th century. This revised edition updates the story to 2008 and the election of President Barack Obama. It is a sweeping interpretation of American political and electoral history.

King, Desmond, and Roger Smith. 2011. *Still a House Divided: Race and Politics in Obama's America*. Princeton, NJ: Princeton University Press.

The authors examine the enduring divisions of American racial politics and how these conflicts have been shaped by distinct political alliances. The book combines historical background with a detailed examination of such contemporary issues as housing, employment, criminal justice, multiracial census categories, immigration, voting in majority-minority districts, and school vouchers. They assess the significance of President Barack Obama's election and the prospects for achieving constructive racial policies for America's future.

Laughlin, Kathleen, and Jacqueline Castledine, eds. 2010. *Breaking the Wave: Women, Their Organizations, and Feminism, 1945–1985*. Abington, UK: Routledge.

The authors review the long history of feminism, both as expressed in the political mainstream and in leftist politics, and the impact of feminist thought on American politics and society. The many contributed essays to the volume cover virtually every feminist organization up to the late 1980s.

Lawless, Jennifer. 2012. *Becoming a Candidate*. Cambridge: Cambridge University Press.

Jennifer Lawless explores the myriad factors that drive political ambition at the earliest stages—those shaping the decision to become a candidate and run for office. She uses data from a comprehensive survey of thousands of eligible candidates. Lawless systematically investigates what compels certain citizens to pursue elective office and others to recoil from the very notion of running for office. She assesses such personal factors as race, gender, and family dynamics to show how those factors affect an eligible candidate's likelihood to consider running for office. Lawless focuses on the professional lives and attitudes toward the political system among those eligible candidates.

Lee, Erika. 2020. *The Making of Asian America*. New York: Simon & Schuster.

Lee's powerful book examines the rich, complicated histories of Asians in the United States and how generations of Asian immigrants and their American-born descendants have made and remade Asian American life. Coverage ranges from the incarceration of Japanese Americans during World War II to the challenges facing Asian refugees trying to rebuild their lives in the United States in the 21st century. It also details how and why Asian Americans are sometimes labeled America's "model minority"—providing eye-opening insights into America itself.

LeMay, Michael C. 2009. *The Perennial Struggle: Race, Ethnicity, and Minority Group Relations in the United States*. 3rd ed. Upper Saddle River, NJ: Prentice Hall.

This is a comprehensive examination of the struggle by ethnic, ideological, racial, and religious minority groups in America to triumph over discrimination and achieve equal civil and voting rights. It distinguishes three overall coping strategies used by a multiplicity of groups from America's founding to post-2000 events. It describes how groups use activism and legal challenges to secure their rights and pursue their political goals.

LeMay, Michael C., ed. 2013. *Transforming America: Perspectives on U.S. Immigration*. Santa Barbara, CA: Praeger Press.

This three-volume set collects essays by 30 scholars to examine how immigrant groups throughout American history have shaped and reshaped American society. Volume 3 focuses on 1945 to date. The essays are multidisciplinary. Several emphasize the role and impact of immigrant groups on politics, political parties, and the electoral process, sometimes forming or re-forming new electoral coalitions.

LeMay, Michael C. 2018. *U.S. Immigration Policy, Ethnicity, and Religion in American History*. Santa Barbara, CA: ABC-CLIO.

This book explores the interrelationships between ethnicity, religion, and immigration policy throughout American history. It shows how all are inextricably linked and influence each other as well as American society and historical political developments, including party coalitions, voter turnout, and issue advocacy that impacted or reflected their unique perspectives.

LeMay, Michael C. 2019. *Immigration Reform: A Reference Handbook*. Santa Barbara, CA: ABC-CLIO.

This book focuses on how immigration policy reform is achieved and the impact it has on American society and on civil rights policy. It examines ethnic and racial groups and explores in-depth the interrelationship between immigration reform politics and civil rights policy concerns, including the fundamental right of citizens to vote and to participate in electoral politics.

Lessig, Lawrence. 2018. *America Compromised.* Chicago: University of Chicago Press.

Lessig argues that the core institutions of America's economic, social, and political life have become corrupted. This sweeping indictment of contemporary American political and cultural institutions presents case studies on Congress, campaign finance, the academy, the media, and the law to show how they are drawn away from their higher purposes and toward money, power, and quick rewards. He brings copious and damning detail gleaned from his years of research to build his persuasive case.

Lessig, Lawrence. 2019. *They Don't Represent Us: Reclaiming Our Democracy.* New York: Dey Street.

In this innovative and provocative book, Harvard Law professor Lawrence Lessig argues persuasively that American democracy is broken due to extreme partisanship in Washington, DC. Lessig argues that because of this destructive partisanship, the American electoral system does not properly ensure representation under the ideal of "one person, one vote." He adroitly discusses what ails the system and how it may potentially be fixed. The book examines how voter suppression, gerrymandering, big-money politics, and the Electoral College, through its winner-take-all system, all serve to undermine democracy. He argues that the American political system is in a state of dysfunction, mired in partisanship, and dominated by special-interest groups.

Levinson, Sanford. 2013. *Constitutional Faith.* Princeton: Princeton University Press.

An eminent constitutional scholar, Sanford Levinson examines the theme of "Constitutional faith" and how since 1788 it has been a central component of America's civil religion. He opens a list of intriguing questions on what it means to be American. Levinson maintains that the Constitution's "sacred role" can result in conflict, fragmentation, and even war. He argues that the Constitution's value lies in the realm of the discourse it sustains and on a uniquely American form of political rhetoric that allows citizens to grapple with every important public issue. Levinson attributes much of the current widespread frustration with the U.S. government to the static nature of the Constitution.

Levinson, Sanford, and Jack M. Balkin. 2019. *Democracy and Dysfunction*. Chicago: University of Chicago Press.

Two leading constitutional law scholars explore the 2016 election and President Donald Trump's first year in office. The authors emphasize the deeply dysfunctional nature of the current political system and their belief that Trump's early presidency was chaotic, turbulent, and disastrous for American democracy. The two scholars disagree on the scope of the crisis and on the remedy required. Levinson believes the Constitution is fundamentally flawed and a new constitutional convention is required. Balkin believes we are suffering from constitutional rot but that less radical solutions are possible. They both agree that it is important to understand how we got here in order to avoid electing other figures such as Trump, whom they describe as a demagogue.

Levinson, Sanford, Paul Brest, and Akhil Reed Amar. 2006. *Processes of Constitutional Decisionmaking*. 5th ed. Riverwood, IL: Wolters Kluwer Law and Business.

This newest edition of a classic casebook of constitutional law traces the historical, political, and social development of constitutional law and considers questions that body of law raises in a broad historical context. The book has chapters on the constitutional treatment of sex equality, race, civil rights, separation of powers, and federalism. It features discussions of legal issues surrounding health care, *Shelby County v. Holder*, sexual orientation, race, and gender. It also traces developments in executive power and national security law through the early 2000s.

Levinson, Sanford, and William Eskridge, eds. 1998. *Constitutional Stupidities, Constitutional Tragedies*. New York: New York University Press.

This volume brings together 27 of the nation's most esteemed constitutional scholars and commentators to address two central questions: What is the stupidest provision of the U.S. Constitution, and what are its most resulting tragedies? All of the 27 contributors apply their own, individual favored theory of constitutional interpretation.

Levinson, Sanford, Mark Graber, and Mark Tushnet, eds. 2015. *The Oxford Handbook of the U.S. Constitution*. New York: Oxford University Press.

This book offers a comprehensive overview and an introduction to the U.S. Constitution from the perspectives of history, political science, law, civil rights, and constitutional themes. It focuses on the Constitution's development, structures, rights, and role in the U.S. political system and in U.S. political culture. The book provides readers with critical comprehension of the extensive literature on the Constitution with accessible and up-to-date analysis.

Levinson, Sanford, and Cynthia Levinson. 2017. *Fault Lines in the Constitution*. Atlanta: Peachtree Publishing.

Cynthia and Sanford Levinson discuss the many political issues of the day that have their roots in flaws in the U.S. Constitution. They discuss the Electoral College, gerrymandering, and gridlock in the U.S. Senate as ramifications of the haggling that took place during the Constitutional Convention. Their provocative book encourages young and old readers alike to explore and discuss this timely and thoughtful exploration of the Constitution's beginnings and how its fault lines reverberate to influence current electoral politics.

Lewis, David. 2009. *W.E.B. Du Bois: A Biography*. New York: Henry Holt.

This biography of W.E.B. Du Bois won a Pulitzer Prize. Lewis traces the long and distinguished career of the African American author, editor, and activist and shows how Du Bois changed forever the way Americans think about themselves.

Mack, Kenneth. 2012. *Representing the Race: The Creation of the Civil Rights Lawyer*. Cambridge, MA: Harvard University Press.

Mack uses law, biography, history, and race relations to examine the first era of civil rights lawyering. In its engaging style, the book brings its subject dynamically alive, both famous and forgotten historical lawyers and the critically important role they played in securing civil rights for Blacks and other racial minorities.

Magleby, David, and Quin Monson, eds. 2004. *The Last Hurrah? Soft Money and Issue Advocacy in the 2002 Congressional Elections*. Washington, DC: Brookings Institution Press.

This book analyzes the role that soft money and issue advocacy played in the 2002 congressional elections. The authors were given insider access to several congressional campaign operations, and they monitored and documented several competitive races. These races were the last national contests before implementation of the Bipartisan Campaign Reform Act and were therefore anticipated to be the "last hurrah" for soft money. The book examines the midterm elections with regard to the activity of political parties, interest groups, and political consultants. The authors note how Republicans defied history by gaining seats in both houses of Congress. The book documents the GOP's emphasis on the "ground war" of voter mobilization. Its case studies, including key Senate races in South Dakota and Missouri, break down the campaign communication of each race, including advertising, get-out-the-vote drives, soft money expenditures, and the increasingly influential role of the national parties on local races. The book discusses trends in the 2002 midterm elections and President Bush's efforts in candidate recruitment, fundraising, and campaign visits.

Manza, Jeff, and Clem Brooks. 1999. *Social Cleavages and Political Change: Voter Alignments and U.S. Party Coalitions*. New York: Oxford University Press.

Now something of a classic of postwar political sociology, this book argues that a key to understanding the political divisions in democratic politics lies with understanding membership in social groups. It examines which social groups supported which political party, how that support changed over time, and incorporates those findings into a systematic, book-length reassessment of the sociological approach to American politics.

Marable, Manning. 2005. *W.E.B. Du Bois: Black Radical Democrat*. Boulder, CO: Paradigm Publishers.

This book is a solid biography of the most gifted Black intellectual of his time. The focus of the book is on the writings of Du Bois—books, essays, and articles. An understanding of Du Bois is central to an understanding of the Black civil rights movement.

Marquez, Benjamin. 2003. *Constructing Identities in Mexican American Political Organization: Choosing Sides, Taking Sides*. Austin: University of Texas Press.

Marquez explores the formation of group identity and whether Mexican Americans seek to assimilate or separate. The book provides a broad cross section of groups to shed light on the process of political identity formation through identity politics.

Marshall, Thurgood, and Mark Tushnet, ed. 2001. *Thurgood Marshall: His Speeches, Writings, Arguments, Opinions, and Reminiscences*. Chicago: Lawrence Hill Books.

The book uses Marshall's speeches, writings, arguments, opinions (both majority and dissenting), and reminiscences to illuminate Justice Marshall and his enduring impact on civil rights law and jurisprudence.

Mayer, Kenneth R. 2001. *With the Stroke of a Pen: Executive Orders and Presidential Power*. Princeton, NJ: Princeton University Press.

Mayer's book is an in-depth study of executive orders from Jefferson to Bush and how presidents have used them to wield their influence on civil rights and foreign policy. Mayer describes a presidential office that is more powerful and active that that typically depicted in political science literature.

McGann, Anthony, Charles Smith, Michael Latner, and Alex Keena. 2016. *Gerrymandering in America: The House of Representatives, the Supreme Court, and the Future of Popular Sovereignty*. New York: Cambridge University Press.

The authors examine the causes and consequences of partisan gerrymandering in the U.S. House of Representatives. The U.S. Supreme Court, in *Vieth v. Jubelirer* (2004), made judicial constitutional challenges on the grounds of partisan gerrymandering next to impossible. The authors use a rigorous analysis of U.S. House district maps to argue that partisan bias increased dramatically in the 2010 redistricting round after the *Vieth* decision, on both the national and state levels. They argue that from a constitutional perspective, unrestrained partisan gerrymandering poses a critical threat to popular sovereignty, a central pillar of American democracy. They demonstrate that state legislatures now, in effect, determine the political composition of the U.S. House of Representatives. They propose a new standard for gerrymandering that is constitutionally grounded and legally manageable.

McGillivray, Alice, Richard Scammon, and Rhodes Cook, eds. 2005. *America at the Polls: A Handbook of American Presidential Elections*. 2 vols. Washington, DC: Congressional Quarterly Press.

This basic text collects statistics from every American presidential election from 1960 to 2000. The copious statistical data are organized by state and by county within a state.

McGillivray, Alice, Richard Scammon, and Rhodes Cook, eds. 2010. *America Votes: A Handbook of Contemporary American Election Statistics*. Washington, DC: Congressional Quarterly Press.

This handbook of contemporary American election statistics of American elections from 1960 through 2010 is a trusted source of complete and reliable information on how Americans vote and is now the longest-running series of election information. It chronicles congressional election cycles and presidential election cycles, and provides detailed election returns for governors, senators, and U.S. representatives. It includes official, state-certified results, summary of primary data, and winner/loser percentages in easy-to-read organized tables.

Meacham, Jon. 2012. *Thomas Jefferson: The Art of Power*. New York: Random House.

This superb biography by the Pulitzer Prize–winning historian brings to vivid life the extraordinary man and his remarkable times. Jefferson's genius, in Meacham's view, is that he was both a political philosopher and political maneuverer. He documents Jefferson's critical role in creating the mass political party in the United States and the mass party's importance for the eventual expansion of the franchise.

Mead, Rebecca. 2004. *How the Vote Was Won: Woman Suffrage in the Western United States, 1868–1914*. New York: New York University Press.

Mead shows that western suffrage came about because of the unsettled state of regional politics and the complex nature of western race relations. She details the broad alliances between suffragists and farm-labor progressive reformers that helped drive public support for passage of the 19th Amendment giving women the right to vote.

Medvic, Stephen. 2021. *Gerrymandering: The Politics of Redistricting in the United States*. New York: Polity Books.

Medvic's book unpacks the complicated process of gerrymandering. It covers its long history and discusses how gerrymandering has been historically reviled, but the author also argues that the process remains poorly understood, which leads to a false sense that there are easy solutions to a complex problem. Medvic adroitly explains its legal status and implementation issues, details the consequences of partisan gerrymandering and proposes some possible options for reform. The book presents a balanced analysis of gerrymandering that acknowledges its most troubling aspects while recognizing that as long as district boundaries have to be drawn (or redrawn), there simply is no easy or perfect way to do so.

Moore, Louis. 2017. *We Will Win the Day: The Civil Rights Movement, the Black Athlete, and the Quest for Equality*. Santa Barbara: Praeger Press.

Moore provides a history of activist African American athletes and their role within the Black community. He profiles a series of athletes who have paved the way for integration in their respective sports and for expanding the political power of the Black community.

Moye, J. Todd. 2013. *Ella Baker: Community Organizer of the Civil Rights Movement*. Lanham: Rowman and Littlefield.

Moye provides a compelling biography of Ella Baker that emphasizes her grassroots community organizing. It is a concise, readable, and current examination of Baker's life and her profound impact on the civil rights struggle, painting Baker as an agent of social change across a wide variety of social issues.

Ness, Immanuel, and James Clement, eds. 2000. *Encyclopedia of Third Parties in America*. 3 vols. Armonk, NY: M. E. Sharpe.

This reference volume is an accessible yet comprehensive resource for information about all major and minor third political parties or candidates in U.S. history. It helps readers understand the role of political parties in changing electoral politics even when they do not achieve majority party status.

Ng, Wendy. 2001. *Japanese American Internment during World War II: A History and Reference Guide*. Westport, CT: Greenwood Press.

Ng's book is a thorough study of the internment experience that Japanese American individuals and families faced during World War II, when U.S. authorities stripped them of their rights and put them in military camps due to anti-Japanese prejudice. It details the historical background and assesses the effects of the policy on Japanese Americans and, ultimately, on the nation. It documents how the denial of naturalization to the Issei generation of Japanese immigrants shaped the politics of the Nissei (native-born immigrants of Japanese ancestry). The latter used the Japanese American Citizens League to advocate for enactment of the McCarran-Walter Act, which granted them a path to citizenship and the right to vote.

Norris, Pippa, and Ronald Inglehart. 2019. *Culture Backlash: Trump, Brexit, and Authoritarian Populism*. Cambridge: Cambridge University Press.

The book explores the concepts of authoritarianism, populism, and cultural backlash theory. It examines the demand side factors of cultural, economic, and societal changes against which populists react, and supply-side factors such as party competition and electoral rules. It elaborates how these factors led to Trump's presidency as well as the Brexit vote in the UK to leave the European Union.

Nownes, Anthony. 2012. *Interest Groups in American Politics: Pressure and Power*. 2nd ed. New York: Routledge.

Nownes's insightful book is grounded in exploring the role of information in interest-group activity. This second edition of his influential book retains its student-friendly tone and adds a new chapter on the connections between interest groups and political parties. Its copious use of figures and tables helps readers visualize important trends and information. The book shows that interest groups represent many members of society who have organized themselves to affect the policy-making process that impacts their daily lives. The book is concise in demonstrating that interest groups are involved in the political system at all levels of government and in all aspects of political activity. Interest groups, he demonstrates, influence election campaigns, agenda setting of government and parties, and lawmaking and policy implementation. Nownes frames interest groups as an entirely normal and healthy function of a pluralist society and of democratic governance. He warns, however, of the dangers posed by unwatched interest-group activity in the realms of electoral process and issue advocacy.

O'Brien, David H. 2017. *Constitutional Law and Politics: Civil Rights and Civil Liberties*, vol. 2. New York: W. W. Norton.

O'Brien's book is a solid text that treats the intertwining aspects of law and politics. It describes how courts weave through both. It discusses the origins of constitutional clauses, covers numerous case opinions, and provides a fuller understanding of constitutional law's strengths and weaknesses.

O'Mara, Margaret. 2017. *Pivotal Tuesdays: Four Elections That Shaped the Twentieth Century*. Philadelphia: University of Pennsylvania Press.

O'Mara's book examines four pivotal presidential elections of the past one hundred years: those of 1912, 1932, 1968, and 1992. She details the four-way race of 1912 between Teddy Roosevelt, William Howard Taft, Eugene Debs, and Woodrow Wilson and focuses on how the candidates grappled with the sweeping changes that industrial capitalism was causing and on how best to respond to those changes. She examines the 1932 election of Franklin D. Roosevelt and how his campaign promises to give Americans a "New Deal" to combat the Great Depression helped him to defeat Herbert Hoover, the beleaguered incumbent. In the dramatic and tragic campaign of 1968, Richard Nixon reflected an America deeply divided by race, region, and war. That pivotal race set in motion the dynamics that persisted to the book's final race—the three-way race that led to Bill Clinton's victory in 1992. Her book explores the personalities, critical moments, and surprises in each of the races. She deftly shows how and why candidates won or lost and examines the effects of their campaigns on subsequent presidencies. The book is about politics and elections but also about the evolution of a nation and how ordinary citizens shaped that history by how they cast their ballots.

Orozco, Cynthia. 2009. *No Mexicans, Women, or Dogs Allowed: The Rise of the Mexican Civil Rights Movement*. Austin: University of Texas Press.

Orozco's book offers a detailed history of the League of United Latin American Citizens (LULAC), placing it in its 20th-century context. The author uses oral histories to probe LULAC's origins and early activism, and against the backdrop of the Mexican Revolution, World War I, gender discrimination, and severe racial segregation, she recasts LULAC at the forefront of civil rights movements in America.

Paulson, Arthur. 2007. *Electoral Realignments and the Outlook for American Democracy*. Boston: Northeastern University Press.

Paulson analyzes the impact of ideological polarization on political parties and electoral realignments. The book is strong on realignment theory and includes the 2000 and 2004 elections and projects the outlook for the 2008 election.

Rabe, Barry. 2004. *Statehouse and Greenhouse: The Emerging Politics of American Climate Change Policy*. Washington, DC: Brookings Institution Press.

Rabe's book is an important early contribution to the growing body of scholarly literature on comparative environmental policy. It combines rich data and empirical analysis with in-depth case-level narratives and assessments. The book's mix of research methods illuminates the similarities and differences in institutional forms through which environmental policy emerges. It covers the spheres or levels of policy action and emphasizes the interplay of politics and policy. The book illuminates the importance of subnational innovation and action in climate change policy, asserting that states often lead the way in shaping national approaches to policy. It also discusses the Kyoto Protocol and the environmental and economic benefits and drawbacks of alternative proposals to reduce greenhouse gasses. Finally, the author shows the growing importance that climate change policy plays in American electoral politics.

Ransby, Barbara. 2003. *Ella Baker and the Black Freedom Movement: A Radical Democratic Vision*. Chapel Hill: University of North Carolina Press.

Ransby chronicles the life of Ella Baker and her long career as a civil rights organizer, an intellectual, and a teacher. Her book reveals Baker as a complex figure whose radical democratic world view compelled her to empower the Black poor and to emphasize a group-centered, grassroots leadership of the civil rights movement that set Baker apart from most of her political contemporaries.

Rawn, James. 2010. *Root and Branch: Charles Hamilton Houston, Thurgood Marshall, and the Struggle to End Segregation*. New York: Bloomsbury Press.

James Rawn provides a riveting story of two fiercely dedicated lawyers, Charles Hamilton Houston and Thurgood Marshall, and details their epic fight from county courthouses to the U.S. Supreme Court to lay the legal foundation for the civil rights movement.

Rosenof, Theodore. 2003. *Realignment: The Theory That Changed the Way We Think about American Politics*. Lanham, MD: Rowman and Littlefield.

Rosenof tells the dramatic story of how a new approach to American politics emerged after 1948. Realignment theory proposes that critical elections shaped politics for decades to come. Rosenof shows how electoral realignment theory emerged as the predominant explanation of electoral change.

Roydhouse, Marion W. 2016. *Votes for Women! The American Woman Suffrage Movement and the Nineteenth Amendment: A Reference Guide*. Santa Barbara, CA: ABC-CLIO.

The book is a detailed account of the long and often bumpy road to suffrage for women, from the Seneca Falls convention to adoption and ratification of the 19th Amendment. It provides extensive coverage of the leaders of the women's suffrage movement, and explores their often-difficult relationships with their counterparts in the abolition and temperance movements.

Rutherglen, George. 2013. *Civil Rights in the Shadow of Slavery: The Constitution, Common Law, and the Civil Rights Act of 1865*. New York: Oxford University Press.

Rutherglen's book recounts the history of the first Civil Rights Act. It offers a reassessment of its deep and continuing influence on constitutional and statutory protections of civil rights. It describes the debates over the act that dealt with controversies such as the scope of federal protection versus private discrimination and the remedies available to victims of civil rights violations that have been at the center of almost all subsequent controversies in courts and legislatures since 1866.

Ryden, David K. ed. 2001. *The U.S. Supreme Court and the Electoral Process*. 2nd ed. New York: Oxford University Press.

This revised and updated edition examines the critical role of the Supreme Court and the judicial branch in U.S. electoral processes. It takes into account famous judicial decisions on the presidency but also a myriad of other decisions made by the Supreme Court that have shaped voting and elections, representation, and political participation in the United States. It examines court actions that directly affect how those who govern are chosen and how those decisions affect electoral politics, constitutional doctrine, and fundamental concepts of democracy, including racial redistricting, term limits, political patronage, campaign finance regulation, third-party ballot access, and state ballot initiatives limiting civil liberties.

Samito, Christian. 2015. *Lincoln and the Thirteenth Amendment.* Carbondale: Southern Illinois University Press.

Samito examines how Lincoln's opposition to amending the Constitution shaped his political views before he became president, and how his perspective changed over the course of his presidency, leading him to support enactment of the 13th Amendment in 1864. Samito contends that Lincoln came to support the amendment to abolish slavery because it worked within the existing constitutional structure, preserving key components of American constitutionalism in the face of radical schemes among some Republicans. He provides an authoritative historical treatment of the amendment, and his book closes with a lively discussion of how the 13th Amendment applies to current events.

Sanders, Bernie. 2016. *Our Revolution: A Future to Believe In.* New York: Thomas Dunne Books.

In this memoir, Senator Bernie Sanders shares his personal experiences from the campaign trail, detailing his historic 2016 primary fight and the people who made it possible. He outlines a progressive economic, environmental, racial, and social justice agenda that he believes can transform America and the world for the better.

Schwartz, Herman, ed. 2003. *The Rehnquist Court: Judicial Activism of the Right.* New York: Hill and Wang.

The book presents essays by 17 distinguished legal scholars who evaluate the Rehnquist Court and its legacy of judicial activism on the political Right.

Sides, John, Michael Tesler, and Lynn Vavrek. 2018. *Identity Crisis: The 2016 Presidential Campaign and the Battle for the Meaning of America*. Princeton, NJ: Princeton University Press.

The authors provide a gripping, in-depth account of the 2016 presidential election that ended in Donald Trump's historic victory. The book discusses how unique characteristics of American self-identity combined with political factors such as the economy, the Obama presidency, and changing demographic trends all interacted with the personalities and rhetoric of Donald Trump and Hillary Clinton to produce one of the most unexpected presidencies in U.S. history. They show how support for the candidates was driven by peoples' racial and ethnic identities—and how the 2016 campaign reinforced and exacerbated those cleavages.

Smith, Bradley. 2001. *Unfree Speech: The Folly of Campaign Finance Reform*. Princeton, NJ: Princeton University Press.

Smith argues that the various reforms of the Federal Election Commission and various state agencies fail to accomplish their stated objectives, instead working to entrench incumbents in office, deaden campaign discourse, burden grassroots organizations with needless regulation, and distance Americans from an increasingly professional, detached political class. The author contends that the legislative cures for the ills of campaign and party fundraising are sometimes worse than the disease.

Stooksbury, Kara E., John M. Scheb II, and Otis W. Stephens Jr., eds. 2017. *Encyclopedia of American Civil Rights and Liberties*. 4 vols. Santa Barbara, CA: ABC-CLIO.

This revised four-volume encyclopedia provides a comprehensive resource for the discussion of American civil rights and liberties. The new edition deals with such topics as gay marriage and government surveillance. The set has seven hundred entries and covers key constitutional provisions, important Supreme Court decisions, social movements and advocacy groups, historical figures, and relevant legal doctrines.

Strang, Stephen E. 2020. *God, Trump, and the 2020 Election.* New York: Frontline.

Strang's book examines how the political climate is affected by what he terms "spiritual warfare." A polemic squarely aimed at Evangelical Christians, it asserts that Donald Trump's campaign can best be understood as a spiritual challenge to secularism.

Stuhler, Barbara. 2003. *For the Public Record: A Documentary History of the League of Women Voters.* Washington, DC: Pogo Press.

Stuhler's book is a concise documentary history of the League of Women Voters. It employs interviews of members of the League of Women Voters (LWV) to tell in their own words the compelling story of the organization and its efforts to support the franchise in American politics. It describes the LWV's work for good government and demonstrates the importance of an informed and active citizenry.

Tarr, Dave, and Bob Benson, eds. 2012. *Elections A to Z: A Ready Reference Encyclopedia.* Washington, DC: Congressional Quarterly Press.

This volume provides more than 225 entries, arranged in alphabetical order, that look at many aspects of the election process. It covers constitutional amendments, qualifications for office, campaign regulation and strategies, political consultants, reapportionment and redistricting, pivotal events, candidates, election rules and regulations, primary scheduling, voter turnout, election scandals, and election trends.

Thomas, G. Scott. 2019. *Presidential Election Record Book*. New York: Niawanda Books.

The book is a counting-the-vote almanac that provides a thorough statistical breakdown of all 58 presidential elections since 1789, including the results of primary elections, conventions, and general elections, and the records of 302 candidates who ran in those races. It also offers statistical profiles of 31 candidates who ran for the presidency in 2020.

Thomas, William H., Jr. 2008. *Unsafe for Democracy: World War I and the U.S. Justice Department's Covert Campaign to Suppress Dissent*. Madison: University of Wisconsin Press.

Historian William Thomas examines the Department of Justice's use of the Espionage Act of 1917 and the Sedition Act of 1918 to suppress dissent. He details how, during World War I, the U.S. Department of Justice (DOJ) targeted isolationists, pacifists, immigrants, socialists, labor organizers, African Americans, members of the clergy, the unemployed, the mentally ill, college students, and schoolteachers. He analyzes documents that show that in case after case, the DOJ used threats and warnings to frighten war critics and silence dissent.

Tushnet, Mark. 2005. *A Court Divided: The Rehnquist Court and the Future of Constitutional Law*. New York: W. W. Norton and Company.

Tushnet examines the Rehnquist Court, arguing that the Court has always followed election returns. He notes that the Warren and Burger Courts never got far out of line with the national political consensus. Tushnet shows the Rehnquist Court reflected the rise of conservatism in the last two decades of the 20th century. He shows how the Court followed the GOP Congress's lead during those decades, striking down several symbols of the New Deal regulatory state. The Court sided with more liberal positions at the margins of the social cultural wars—on gay rights, affirmative action, and early-term abortions. As Tushnet notes, in the arena of politics, economic conservatives were winning, and cultural conservatives were losing.

Vile, John. 2014. *Essential Supreme Court Decisions: Summaries of Leading Cases in U.S. Constitutional Law.* 16th ed. Lanham, MD: Rowman and Littlefield.

John Vile's book has become a standard of the most important Supreme Court cases in U.S. constitutional law. His book includes every facet of constitutional law, including powers and privileges of the three branches of the national government, federalism, war powers, and extensive briefs on civil rights and civil liberties.

Vile, John R. 2015. *Founding Documents of America: Documents Decoded.* Santa Barbara, CA: ABC-CLIO.

Vile offers historic documents key to the foundation of the national government, with introductions that supply the background information and analysis that highlight key provisions and provide historical context. He covers the Declaration of Independence, the Constitution, the Bill of Rights, private diary entries, and political polemics organized chronologically into four sections. The book includes coverage of more than 50 primary source documents.

Wilentz, Sean. 2004. *Chants Democratic: New York City and the Rise of the American Working Class.* New York: Oxford University Press.

Wilentz presents a classic narrative of the rise of organized labor and its impact on American democracy. His book explores the dramatic social and intellectual changes that came with the early industrialization of New York City and how those changes affected city politics and the Democratic Party.

Williams, R. Hal. 2010. *Realigning America: McKinley, Bryan, and the Remarkable Election of 1896*. Lawrence: University Press of Kansas.

Williams provides a detailed study of the presidential election of 1896, showing how new voting patterns replaced old ones and a new majority party came to power.

Witcover, Jules. 2003. *Party of the People: A History of the Democrats*. New York: Random House.

Witcover traces the evolution of the Democratic Party from its roots to its emergence as today's progressive party of social change and economic and racial justice. He documents its sweeping impact on American electoral politics and how several of the party's leaders played transformative roles in U.S. politics and elections by building new coalitions of voting blocs and new avenues for fundraising and voter mobilization.

Wolbrecht, Christina, Karen Beckwith, and Lisa Baldez, eds. 2008. *Political Women and American Democracy*. New York: Cambridge University Press.

This edited volume provides a critical synthesis of the scholarly research of leading experts in the field of women in politics to chronicle the dramatic increase in women's political participation since the 1970s—in mobilization and activism, in voting, in running for office, and in serving in elective offices at all three levels of government. Book chapters examine women as citizens, voters, participants, movement activists, partisans, candidates, and legislators. The chapters focus on theory, methodology, and empirical debates, and they map out productive directions for future research.

Wolbrecht, Christina, and Rodney E. Hero. 2005. *The Politics of Democratic Inclusion*. Philadelphia: Temple University Press.

The authors contribute to our understanding of the processes and mechanisms by which underrepresented groups have or have not achieved political influence. They collect essays from contributors that trace the issue of political inclusion from colonial times to the present. They give particular emphasis to the institutions, processes, and rules that encourage, mediate, or hamper the representation and incorporation of different socioeconomic and political constituencies into the mainstream of American political life.

Woods, Randall. 2006. *LBJ: Architect of American Ambition*. New York: Free Press.

Distinguished historian Woods offers a wholesale reappraisal and sweeping authoritative account of Lyndon B. Johnson, whose leadership in enacting the Civil Rights Acts of 1964, 1965, and 1968 had a profound impact of U.S. elections, on the expansion of the vote, and on the importance of minority groups in Democratic politics. The author uses thousands of newly released documents, White House tapes, and extensive interviews with key aides to bring crucial new evidence to bear on key aspects of the man and the politician and his impact on American society.

Zentner, Scot, and Michael LeMay. 2020. *Party and Nation: Immigration and Regime Politics in American History*. Lanham, MD: Lexington Books.

This book blends three topics: a history of American political development, a history of American political parties, and a history of the politics of immigration. It covers these themes, noting how they intertwine and influence one another, from America's founding through the first two decades of the 21st century.

Zolberg, Aristide. 2006. *A Nation by Design: Immigration Policy and the Fashioning of America*. Cambridge, MA: Harvard University Press.

The late Harvard professor explores American immigration policy from colonial times to the present, describing how it has been used as a tool of nation building, covering policy at the state and local levels, and describing how the oscillating currents of immigration throughout American history shaped the nation, its elections and politics, and the values and priorities of both major and minor political parties.

Leading Scholarly Journals

American Journal of Sociology was established in 1895 and is the oldest academic journal of sociology in the United States. It is attached to the Department of Sociology at the University of Chicago and is published bimonthly. It is a leading voice in all areas of sociology, with an emphasis on theory building and innovative methods, and is open to interdisciplinary contributions from anthropologists, economists, educators, historians, and political scientists. It publishes book reviews and commissioned book review essays.

American Journal of Political Science is a peer-reviewed academic journal published by the Midwest Political Science Association. It has been published quarterly since 1973. It publishes original research articles in all areas of political science.

American Political Science Review is a quarterly, peer-reviewed academic journal covering all areas of political science. It is the official journal of the American Political Science Association and is published by Cambridge University Press. It was established in 1906 and is widely considered to be the field's premier research journal.

American Politics Research is a quarterly, peer-reviewed journal that has been published bimonthly for more than 30 years. It covers research analysis in all areas of American politics.

Annals of the American Academy of Political and Social Science was founded in 1889 to promote progress in the social sciences. Today, it is headquartered at the Annenberg Public Policy Center in Philadelphia, and it offers interdisciplinary perspectives on important social science issues.

Annual Review of Political Science has been published since 1998. It covers significant developments in the field of political science, including political theory and philosophy, international relations, political economy, political behavior (with many articles on voting and electoral behavior), American and comparative politics, public administration, and policy (including election administration and voting-related regulatory policy at the state and local levels), and methodology. It publishes reviews commissioned by the journal's Editorial Committee.

Columbia Law Review has been published since 1901 and is a leading publication of legal scholarship that publishes eight issues a year. Produced by the Columbia University Law School, it also has featured an online supplement, *Columbia Law Review Online,* since 2008.

Election Law Journal is a quarterly, peer-reviewed journal published in print and online. It covers legal, policy, and administrative issues concerning all matters of elections and voting rights, including redistricting, gerrymandering, election monitoring, contested elections, voting technology, political parties, ballot access, the initiative process, and campaign finance and ethics. It is published by Mary Ann Liebert Inc.

Electoral Studies is a refereed international journal concerning all aspects of voting and electoral systems and strategies. It publishes research from diverse approaches, both theoretical and empirical, and is published by the Elsevier Publishing Group.

Emory International Law Review is a leading quarterly journal of international legal scholarship known for its excellence in scholarship, legal research, analysis, and professionalism. It publishes articles on a vast array of topics, from human rights to international intellectual property issues.

Emory Law Journal was founded in 1952 as the *Journal of Public Law*. It has been publishing academic, professional, and student-authored legal scholarship on the full range of legal subjects since 1978. It publishes six issues annually.

Georgetown Journal of Legal Ethics was founded in 1987. It is published quarterly. It publishes interdisciplinary scholarship related to the future of the legal profession, issuing cutting-edge articles on ethical issues from diverse practical areas.

Georgetown Law Review is headquartered at Georgetown University Law School in Washington, DC. It has published more than 500 issues since its inception in 1912. It employs 100 law students. It publishes articles across the full spectrum of legal issues and cases and an *Annual Review of Criminal Procedure.*

Harvard Law Review publishes eight regular annual issues of various legal articles by professors, judges, practitioners, and law students, and leading case summaries. It is run by an independent student group at Harvard Law School. It also publishes an online *Harvard Law Review* Forum. One of the nation's oldest law reviews, it has been published since 1887. It is one of the most prestigious law reviews, and its published alumni include President Barack Obama, seven Supreme Court justices, and a host of federal court judges and other high-level federal government officials.

Hastings Law Journal has been published since 1949. It is the flagship law review of the University of California–Hastings. It is published six times per year. Its scholarly articles span a wide variety of legal issues and are written by experts in the legal community. It also publishes an occasional law symposium issue. It is run by 90 student members, and it reaches a large domestic and international audience.

Journal of American Ethnic History is the official journal of the Immigration and Ethnic History Society. Since 1981, its articles, review essays, and book reviews have been published quarterly. It also publishes special issues that group articles and essays on specific topics or themes. It is published by the University of Illinois Press in print and online.

Journal of American History is the official academic journal of the Organization of American Historians. Originally founded in 1914 as the *Mississippi Valley Historical Review*, it is published quarterly by Oxford University Press.

Journal of Democracy is a quarterly academic journal established in 1990 as the official publication of the National Endowment for Democracy's International Forum for Democratic Studies. It covers studies of democracy, democratic regimes, and pro-democracy movements worldwide for activists and intellectuals. It is one of the most cited social science journals and is published by the Johns Hopkins University Press.

Journal of Politics is a peer-reviewed academic journal of political science established in 1939 and now published quarterly by the University of Chicago Press for the Southern Political

Science Association. It publishes original research studies in all fields of political science.

Journal of Politics and Society has been published since 1989 by Columbia University, and it covers issues concerning law and public policy by undergraduates in a process comparable to that of a peer-reviewed journal.

Journal of Social History is a scholarly, peer-reviewed journal that has been published since 1967. It covers social history in all regions and time periods. It is published quarterly by Oxford University Press and is a top-ranked journal in the field of social history.

Journal of Women, Politics, and Policy has been published since 1980, when it was known as *Women & Politics*. It was renamed in 2005. Published for the Institute for Women's Policy Research at George Washington University, the journal covers new research on politics and policy of special interest to women.

Legislative Studies Quarterly, published since 1976 by Washington University, publishes articles on legislative systems, procedures, behavior, and parliaments, and their relation to other institutions, their functions in political systems, and activity by members. It is a quarterly, peer-reviewed academic journal of the Legislative Studies section of the American Political Science Association (APSA) and is published by Wiley-Blackwell.

Michigan Law Review publishes eight issues annually, seven of which are comprised of articles by legal scholars and practitioners and notes by law students. One issue is devoted to book reviews. The review publishes important judicial decisions and legislative developments. It has been published by the University of Michigan Law School since 1902.

Northwestern University Law Review was founded in 1906 as the *Illinois Law Review*. It is published quarterly in print and online. It features articles on general legal scholarship written by professors, judges, legal professionals, and students.

Notre Dame Law Review was founded in 1925 and known as the *Notre Dame Lawyer* until 1982. It is a student-edited quarterly that fosters scholarly discourse within the legal community mindful of its Catholic tradition. It also publishes an annual "Federal Courts, Practice and Procedure" symposium issue as a forum exploring civil practice and procedures in the federal courts.

Party Politics is an international journal for the study of political parties, party systems, and organizations. It is the official journal of the Political Organizations and Parties section of APSA. Founded in 1995, it publishes six times per year.

Perspective on Politics is a quarterly, peer-reviewed academic journal established in 2003. Published by Cambridge University Press, it covers the political science profession and the impact of politics on broader society. It seeks to nurture political science as an academic field by publishing important scholarly topics, ideas, and innovations.

Political Behavior is an interdisciplinary journal publishing peer-reviewed articles about political attitudes and behavior by individuals and institutions.

Political Research Quarterly is a peer-reviewed academic journal covering the field of political science. Founded in 1948, it is a SAGE publication for the University of Utah, a COPE (Committee on Publication Ethics) publication, and the official journal of the Western Political Science Association.

Political Science Quarterly is a peer-reviewed academic journal covering government, politics, and policy. It has been published since 1886 by the Academy of Political Science.

Politics and Gender is an agenda-setting journal publishing high-quality scholarship on the intersection of gender and politics. The journal of the Women and Politics section of the APSA, it is published by Cambridge University Press.

Politics and Society is a peer-reviewed quarterly that publishes scholarship that explores how the world is organized politically, economically, and socially. It began in the 1960s as an alternative critical voice in the social sciences. It regularly features debates on the theory of the state, class analysis, politics of gender, methodology, rational choice, and the future of capitalism and socialism. Published by SAGE, it is also a COPE publication.

Polity is a Palgrave Macmillan journal published on behalf of the Northeastern Political Science Association since 1968. It publishes articles of original research of general interest to political scientists across all fields.

Presidential Studies Quarterly is an interdisciplinary journal of theory and research on the American presidency by the Center for the Study of the President and Congress. Published by Blackwell Publishing, it is the official journal of the Presidential Research section of the APSA.

Public Choice is a peer-reviewed academic journal on economics and political science, established in 1955, it is published eight times per year by Springer Science and Business Media.

Public Opinion Quarterly is an academic, peer-reviewed journal published by Oxford University Press for the American Association of Public Opinion Research. It covers communication studies and political science and has been published since 1937.

Publius: The Journal of Federalism is the world's leading journal devoted to federalism. It publishes original empirical and theoretical work on federalism and intergovernmental relations. It is published by the Center for the Study of State and Local

Government, Lafayette College, in Easton, Pennsylvania. It is the official journal of the section on federalism of the APSA.

Research and Politics is a peer-reviewed academic journal of political science and related fields. It is both a SAGE and a COPE publication. It is now an open-access political science journal.

Review of Politics publishes articles primarily on political theory, interpretive studies of law, and historical analysis on all aspects of politics: institutions, techniques, literary reflections on politics, and constitutional theory and analysis. It has been published quarterly since 1939. It is published by Cambridge University Press for the University of Notre Dame.

Social Science History is an interdisciplinary journal aimed at historians, sociologists, political scientists, anthropologists, and geographers. It has been published since 1976 by Cambridge University Press and is the official journal of the Social Science History Association.

Social Science Quarterly is a quarterly academic journal nationally recognized as one of the top journals in the field of all social sciences. It is the official journal of the Southwestern Social Science Association. It began in 1919. It has been published by Wiley and Blackwell since 2004 and publishes an annual special issue.

Stanford University Law Review is published both in print (since 1948) and online (since 2011). It fosters intellectual discourse among student members and contributes to legal scholarship by addressing important legal and social issues. It publishes six issues per year.

Supreme Court Review is published by the University of Chicago Law School since it first appeared in 1910. An annual publication, it provides a sustained and authoritative survey of the Court's most significant decisions. It provides an in-depth critique of the Supreme Court and its work and of the ongoing reforms and interpretations of American law. It is written by and for legal academics, judges, political scientists, journalists, and sociologists.

University of California Law Review is the preeminent legal publication of the University of California–Berkeley School of Law. Founded in 1912, it is published six times annually and covers a wide variety of topics of legal scholarship. Edited and published entirely by students at Berkeley Law, it includes contributions from the Berkeley Law faculty, centers, students, judges, and legal practitioners.

University of Chicago Law Review was founded in 1933. It is edited by the law school's students and is one of the most prestigious and often-cited law reviews. Its authors include a host of Supreme Court justices, federal court judges, state supreme court judges, and preeminent legal scholars. It is published quarterly.

University of Pennsylvania Journal of Constitutional Law provides a forum for the interdisciplinary study and analysis of constitutional law. It cultivates legal scholarship, promotes critical perspectives, and reinvents the traditional study of constitutional law. It has been published quarterly since 1998.

University of Pennsylvania Law Review is a law review focusing on a wide range of legal issues. It was founded in 1852. It serves the legal profession, the bench, the bar, and the legal academy by providing a forum for publication of legal research.

University of Virginia Law Review has been one of the most prestigious publications in the legal profession since its founding in 1913. The Virginia Law School was founded by Thomas Jefferson in 1819. The *Review* is published eight times annually. It covers law-related issues by and for judges, practitioners, teachers, legislators, students, and others interested in the law.

Western Political Quarterly is published by the University of Utah on behalf of the Western Political Science Association, the Pacific Northwest Political Science Association, and the Southern Political Science Association. It has been published since 1948.

Yale Law Journal has been published since 1891. It has been at the forefront of legal scholarship and shapes discussion of the most important and relevant legal issues through rigorous scholarship. It is published eight times per year, and its online companion has been published since 2005.

Websites

Act Blue: https://secure.actblue.com
AFL-CIO: https://www.afl-cio.org
American Archive: https://americanarchive.org
American Civil Liberties Union: https://www.aclu.org
American Constitution Society: https://www.acslaw.org
Americans for Prosperity: https://americansforprosperity.org
Ballot Access: https://ballot-access.org
Ballotpedia.org: https://ballotpedia.org
Brennan Center for Justice: https://www.brennancenter.org
Cato Institute: https://www.cato.org
Census.gov: https://www.census.gov
Center for American Progress: https://www.AmericanProgress.org
Center for Politics: https://centerforpolitics.org
Club for Growth: https://www.ClubforGrowth.org
Congressional Quarterly: https://info.cq.com
Democratic National Committee: https://democrats.org
Emily's List: https://www.Emilyslist.org
Federal Election Commission: https://www.fec.gov
Federalist Society: https://fedsoc.org
Green Party of the United States: https://www.GP.org
Heritage Society: https://www.heritage.org

League of Women Voters.org: https://www.lwv.org
Library of Congress.gov: https://www.loc.gov
Lincoln Project: https://www.lincolnproject.us
NAACP: https://www.naacp.org
National Conference of State Legislatures: https://www.ncsl.org
National Democratic Redistricting Committee: https://democraticredistricting.com
Oyez.org: https://www.oyez.org
Pew Research Center: https://www.pewresearch.org
Republican National Committee: https://www.GOP.com
U.S. Elections Assistance Commission: https://www.eac.gov
U.S. Supreme Court: https://www.supremecourt.gov
Vote.org: https://www.vote.org
WinRed: https://winred.com

Documentaries

Bush Family Fortunes, 2004, 61 minutes, color. Greg Palast has been following the Bush family around for years as an investigative reporter for the BBC. This documentary is based on his book *The Best Democracy Money Can Buy*.

Citizen Koch, 2013, 90 minutes, color. This documentary follows the use of "dark money" behind the rise of the Tea Party.

Electoral Dysfunction, 2012, 90 minutes, color. This documentary follows political humorist Mo Rocca on an irreverent road trip across America to see how voting works—and doesn't work—in the United States.

Gerrymandering, 2010, 81 minutes, color. This documentary film takes a critical look at American democracy and how it provides for a perfectly legal way to control electoral outcomes. It focuses on how Republican-dominated state legislatures, in particular, have "weaponized" gerrymandering for political advantage.

The Great Hack, 2018, Netflix, 114 minutes, color. This compelling documentary examines in detail the Facebook-Cambridge Analytica scandal, in which it was revealed that private Facebook data of 87 million users was acquired by Cambridge Analytica for political advertising in the months prior to the 2016 U.S. presidential election.

Stealing America: Vote by Vote, 2008, 90 minutes, color. Filmmaker Dorothy Fadiman examines charges of voter disenfranchisement, data breaches, and election fraud in the 2004 presidential election.

Unprecedented: The 2000 Presidential Election, 2002, 50 minutes, color. This riveting documentary examines the undermining of democracy by focusing on the events leading up to Election Day 2000 and on the failed attempt to count all the legally cast votes in Florida. It examines the suspicious pattern of irregularities, injustices, and voter roll purges that took place in the state at a time when Jeb Bush—brother of Republican candidate George W. Bush—was governor.

With God on Our Side: George W. Bush and the Rise of the Religious Right in America, 2004, 50 minutes, color. This well-made, comprehensive BBC television documentary is an extensive examination of the conservative Evangelical movement that came to be known as the "religious Right." It covers the prehistory and history of the Evangelical movement, culminating in the "stolen" election of George W. Bush in 2000. It is packed with historical, sociological, and cultural context.

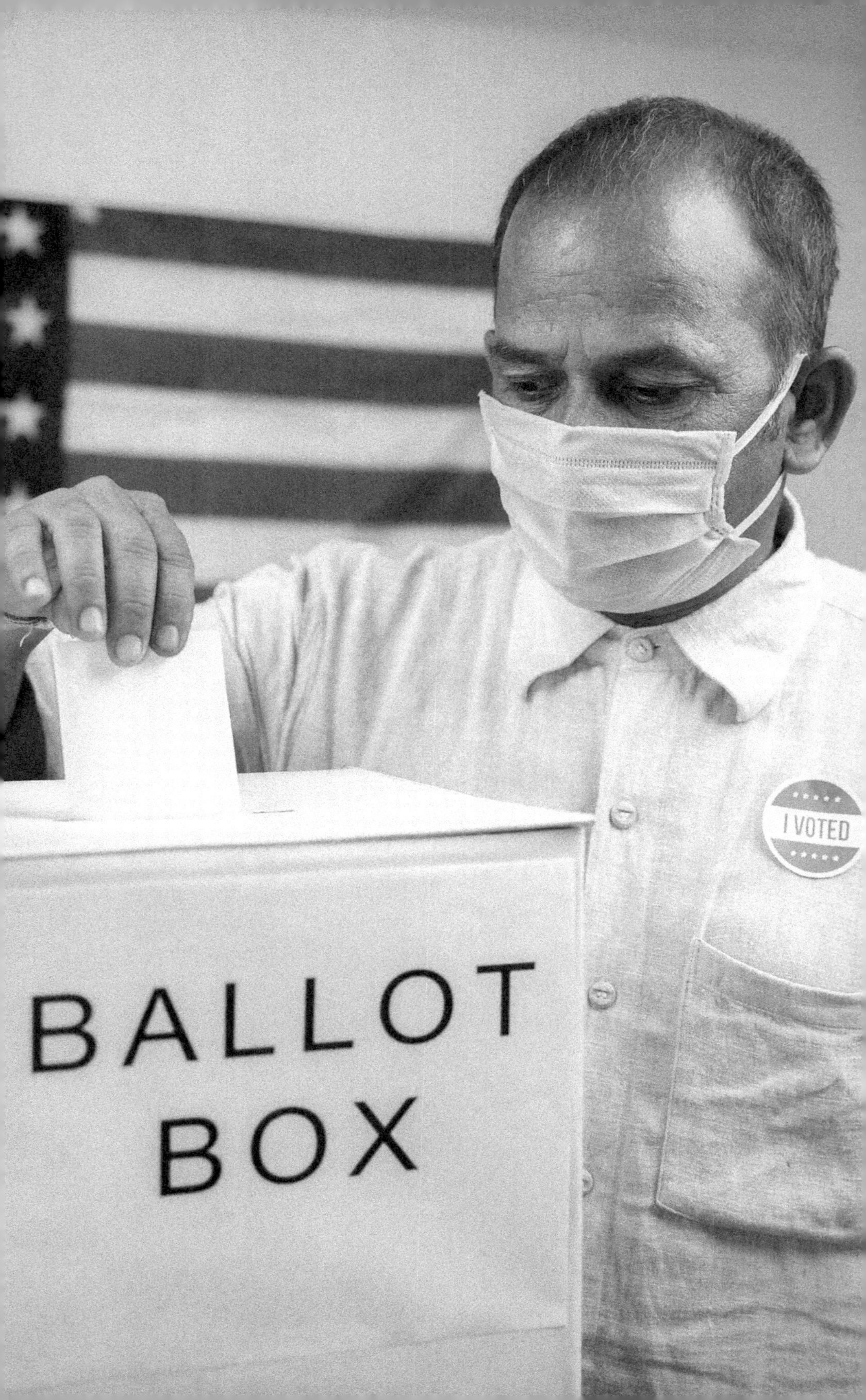
I VOTED
BALLOT
BOX

7 Chronology

1776 Declaration of Independence written and signed on July 4.

1776 George Mason drafts Virginia's Declaration of Rights, which later becomes a model for the U.S. Bill of Rights. Voting rights are affirmed: just powers are derived from the consent of the governed.

1777 Articles of Confederation drafted without Bill of Rights.

1781 Articles of Confederation ratified without Bill of Rights. A weak central government established.

1787 Second Constitutional Convention held to revise the Articles of Confederation. It results in proposing the new Constitution. Voting rights are reserved to the states.

1788 June 21: voting left to the states; Article II establishes the Electoral College.

1789 Constitution is ratified; a new government begins that drafts Bill of Rights amendments. Ten of the 12 proposed amendments are adopted.

1791 The Bill of Rights—comprised of the first 10 amendments—is ratified.

1801 Thomas Jefferson begins his presidency.

In the 2020 elections, voters who opted to vote in person on Election Day took extra precautions to do so safely during the pandemic. Pictured here is a male voter wearing a medical-grade mask while placing his ballot into the ballot box. (Lakshmiprasad S/Dreamstime.com)

1801 The Democratic-Republican Party is created.

1803 Louisiana Purchase adds territory and Catholics to the U.S. population.

1803 *Marbury v. Madison* decision is handed down, establishing judicial review power.

1820 Missouri Compromise regarding entry of slave states and free states passed.

1820 Property rights requirements to vote begin to be eliminated.

1845 Congress enacts National Election Day as first Tuesday in November.

1848 Treaty of Guadalupe Hidalgo signed.

1848 Irish potato famine brings a wave of immigrants, many Catholics among them, to the United States and spurs anti-Catholic discrimination.

1848 California gold rush begins bringing thousands of Chinese immigrants to the West Coast, sparking a rise in anti-Chinese sentiment and discrimination.

1848 Seneca Falls Convention is held and women's suffrage movement begins.

1849 Order of the Star-Spangled Banner/Know Nothing Party begins.

1850 Congress passes the Compromise of 1850 that delayed the Civil War by a decade. It included a provision known as the Fugitive Slave law.

1854 Republican Party established with an antislavery platform.

1860 President Abraham elected.

1860 Civil War begins.

1861 Lincoln suspends writ of habeas corpus.

1862 Homestead Act passed.

1862 Transcontinental Railroad construction begins, further opening western states to settlement.

1862 States allow noncitizens to vote in local elections.

1863 President Lincoln issues Emancipation Proclamation order freeing slaves in 10 Confederate states.

1863 Lincoln gives his famous Gettysburg Address.

1864 Lincoln is reelected.

1865 The Civil War ends.

1865 On December 6, the 13th Amendment is ratified.

1865 President Abraham Lincoln assassinated on April 15.

1865 Reconstruction era (1865–1877) begins in the South.

1866 Civil Rights Act enacted on April 6.

1868 The 14th Amendment is ratified, granting citizenship to all U.S.-born or naturalized.

1869 National Women's Suffrage Association is founded.

1870 The 15th Amendment is ratified. Black men are guaranteed the right to vote.

1875 Civil Rights Act of March 3, 1875, is enacted—a.k.a. "the Enforcement Act."

1877 Post-Reconstruction era begins (1877–1890).

1879 *Reynolds v. Sims* upholds polygamy laws against Mormons.

1896 *Plessy v. Ferguson* decision establishes "separate but equal" doctrine, legally justifying segregation and spurring use of Jim Crow laws throughout the South.

1896 William McKinley elected president, beginning the Progressive era.

1898 Spanish-American War results in the acquisition of new territory and citizens.

1909 NAACP (National Association for the Advancement of Colored People) is founded.

1910 The Urban League is founded.

1913 The 17th Amendment, calling for the direct election of U.S. senators, is ratified.

1914 Marcus Garvey founds the Universal Negro Improvement Association promoting Black separatism.

1917 The Espionage Act is passed.

1917 The United States enters World War I.

1918 The Sedition Act is passed.

1919 Attorney General Palmer uses "Red Scare" raids to round up radical socialists and communists.

1919 *Schenck v. United States* upholds convictions of socialists under the Espionage Act.

1919 Several hundred immigrants are deported to Russia.

1920 The 19th Amendment is ratified, granting women the right to vote.

1920 The American Civil Liberties Union is founded.

1920 The League of Women Voters is founded.

1920 Many southern states restrict minority women from voting through enactment of Jim Crow discriminatory laws.

1921 Supreme Court decides *Newberry v. United States.*

1922 *Leser v. Garnett* upholds the constitutionality of the 19th Amendment.

1922 The Cable Act is passed on September 22, granting citizenship to women when their husband is naturalized—but also stripping citizenship from women who marry foreigners who cannot become citizens.

1922 *Ozawa v. United States* rules that the law banning Japanese immigrants (Issei) from naturalization is constitutional.

1923 Court holds in *United States v. Bhagat Singh Thind* that "free white persons," who qualify for citizenship, only refers to individuals who look white; East Indians are therefore not considered white and cannot naturalize.

1924 In recognition of Native Americans' military service in World War I, Congress enacts the Act of June 4, "Citizenship for Non-Citizen Indians" a.k.a. the Indian Citizenship Act.

1929 Japanese American Citizens League is founded.

1929 League of United Latin American Citizens is founded.

1929 *United States v. Schwimmer* decides that a woman who refuses to swear oath because of pacifism can be denied citizenship.

1929 New York passes law requiring literacy test for new voters.

1929 The stock market crash leads to the Great Depression and President Franklin D. Roosevelt's New Deal, which emphasizes economic rights.

1931 Act of March 3 restores citizenship to women who lost it because of the Cable Act of 1922 and their having married a foreign man and/or residing abroad.

1935 Act of June 24 allows for naturalization of aliens who were veterans of World War I, explicitly granting citizenship to Asian veterans.

1936 Repatriation granted to native-born women who lost citizenship due to marriage, revising the Cable Act and Act of March 3, 1931.

1941 Pearl Harbor attacked; United States enters World War II.

1942 Japanese Americans relocated and internship camps opened by Executive Order 9066 and Act of March 21, 1942. 120,000 are incarcerated.

1942 The Congress of Racial Equality (CORE) is founded.

1943 *Hirabayashi v. United States* upholds constitutionality of relocation order by virtue of "military necessity." Congress enacts the War Labor Dispute Act.

1943 Chinese Exclusion Act repealed, and China is given a quota of just over 100 annual immigrants to enter as legal resident aliens. Chinese immigrants are permitted to naturalize.

1944 Ex parte *Mitsuye Endo*, the Supreme Court rules that Endo and others cannot be detained in internment camps.

1944 The National Congress of American Indians is founded.

1945 World War II ends.

1947 Community Service Organization, a Latino civil rights group, is founded in California.

1950 Mattachine Society, an early national gay rights organization, is founded.

1952 The McCarran-Walter Act is passed, giving, among other provisions, the right to the Issei (meaning "firstborn," that is, immigrants born in Japan) to become naturalized citizens.

1953 Earl Warren appointed chief justice of the Supreme Court.

1955 Daughters of Bilitis, America's first formal lesbian rights organization, is founded.

1957 Montgomery bus boycott starts, and Montgomery Improvement Association begins.

1957 Southern Christian Leadership Council is founded by Martin Luther King Jr., Ralph Abernathy, Ella Baker, and others.

1957 President Eisenhower sends troops to protect the first wave of Black students desegregating a public school in Little Rock, Arkansas.

1957 Eisenhower signs the Civil Rights Act of August 9, a.k.a. the Eisenhower Civil Rights Act.

1958 AARP (originally the American Association of Retired Persons) is founded.

1960 The Student Nonviolent Coordinating Committee (SNCC) is founded.

1960 The Civil Rights Act of May 6, 1960, is enacted, banning the poll tax and setting up conditions for federal voter registration efforts.

1961 The National Indian Youth Council is founded.

1961 The 23rd Amendment, allowing residents of the District of Columbia to vote in presidential elections, is ratified on March 29, 1961.

1962 The United Farm Workers (UFW) is founded by Cesar Chavez and Dolores Huerta.

1963 La Alianza Federal de Mercedes, a Latinx civil rights group, begins.

1963 On February 21, Malcolm X is assassinated.

1963 On November 22, President John F. Kennedy is assassinated.

1964 Civil Rights Act of 1964 passed.

1964 Supreme Court decides the courts can hear cases on redistricting in *Reynolds v. Sims* and issues "one man, one vote" doctrine.

1964 Poll taxes banned by the 24th Amendment.

1965 Civil Rights Act of August 6 enacted.

1965 Voting Rights Act signed by President Lyndon Johnson on August 6.

1966 The Black Panther Party is founded.

1966 The Crusade for Justice, a Chicano minority protest group, starts in Colorado.

1967 The U.S. Supreme Court rules in *Afroyim v. Rusk* that an American citizen may have dual citizenship with another country and that Americans can't be stripped of their citizenship involuntarily.

1967 The Mexican American Youth Organization is founded.

1968 The Mexican American Legal Defense and Education Fund is founded.

1968 The National Council of La Raza begins.

1968 The American Indian Movement begins.

1968 The Civil Rights Act of April 11 is passed, containing provisions known as the Fair Housing Act and the Indian Civil Rights Act.

1968 Martin Luther King Jr. is assassinated.

1968 On June 5, former attorney general, senator, and presidential candidate Robert F. Kennedy is assassinated.

1970 The 26th Amendment is ratified, lowering the voting age to persons 18 years or older.

1971 The National Women's Political Caucus is established.

Congress passes the Federal Election Campaign Act.

1971 The Southern Poverty Law Center is established.

1972 Congress enacts the Federal Election Campaign Act (FECA).

1974 The Asian American Legal Defense and Education Fund is established.

1974 Chief Justice Earl Warren dies.

1975 Congress enacts Voting Rights Act of 1975

1976 Supreme Court decides case of *Buckley v. Valeo,* holding 7–1 that provisions of the Federal Election Commission Act are violations of the Constitution.

1984 On September 28, Congress enacts the Voting Accessibility Act for the Elderly and Handicapped.

1991 Civil Rights Act of November 21—a.k.a. the Equal Opportunity Act—is passed.

1993 Civil Rights Act of May 20, also known as the National Voter Registration Act and the "motor voter" law, is passed.

1993 Cesar Chavez dies.

1993 Justice Thurgood Marshall dies.

1995 The American Association of People with Disabilities is founded.

1997 *Chandler v. Miller* decides on a Georgia law requiring candidates for office to take a drug test to run for office.

1997 Supreme Court decides *Colorado Republican Federal Campaign Committee v. Federal Election Commission,* ruling in favor of the Colorado Republican Party against restrictions imposed by the Federal Election Commission (FEC).

2000 In the case of *Bush v. Gore,* Supreme Court decides in a 5–4 ruling split down partisan lines that Republican presidential candidate George W. Bush won the Electoral College vote despite losing the popular vote to Democratic nominee Al Gore.

2002 Help America Vote Act is passed and signed into law, establishing the Election Assistance Commission to improve and certify voting equipment, maintain the National Voter Registration form, and administer a national elections clearinghouse.

2002 Congress enacts the Bipartisan Campaign Reform Act, known as the McCain-Feingold Act, on campaign finance reform to address some "soft money" loopholes.

2003 Supreme Court decides *McConnell v. FEC* upholding the constitutionality of the Bipartisan Campaign Reform Act.

2005 Chief Justice William Rehnquist dies.

2007 Supreme Court decides by 5–4 vote in *FEC v. Wisconsin Right to Life, Inc.* that so-called "issue ads" may not be banned in months preceding a primary or general election.

2010 Supreme Court issues 5–4 decision in *Citizens United v. FEC,* further tilting political influence toward wealthy donors and corporations via "dark money." The ruling by the conservative Court that unlimited campaign spending is protected by First Amendment free speech rights overturns long-standing election spending restrictions. The decision spurs the creation of a flood of powerful new political action committees (PACs) and super PACs.

2011 *Bond v. United States* holds that individuals have standing to raise 10th Amendment challenges to federal laws.

2013 In a narrow 5–4 decision, in *Shelby v. Holder*, the Supreme Court's conservative majority strikes down major provisions of the 1965 Voting Rights Act, giving individual states latitude to pass discriminatory voting laws. Since the decision, dozens of states have enacted newly restrictive statewide voter laws, including strategic polling place closures, voter ID laws, and limiting early voting.

2014 The National Center for Civil and Human Rights is established.

2014 In *McCutcheon v. FEC*, the Supreme Court rules that aggregate campaign contribution limits are unconstitutional.

2019 U.S. Supreme Court rules on *Rucho v. Common Cause,* essentially upholding political gerrymandering.

2020 In response to the COVID-19 pandemic, numerous states change voting procedures to expand early voting, mail-in voting, and drop box provisions, and to extend the date by which mail-in ballots must be received.

2020 Joseph Biden defeats Donald Trump in presidential election; Trump alleges widespread voter fraud but loses 59 court cases challenging election.

2021 On January 6th, an insurrection attempts to stop the certification of President Biden. It fails to do so, but it is the first time in U.S. history that the peaceful transfer of power is attempted to be blocked. President Biden in certified and inaugurated.

Glossary

Ballot A form (either paper or electronic) used for voters to make their selections for candidates running for office and to vote on initiatives, referenda, and other public policy questions decided by popular vote.

Bill of Rights A bill or declaration of rights delineated as fundamental rights and consisting of the first 10 amendments to the 1789 Constitution of the United States. These and later amendments specify the fundamental rights of American citizens.

Bloc voting The action by which an ethnic, racial, or religious group of voters overwhelmingly casts its ballots for a particular party or candidate based on ethnic, racial, or religious affiliations, as in Irish Catholic Democrats.

Blue states States that are generally considered to be reliably Democratic states, mostly clustered on the East and West Coasts.

Citizenship The legal concept identifying a full member of a nation.

Civil liberties Basic freedoms contained in the First Amendment, such as freedom of religion, speech, press, assembly, and to petition the government; together these liberties are regarded as cornerstones of democracy.

Civil rights The rights of citizens to political and social freedom (including voting) and equality, and against discrimination on grounds such as race, gender, sexual orientation, national origins, color, age, ethnicity, religion, and disability.

Cracking A form of gerrymandering in which electoral districts are drawn to divide communities or constituencies in ways that reduce the political power of those communities or constituencies.

Dark money Money coming from unknown sources or donors and used by political groups (corporations and specially created political action committees) for campaigns.

De facto A Latin phrase meaning "by action."

De jure A Latin phrase meaning something being done "by law."

Direct election Any election resulting in a candidate being selected to hold an office.

Disenfranchise To deprive someone of the right to vote; or to deprive someone of the legal rights and privileges bestowed by a locality, state, or country.

Doctrine of Incorporation The legal theory allowing the Supreme Court to apply the Bill of Rights to the states under the 14th Amendment's due process clause.

Electoral college A body of electors chosen by the voters in each state to select the presidential ticket that won their state.

Ethnocentrism The evaluation of other cultures according to preconceptions that are based in the standards and customs of one's own culture; the belief in the inherent superiority of one's own ethnic group.

Filibuster rule A procedural rule of the U.S. Senate requiring 60 votes for cloture (to close debate on a bill) that is often used by the minority party in the Senate to block passage of a bill supported by the majority.

Fourteenth Amendment The Civil War amendment, ratified in 1868, that declared that all persons "born or naturalized in the United States" are citizens. It overturned the 1857 decision in *Dred Scott v. Sandford*, which had declared that Blacks were not and could not be citizens.

Franchise The right to vote in elections.

Gerrymandering The drawing of district boundaries into odd shapes to benefit one political party and weaken the chances of candidates of the other party.

Gilded Age An era of U.S. history between 1870 and 1900 when outer wealth masked inner corruption and poverty; an era of abject poverty when millions of immigrants from the impoverished regions of Eastern and Southern Europe poured into the nation and the high concentration of wealth among a small percentage of the U.S. population became more visible and politically contentious.

GOP The Grand Old Party—the nickname for the Republican Party coined after the Civil War.

Grassroots The base of voters at the local level (for example, a precinct) who support a political party.

Gubernatorial election An election to select a candidate for the office of governor of a state.

Identity politics A tendency for people of a particular religion, race, sexual orientation, or social background to form exclusive political alliances on that basis, moving away from traditional, broad-based party politics.

Individualistic political culture In Elazar's typology of political cultures, it is the culture that sees government as a marketplace of competing individual interests that use politics to better their own causes and are focused on private concerns. This culture accepts strong political parties based on patronage and constituent services, with a high tolerance for corruption.

Jim Crow The former practice of segregating Black people in the United States. It involved laws and practices that were used to justify disenfranchisement of Black citizens across the American South.

Judicial review A power, exercised by U.S. courts, to examine legislation and strike down those laws that judges believe violate the U.S. Constitution.

Jus sanguinis Citizenship based on blood or parentage.

Jus soli Citizenship based on place of birth.

Landmark decision A Supreme Court decision that sets an important legal precedent and serves as a guidepost for settling subsequent legal cases and challenges.

Litigation The process of taking legal action.

Money primary Also known as the invisible primary, it refers to a period of some months' duration when potential candidates test the waters for a possible run by raising funds for their candidacies.

Moralistic political culture In Elazar's typology, it is a culture that values collective action through politics and views politics as fulfilling the objectives of a government that acts for the betterment of the greater good. It opposes individual enrichment and is policy/issue driven. Parties are secondary, and nonpartisan solutions are sought. It eschews corruption.

National Election Day Established by an 1845 act of Congress to set a day for national elections, it is the first Tuesday in November.

Naturalization The legal act of making an individual born in another country a citizen of that individual's adopted country.

Packing A form of gerrymandering in which district boundaries are modified in such a way that the opponent's voters are confined to a smaller number of districts, to dilute their voting power.

Pluralism A theory of group behavior that argues that competition among groups counterbalances them and leads to better policy by "competitive equilibrium."

Political culture Underlying semipermanent characteristics that help explain the functioning of states and localities.

Political interest group Any organization of individuals who share a common interest in certain public policy issues and who make policy-related appeals and lobbying efforts to government agencies, officials, or lawmakers to promote or further those interests. It is also known as a special-interest group, an advocacy group, or a pressure group.

Poll auditors Also known as independent auditors, they are used to carry out vote recounts and confirm election results in a nonpartisan manner.

Poll judges Also called election judges, they are nonpartisan officials who oversee voting at a local station or precinct and are responsible for ensuring that everyone who is eligible to vote at a location can do so. They distribute provisional ballots, set up polling stations, and ensure voting integrity of polling places, ballots, and voting machines.

Poll tax A tax imposed on individuals to vote. It was originally developed in Northern states to suppress the votes of naturalized citizens considered "less desirable" immigrants, mostly from Southern and Eastern European nations, but the practice became most notorious during the Jim Crow era, when it widely used in the South to suppress the vote of Blacks. Poll taxes were made unconstitutional by the 24th Amendment.

Poll watchers Private citizen observers or poll challengers who represent political parties, candidates, or groups in monitoring activities at poll locations; nominally defended as individuals seeking to ensure the integrity of elections, poll watchers are increasingly criticized for engaging in intimidation and other tactics to reduce turnout of voters seen as likely to support opposing parties or candidates.

Presidential coattails The effect whereby the candidate at the top of the ticket in national elections garners votes for down-ticket candidates in the same party.

Primary elections A type of election used by political parties to select their nominees for general elections, or those in which the nominees run against nominees from other political parties.

Privileges and Immunities Clause This clause in the 14th Amendment establishes basic rights of citizenship and ensures that they are protected against discriminatory state laws.

Racial profiling A pattern of discriminatory behavior of police officers based on the race of members of the public with whom they interact.

Racism The discriminatory treatment of people who belong to a different race from one's own. It often is used to justify prejudicial behavior toward them, such as enacting laws designed to suppress their voting rights.

Ranked choice voting An electoral system in which voters rank candidates by preference on their ballots. A candidate who wins a majority of first-preference votes is declared the winner. If no candidate wins a majority of first-preference votes, however, the candidate with the fewest first-preference votes is eliminated, and those votes are distributed to the remaining candidates based on second-preference choices of those ballots. The process is repeated until a candidate wins an outright majority of votes.

Recall election An election at the state level in which an incumbent officeholder is required to seek voter approval to retain the office for the remainder of an elected term.

Red states States that are generally considered to be reliably Republican states and are often mapped as red; they are mostly clustered in the South, the Midwest, and the mountain states.

Referendum election A type of special election in a state whereby local voters—instead of lawmakers—approve or disapprove the enactment into law of a bill.

Regime politics A form of government and associated rules, culture, or social norms that regulate the operations of government and its interactions with society.

Reserved powers Authority and powers not granted to the national government that are thereby retained by the state governments unless specifically prohibited by the Constitution.

Runoff elections Elections that are held between the two leading vote getters for an office when the prior election failed to produce a candidate who won a majority vote.

Special election Any election held at a time different from a general election, typically used to fill an office that has become vacant due to death, resignation, or removal from office.

Split-ticket voting A practice whereby individual voters vote for members of different political parties on their ballot.

Stare decisis A Latin phrase meaning "let the decision stand"; it is the doctrine or policy of following the rules or principles of determining points in litigation according to precedent. It is a doctrine that has been used regarding the right to vote and to participate in electoral politics.

Straight-ticket voting A practice whereby a voter casts all votes for members of the same political party.

Suffrage The right to vote in political elections.

Traditionalistic political culture In Elazar's typology, it is a culture in which governments are designed to protect and preserve the status quo to benefit elites. Political and government positions are held by groups of wealthy landholders and business families who rule through an elitist conception of the common good. Political participation by nonelites is discouraged and low. Political competition is primarily among factions of the dominant party.

Tribalism An attitude where loyalty to the political party is more important than loyalty to anything else; a total "us" versus "them" mentality.

Writ A form of legal command in the name of a court or other legal authority to act or to abstain from acting in some way, for example, an injunction, or a writ of certiorari.

Xenophobia The excessive fear of the foreign or foreigners; often a driving factor in efforts to suppress or restrict the vote of ethnic groups.

Index

Note: Page numbers followed by *t* indicate tables.

About the Author

Michael C. LeMay, PhD, is professor emeritus of political science at California State University–San Bernardino with 35 years' experience teaching at the university level. He is author of more than two dozen academic books and has authored many books with ABC-CLIO, including *Global Pandemic Threats*; *Illegal Immigration*, first and second editions; *Doctors at the Borders*; and *Transforming America: Perspectives on Immigration*, three volumes. His book *The American Political Party System* was selected by Choice as a 2017 Outstanding Academic Title.